Obama vs Trump

New Perspectives on the American Presidency
Series Editors: Michael Patrick Cullinane and Sylvia Ellis, University of Roehampton

Published titles
Constructing Presidential Legacy: How We Remember the American President
Edited by Michael Patrick Cullinane and Sylvia Ellis

Presidential Privilege and the Freedom of Information Act
Kevin M. Baron

Donald Trump and American Populism
Richard S. Conley

Trump's America: Political Culture and National Identity
Edited by Liam Kennedy

Obama vs Trump: The Politics of Presidential Legacy and Rollback
Clodagh Harrington and Alex Waddan

Obama's Fractured Presidency: Policies and Politics
Edited by François Vergniolle de Chantal

Forthcoming titles
The White House, the War on Poverty and the GOP
Mark McLay

Midterms and Mandates
Patrick Andelic, Mark McLay and Robert Mason

Harry S. Truman and Higher Education
Rebecca Stone

Series website: https://edinburghuniversitypress.com/new-perspectives-on-the-american-presidency.html

OBAMA vs TRUMP

The Politics of Presidential Legacy and Rollback

Clodagh Harrington and Alex Waddan

EDINBURGH
University Press

Edinburgh University Press is one of the leading university presses in the UK. We publish academic books and journals in our selected subject areas across the humanities and social sciences, combining cutting-edge scholarship with high editorial and production values to produce academic works of lasting importance. For more information visit our website: edinburghuniversitypress.com

© Clodagh Harrington and Alex Waddan, 2020, 2022

Edinburgh University Press Ltd
The Tun – Holyrood Road, 12(2f) Jackson's Entry, Edinburgh EH8 8PJ

First published in hardback by Edinburgh University Press 2020

Typeset in 11/13 Adobe Sabon by
IDSUK (DataConnection) Ltd,

A CIP record for this book is available from the British Library

ISBN 978 1 4744 4700 3 (hardback)
ISBN 978 1 4744 4701 0 (paperback)
ISBN 978 1 4744 4702 7 (webready PDF)
ISBN 978 1 4744 4703 4 (epub)

The right of Clodagh Harrington and Alex Waddan to be identified as the authors of this work has been asserted in accordance with the Copyright, Designs and Patents Act 1988, and the Copyright and Related Rights Regulations 2003 (SI No. 2498).

Contents

Acknowledgments		vi
1.	Introduction: Presidential legacy in the era of Obama and Trump	1
2.	A "hard" legacy, under pressure	38
3.	An uncertain "soft" legacy, under fire	77
4.	America and the world	116
5.	Exercising presidential power	154
6.	Public communication and vision	198
7.	Conclusion: From "Renegade" to "Mogul"	232
Index		250

Acknowledgments

The authors would like to thank first and foremost Sarah Foyle and her colleagues at Edinburgh University Press for their patience and professionalism throughout this process. In addition, thanks go to Sylvia Ellis and Mike Cullinane, editors of the excellent *New Perspectives on the American Presidency* series, for their roles in initiating this project. We are grateful for their enthusiasm and support.

We also want to express our gratitude to kind colleagues who took the time to read sections of the work and offer informed comments. In particular we would like to thank John Berg (Suffolk University, MA) for his expertise on environmental issues and Jeremy Shapiro, Research Director of the European Council on Foreign Relations, who provided helpful insights into the mechanics of Obama-era foreign policy delivery. In addition, thanks go to colleagues and friends in the American Politics Group for feedback on various draft chapters. All errors and misjudgments are entirely the authors' own.

And finally, Clodagh would like to thank Zara for her patience, and promises to make up that missed time.

1
Introduction: Presidential legacy in the era of Obama and Trump

As Barack Obama took the oath of office to become the 44th president of the United States on January 20, 2009, he immediately left a distinct imprint on the history of the institution. The presidency was no longer the exclusive preserve of white men. As the first African American to win the White House, Obama, by virtue of becoming president, had established a legacy that could not be repeated or undone. In itself this was a moment of consequence for a nation with a history steeped in racial division, but it did not automatically bestow a record of achievement that would last beyond his presidency. On that day, however, it was unsurprising that the historic nature of events generated even more excitement, especially amongst supporters of the President, than is always present as someone newly elected takes office. That enthusiasm also came with raised expectations for what would be achieved and Obama's inheritance suggested that there was much that needed to be done.

By the end of 2008 it was evident that the financial crisis, which had already left many of the Wall Street giants diminished and gasping for survival, was going to extend its toxicity and cause damage well beyond the world of investment bankers into the wider economy. That damage, in turn, brought into sharper relief other long-standing problems, such as the number of Americans without, or with inadequate, health insurance. Moreover, Obama's victory along with Democratic control of both chambers of Congress gave hope to all those progressive activists whose voices had been marginalized in recent years. Hence climate change campaigners jostled with representatives of other liberal causes, such as those championing an expansion of same-sex rights, to get their place near the front of the line to advocate for their preferred policies. In addition to domestic challenges Obama faced a complex international situation, with the nation wearied by the loss of blood and treasure resulting from extended engagements in Iraq and Afghanistan.

Inevitably the burst of enthusiasm accompanying his entry to the White House at the start of 2009 wore off. The realities of compromising in an effort to find solutions to complex real-world problems on the home front and dealing with, to paraphrase Donald Rumsfeld, unexpected as well as expected problems and fractures in the international order took its toll on Obama's approval ratings. Moreover, his political opponents quickly regained their mojo and organized resistance to the administration's initiatives. In fact, the backlash was soon manifested with the rise of the so-called Tea Party in 2009 and the surprise victory of Republican Scott Brown in a Massachusetts Senate special election in January 2010, providing a harbinger of what was to come in the 2010 November midterm elections.[1] In institutional terms, the Republican takeover of the House of Representatives in those elections and the continued GOP control of that chamber throughout the rest of Obama's presidency meant that the administration effectively had only two years to push through its most ambitious legislative goals.

Much of the presidential literature in the latter part of the twentieth century correctly pointed to the importance of the negotiation process between executive and legislative branches and the capacity of the former to bring together enough votes in the latter to form a majority coalition, be that on a case-by-case basis or over a series of measures.[2] But the increase in partisan polarization in Washington, DC—so evident from the early 1990s—made cooperation between an executive branch run by one party and a legislature with at least one chamber controlled by the opposite party ever more unlikely.[3] As the 2010 midterm elections approached, Republican leaders, anticipating victory in at least one chamber, made their intentions plain. Then Senate Minority Leader Mitch McConnell (Kentucky) somewhat infamously reflected: "The single most important thing we want to achieve is for President Obama to be a one-term president."[4] In reality, it is hardly surprising that leaders of the "out" party should wish for an incumbent to be defeated by their own party's candidate in the next election, but it was nevertheless unexpected to hear such an explicit expression of that sentiment. As it was, the words of soon-to-be-Speaker of the House John Boehner (Ohio) were more ominous for the President. With regard to Obama's ongoing agenda, he commented, "We're going to do everything—and I mean everything we can do—to kill it, stop it, slow it down, whatever we can."[5]

Yet, for all the frustration and disappointment that Obama and his supporters felt as his time in office drew to a close, on the eve of the 2016 presidential election it did look as if the next occupant of the White House would be Obama's first secretary of state, Hillary Clinton, who would continue to push most areas of policy in the same direction—and that the stand-out legacies of Obama's time in office would become a direction of travel rather than an end point. Health care reform, the expansion of LGBT+ rights, and the nuclear deal with Iran would not just be preserved but would be further consolidated.[6] That, as everyone knows, is not how things turned out: Not only did Donald Trump win the White House, but he entered office reinforced by a unified Republican government in Washington, DC. The GOP's congressional majorities in 2017 were not as big, especially in the Senate, as Obama's had been in 2009, but Trump and congressional Republicans had the apparent institutional capacity to deliver on some of their major promises. These included repealing the signature health care reform, rolling back the expansion of the regulatory state that had taken place over the previous eight years, and rowing the US back from a range of international agreements—such as the Iran deal—that had been negotiated by the Obama administration. Yet, just as President Obama had often found himself thwarted by the fragmented institutions of US government and the capacity of opponents to turn to the courts to challenge executive authority, so too President Trump found that resistance could not always be overcome. Some aspects of Obama's legacy could be straightforwardly reversed and others picked apart, but other parts of that legacy proved more resilient. Moreover, and just as with Obama, Trump's party lost control of the House in the first midterm elections of his presidency, making major legislative action explicitly to undo the remaining legacy highly unlikely.

It is the purpose of this book project to come to an understanding of the nature and substance of the Obama presidency's legacy and President Trump's repudiation of that legacy. In discussing President Obama's legacy and the efforts of the Trump administration to roll back much of that inheritance, this project seeks to shine light on some broad questions about the nature of the modern presidency, but the fundamental clash of philosophies of governance, both in terms of substance and style, thrown up by the juxtaposition of Presidents Obama and Trump is also very particular. It became a staple of political journalism to point to President Trump's obsessive efforts to undo the record of his predecessor, and justifiably so, with some journalists even stretching to contrast their approaches to visiting US forces serving in Iraq.[7] Even 30 months into his presidency, Trump displayed a continuing desire to dismiss not just the record but the person and popularity of his predecessor. In an interview with *Meet the Press* in June 2019, President Trump referred to the Obamas and Obamacare twenty-three times.[8] In the summer of 2019, leaked memos revealed that the UK ambassador to the US thought that the Trump administration's decision to withdraw the US from the nuclear deal with Iran was at least partly motivated by "personality reasons," since the agreement was "Obama's deal."[9] The personal antagonism between the two, unsurprising given Trump's promotion of so-called "birtherism," was self-evident and on public display as early as the 2011 White House Correspondents' Dinner.[10] As Trump emerged as a serious political figure in 2016, President Obama broke with convention and angered conservatives by attacking Trump while overseas at the G-7 summit in Japan.[11] Later he aggressively mocked the Republican nominee a month before the 2016 election on the Jimmy Kimmel show.[12]

Obama campaigned ferociously for Clinton, certainly surpassing the recent efforts of George W. Bush on John McCain's behalf or Bill Clinton for Al Gore. In doing so he often invoked his own actions as reasons for supporting her candidacy.[13] The day prior to the election, he told an audience in Michigan: "I think I've earned some credibility here," as he referred back to the efforts to save jobs in the automobile industry. He also made clear that he saw the clash between Clinton and Trump as one that would help define his legacy: "Tomorrow, you will choose whether we continue this journey of progress, or whether it all goes out the window."[14] The reporting told of a cheering crowd, repeatedly declaring its affection for the outgoing president—but fatefully, that mood was not matched across the whole state. The theme was a regular feature of Obama's stump speech in the closing stages of the campaign as he tried to sound the alarm that his legacy was at stake in the election: "All the progress we've made over these last eight years . . . goes out the window if we don't win this election."[15]

After the election, however, in an interview with the *New Yorker*'s editor, David Remnick, Obama was more sanguine about his legacy lasting through Trump's time in office. He explained just how difficult it was for any president to get done what they wanted to get done:

> I think that the possibility of everything being out the window exists. But, as a practical matter . . . the federal government is an aircraft carrier, it's not a speedboat. And, if you need any evidence of that, think about how hard we worked over the last eight years with a very clear progressive agenda, with a majority in the House and in the Senate, and we accomplished as much domestically as any president since Lyndon Johnson in those first two years. But it was really hard.

Obama added that "maybe fifteen percent . . . gets rolled back, twenty percent, but there's still a lot of stuff that sticks."[16]

For his part, Trump constantly made clear his disdain for the incumbent president. It is unsurprising that a presidential candidate from the "out" party would attack the record of the incumbent and their party, but there was an edge to Trump's rhetoric beyond standard political rebukes. That was evident before he was recognized as a serious political figure when he became a leading booster of the "birther" movement, which cast doubt on whether Obama had been born in the US and hence whether he was ever a legitimate president. Very late in the 2016 campaign, Trump did acknowledge the fact that Obama had been born in the country; but it is important to understand the importance of Trump's embrace of birtherism in winning him support amongst Republican voters.[17] That movement, denounced by many as racist at the time, was clearly seen by the Obamas as such even if they did not say so publicly until after they had left the White House.[18] Beyond that personal attack, candidate Trump's portrayal of Obama's America was not simply of a country on "the wrong track," but one that had derailed and crashed. This message was at its sharpest in his inaugural address, when he used language that spoke of "American carnage" that "stops right here and stops right now."[19]

More specifically, throughout the campaign, candidate Trump promised to revoke Obama-era initiatives. His acceptance speech at the Republican National Convention pledged to "repeal and replace disastrous Obamacare," to stop the Trans-Pacific Partnership (TPP), and to end "Excessive regulation . . . very quickly." He declared that the Iran nuclear agreement signed by the Obama administration would "go down in history as one of the worst deals ever negotiated." He reflected that he was "certain" that naming Hillary Clinton as secretary of state was a decision that Obama "truly regrets." Tying Clinton and Obama together, he denounced "the legacy of Hillary Clinton: Death, destruction and terrorism and weakness."[20] In May 2016 he had announced that he would "cancel" the Paris climate agreement if he became president, arguing that the pact would give "foreign bureaucrats control over how much energy we use."[21] In August 2016, in a speech recounting stories of Americans who, left vulnerable by "Obama–Clinton open borders policies," were murdered by illegal immigrants, he made a more particular commitment:

> We will immediately terminate President Obama's two illegal executive amnesties, in which he defied federal law and the constitution to give amnesty to approximately 5 million illegal immigrants.[22]

This referred to two programs the Obama administration had introduced through executive actions: Deferred Action for Childhood Arrivals (DACA) and Deferred Action for Parents of Americans and Lawful Permanent Residents (DAPA). As it was, legal challenges prevented DAPA, which was the wider-ranging of the two actions, from ever coming into effect, but DACA was in force when Trump took office.

Here, in the cases of the Affordable Care Act (ACA), the Iran deal, environmental regulations, DACA, the TPP, and the Paris accord, Trump was speaking of identifiable actions taken by the Obama administration (though, it should be noted, the last two had not come into effect). Yet, to boil Obama's legacy down to such a limited range of features misses much of the story and impact of his presidency. In turn, this leads to the question of what we mean by "legacy," which is something that is assumed but relatively undefined in much writing about individual presidents and the institution of the presidency.

Defining legacy

Presidential legacy is something that generates debate and controversy almost from the moment a new president enters the White House, reaching a fever pitch as their time in office draws to a close. Historians and social scientists periodically update their league tables that rate and rank presidents, presumably based largely on the significance of their legacy, be that positive or negative.[23] Yet, for all the discussion of each president's legacy, there is little formal analysis of what criteria we should use to judge legacy, nor even of when it is fair to make any judgment at all. The weighty *Oxford Handbook of the American Presidency* has no chapter dedicated to the study of presidential legacy, nor even any index references to "legacy."[24] Nevertheless, book and journal article titles will often include the word "legacy" as they seek to assess the record of any particular president, sometimes even before that president has left office.[25]

Hence, before moving on to look at particular examples of Obama's legacy and the Trump administration's efforts to roll that back, it is important to think through the complexities of defining presidential legacy, the means of establishing and consolidating a legacy, and then the factors that facilitate or hinder later moves to undo that legacy. In this context, the purpose of the rest of this chapter is twofold. Firstly, we offer some thoughts on the difficulty of defining legacy and thinking about the ways in which legacies do, or do not, become institutionalized and the different ways in which legacies can, or cannot, be rolled back. Secondly, we move on to look at legacy reversal and Trump's repudiation of Obama's legacy. The chapter aims to provide a framework for moving on to looking at what we can think of as Obama's legacy and how successfully the Trump administration has instigated moves to undo that legacy.

When considering the meaning and impact of presidential legacy, a range of questions present themselves. How do presidents choose to articulate their ambitions, and then what means do they use to pursue those objectives? What factors facilitate or hinder their efforts? And, given that presidents rarely get all that they ask for in any particular political or policy episode, how should we assess compromise and incremental movement? What circumstances make a president's "positive achievements" most likely to prove resilient over time, particularly if a successor perceives those changes through a more negative lens and seeks to undo or remake them? And, in turn, what factors facilitate or impede a president's efforts to repeal the legacy of their predecessor? Our intent is to think through these questions across a range of presidential activity. So we look not only at key aspects of domestic and foreign policy, but also at how the institution of the presidency is molded by its occupant and their vision of how leadership is most effectively displayed.

This is not a book about presidential power per se, but when looking at a president's legacy the institutional capacity to establish that legacy, as well as the skills used to maximize that capacity, clearly matter. In this context, some of the recent literature on presidential authority has emphasized the limits of powers to bring about change. George Edwards has pointed to the overconfidence of presidents, who misunderstand the restraints on their power and misinterpret their mandate.[26] Jeremi Suri notes how the responsibilities of the modern presidency, defined as the post-Franklin Roosevelt world, have become so sprawling that it is now an "impossible" job, while the presidential scholars William Howell and Terry Moe lay the blame for presidential weakness on the Constitution.[27] For these last authors, "blame" is an operative word: They lament the manner in which institutional barriers have enfeebled the occupant of the White House, whom they see as the political actor who is most able to take a national perspective.

For all the constraints on presidential power, however, it is clear that presidents strive to leave a legacy. As Howell and Moe assert, "If there is one motivator that most forcefully drives presidential behavior, it is their concerns about legacy."[28] This results from their "burning desire to be remembered as great leaders." Presidents, of course, do not get to choose which aspects of their legacy historians and political scientists focus on. Lyndon Johnson, for example, clearly wanted to be judged according to his domestic policy record, but however ranging his achievements on the home front, his presidency will be remembered as much, if not more, for the calamitous engagement in Vietnam[29]—which Johnson himself implicitly recognized, as his memoir of his time in the Oval Office spends disproportionate space attempting to rationalize his actions with regard to that war.[30] Further, while there have been scholarly attempts to rehabilitate Richard Nixon's reputation and deal with important policy aspects of his presidency, his presidency will forever be framed by the Watergate scandal and his resignation from office.[31] Indeed, one lasting legacy of his presidency is the term "Nixonian," meaning deceptive and corrupt. Yet the examples of Johnson and Nixon also illustrate that we do need to look at legacies in terms of their complex parts as well as a perhaps oversimplified sum.

Hence, while legacy is a construct that does have a meaningful everyday use, it is simultaneously somewhat intangible. Onlookers can intuitively grasp that a legacy is what a president passes on to their successor, but that does not always mean that any onlooker can see all that there might be to see, and it is likely that different onlookers will see different things and come to quite different judgments about the merits of a presidential legacy. Nor does it tell us what a presidential successor will make of what they have been left by their predecessor. Here, rather obviously, the two candidates in 2016 offered profoundly different verdicts on the virtues of the Obama presidency and its legacy. Hence, those 80,000 votes cast across Pennsylvania, Wisconsin and Michigan, which gave Trump victory in the electoral college, meant that the US had elected a president whose political identity was based not only on a rejection of Obama-ism but also a personal repudiation of Obama.

As Bert Rockman notes, to talk of legacy "implies that something durable" has been passed from one administration to the next, which the latter "will benefit by or have to deal with as a set of problems well into the future." Rockman adds that almost "every presidential administration has something to leave, either by design, circumstance, or ineptitude."[32] Also helpful are Hugh Heclo's comments in his review of Ronald Reagan's presidency, when he notes that for all major leaders, "legacy is a complex thing. It is a mixture of intended accomplishments and unintended by-products, of actions taken and things left undone."[33]

Using the framework provided by these insights, it is possible to identify a series of different ways in which we can think about what should be included when discussing a president's legacy. Given that new Presidents arrive in office touting their agenda for change, be that major change to set the country in a new direction or just to leave their own imprint while improving what is already working, one test of legacy is to ask how much of that agenda they were able to put in place.[34] In short, does a president leave office with a series of White House policy initiatives having become legislative accomplishments? Or, if not codified by legislation, does a president at least manage to secure some of a preferred agenda through exercising the powers of the administrative presidency?[35]

Crafting legacy

Some presidents clearly leave legacies that are truly unique and arise from circumstances that cannot be replicated. George Washington's initial shaping of the institution and Abraham Lincoln's leadership through the Civil War provide examples of presidencies whose legacies owed much to a particular time and place. Similarly it is unlikely that the conditions seen during Franklin Roosevelt's tenure, which included combating an economic depression that ravaged politics in Europe, managing the US's role in a global conflict, and helping shape the emerging post-war international environment, will be repeated. Those conditions created almost a perfect storm for a president of "reconstruction."[36] As it was, Roosevelt's time as president left transformative policy legacies across a range of socio-economic and foreign affairs, re-cast the nature of the institution he occupied, and established the Democrats as the majority party, if in an inherently unstable coalition. Hence, Roosevelt's was a legacy of a scope that has not been matched since. If nothing else, the passage of the 22nd Amendment to the Constitution means that no future president can be in office as long as Roosevelt.

Yet, even Roosevelt faced considerable institutional obstacles in terms of both his domestic and foreign policy agenda.[37] At home, his administration's early troubles with a recalcitrant Supreme Court caused much frustration and abroad, while measures such as Lend-Lease nudged the US away from neutrality with regard to the conflict engulfing much of the world throughout 1940 and 1941, Roosevelt remained thwarted from adopting a more decisive response by isolationist sentiment through to the attack on Pearl Harbor. Moreover, scholars still debate the long-term consequences and policy legacies of choices and compromises that were made, and why they were made, by the Roosevelt administration.[38] For example, it is clear that the early rollout of the Social Security program distributed pensions inequitably, as a disproportionate number of the workers excluded from the program were African American. Whether this was an unfortunate but unintended consequence of program design or a reflection of how the administration conceded ground to pressure from Southern congressional forces through the policy-making process remains contested.[39] The long-term legacy of the Social Security Act was to establish a program that covers virtually all of the nation's seniors, but these alternative accounts of the decision-making process clearly frame the actions of the Roosevelt administration quite differently.

As it is, presidents who leave the most significant legacies are clearly likely to have many of their favored policy initiatives enacted into law, even in adulterated form, although it is worth distinguishing between quantity and quality. In this context, measuring presidential success by relying too heavily on roll-call votes or support scores for a president in Congress is potentially misleading, certainly if we are thinking about the significance and what might be thought of as the weight of legacy. President Carter, for instance, scores better on these voting indicators than President Reagan, but there are few tomes dedicated to explaining the age of Carter or reflecting on his lasting imprint on Democratic Party development. In contrast, Reagan is often seen as the dominant political figure of his time, with Republicans consistent in their continuing praise of his leadership and promising to maintain his legacy.[40] Hence, crafting a substantive legacy is different from winning numerous legislative skirmishes.

Clearly, given the sausage-making machine nature of the legislative process in Washington, DC, presidents very rarely get exactly what they want from Congress, even in times of unified partisan government, but they can still get more or less of what they initially wanted.[41] In most cases, assuming a president chooses to take ownership of the final product upon signing it, then it seems reasonable to label that outcome as part of their *legacy*, though that might be different from ascribing any particular legislative episode that culminates in a presidential signature as a success for the executive branch. Sometimes this is very straightforward to judge, as a compromise might affect the choice of side dish but the executive branch's choice of main course prevails; for example, President Obama may have supported the idea of including the "public option" in the health reform package as it developed through 2009, and he later lamented the absence of such a measure, yet the Affordable Care Act, minus the public option, was very obviously the major aspect of *his* social policy legacy.[42] Equally, the tax cuts enacted in 2001 did not match the Bush administration's initial plans, but they were clearly an accomplishment from the White House's perspective, leaving a lasting legacy.[43]

Sometimes, though, it is potentially more problematic to decide on whether the president's role in the legislative process warrants that the White House explicitly be seen as responsible for the final product. A presidential focus can certainly lead to an overly top-down perspective on what drives political development. For example, historians may disagree about how much direct credit President Johnson deserves for the passage of the Civil Rights Act in 1964, suggesting that emphasizing Johnson's role diminishes the role of the civil rights movement.[44] Yet, acknowledging Johnson's role while appreciating the wider social movements and the force for change that the latter created are not intellectually incompatible. Moreover, in this case it is important to reflect that there was still political opposition to be overcome in Washington, and Johnson showed bolder leadership than President Kennedy had previously done and set a direction in pushing for a strong and unambiguous law in a manner that would not have come from congressional leadership alone.[45] Hence, whether Johnson should be regarded as the prime mover or as playing a more limited facilitator role, the Civil Rights Act should clearly be seen as a legacy of his time in office.

A more problematic, if narrower, case of where to attribute credit—or blame—for a particular law comes with the passage of the Personal Responsibility and Work Opportunity Act (PRWORA) into law in August 1996. At issue here is whether this law should be seen primarily as the work of the Republican-controlled Congress that crafted the final bill. At the time, President Clinton could claim to be fulfilling a campaign promise from 1992 when, as a candidate, he had famously embraced the slogan "Ending welfare as we know it" on the campaign trail; but the actual plans he set out during the campaign and the plan advanced by the administration, if to little avail, in the summer of 1994 were different in kind from the welfare reform package that he ended up signing. PRWORA was the product of the work of congressional Republicans and Clinton had in fact twice vetoed very similar plans, though he was given political cover to do so by additional measures attached to those bills. When a stand-alone measure came to his desk, the White House divided over the issue, but Clinton signed the bill, angering his welfare policy advisors.[46] George Stephanopoulos was one of those preferring another veto, but he acknowledged that his mood was "tempered by my complicity" as he had been part of the 1992 campaign team that was happy to let the public over-interpret the campaign's welfare reform promises.[47] As it was, Clinton not only signed PRWORA, but demanded that he be seen as an equal parent to congressional Republicans.[48] Hence, welfare reform properly should be seen as part of his legacy, even though he signed on to crucial policy elements that were as much a product of unintended political consequences and circumstance as of design.[49]

Another layer of complexity comes when we consider legacies that arise from a president acting, partially at least, in order to deny political opponents an opportunity to exploit an issue. For example, George W. Bush did not simply sign into law the Medicare Modernization Act (MMA) of 2003: He aggressively pushed its passage in Congress, including making 4.00 a.m. calls to hesitant Republicans preparing to vote and withholding revised higher cost estimates of the bill.[50] Yet the MMA, in contrast to conservative orthodoxy, expanded the welfare state by introducing a prescription drug program to Medicare. It should also be emphasized that the bill did many other things, much more amenable to conservative thinking, but the drug benefit was a response to political pressure as Democrats attempted to develop this popular measure into a wedge issue to their partisan advantage.[51] Clearly the MMA is part of Bush's legacy, but whether the prescription drug benefit included in it should primarily be regarded as a new welfare state program offering some help to seniors or as a cheaper and less expansive arrangement to the alternatives on the table is less certain.

Another muddying example comes from the Nixon era and the passage of the Occupational Safety and Health Act of 1970, which established the Occupational and Safety Health Administration (OSHA). The law itself, passed by overwhelming margins in both chambers of Congress, was a compromise between Democrat and Republican alternatives, pushing respectively for relatively stronger and more limited powers of regulation and intervention to be given to government. The new agency exercised its authority uncertainly in its opening years under the eyes of presidents Nixon and Ford, but did bare its teeth and antagonize industry under the leadership of Eula Bingham, who was asked to lead OSHA during the Carter administration. When Reagan appointee Thorne Auchter replaced Bingham, however, OSHA adopted a much lighter touch in its enforcement of worker protection measures and has not subsequently re-emerged as an aggressive agency, lacking confidence in its remit when pressured by other government bodies and business interests to tread softly.[52] Thus, there is no straightforward narrative that accounts for how the creation of OSHA should be assessed as part of Nixon's legacy.

An even more perplexing, if rare, category of legislation is one where a president subsequently explicitly denounces a law that they signed. For example, President Clinton signed the Defense of Marriage Act into law in September 1996. Yet, even as the House passed its version of the bill, White House spokesperson Michael McCurry called the bill "gay baiting, pure and simple" while simultaneously saying that the President believed that marriage was something that should be between a man and a woman and that he would sign the bill.[53] Clinton may have felt compelled rather than heartened to sign the law, passed with veto-proof majorities, in the context of the looming presidential election, but he did then invoke his signing of the bill on advertisements broadcast, if briefly, on Christian radio stations the following month.[54] And, if this makes it difficult to discern a clear legacy when Clinton left office, it became even more difficult to categorize when he later declared that the law should be declared "incompatible with our Constitution."[55]

The complexities embedded in these examples of legacy-making owe much to the bargaining inherent to the legislative process, but if presidents find themselves frustrated by the obstacles embedded in that process they can turn to use more unilateral powers afforded their office, and presidential scholarship has paid greater attention in recent years to this aspect of executive authority.[56] This "unilateralism" may be a consequence of frustration with the legislative process, though it is misleading to think of executive action as signaling a retreat from attempting to get legislation enacted.[57] The effort to expand the remit of executive authority is likely to draw ire from the "out" party, but it is unlikely that future presidents will walk too far back from employing the same institutional tools, however much they may have criticized the behavior of their predecessor for its violation of constitutional norms. And unilateralism can be an effective means of baring presidential teeth.[58] As Andrew

Rudalevige charts, the Obama administration carried through a range of actions, some of considerable consequence, such as the Deferred Action for Childhood Arrivals (DACA) program, the use of drones to carry out targeted killings, and selective delayed implementation of aspects of the ACA. To illustrate the variety of tools available, none of these examples were accomplished through the use of an executive order.[59] One critic of this use of executive power was citizen Donald Trump. In February 2016, at a debate for Republicans seeking the party's presidential nomination, he declared: "Obama goes around signing executive orders. He can't even get along with the Democrats. He goes around signing all these executive orders. It's a basic disaster. You can't do it."[60] President Trump, however, found executive action an attractive tool, leading Rudalevige to conclude at the end of his first year in office that "on the whole, the major policy changes Trump achieved in his first year came mostly from the use of administrative power, not via Congress."[61]

Nevertheless, when assessing the impact of executive action it is important to distinguish between quantity and quality, as often these actions are symbolic or instruct agencies to develop plans for action rather than implementing action in the short term.[62] Furthermore, the limits of unilateral action to establish a legacy that will be consolidated over time sit in the very existence of those powers. "Incoming presidents regularly relax, or altogether undo, the regulations and orders of past presidents; and in this respect, the influence a sitting president wields is limited by the anticipated actions of their successors."[63] Furthermore, as President Obama and subsequently President Trump have found, opponents are sometimes able to use the judiciary as a check on the potential excessive exertion of executive authority. Hence, as we will discuss later in the book, the Obama legacy did not include the Clean Power Plan or DAPA.

The judiciary's role in downsizing the Obama administration's imprint on immigration and climate policy highlights another area of uncertainty in terms of defining presidential legacy. What of the relationship between a president and the Supreme Court? Firstly, while presidential nominations to the Supreme Court are a means by which a president's favored perspectives can influence

American life long after the White House has a new occupant, the opportunity to nominate a new justice to the Court for each individual president arises as much by chance as design, or is dependent on where they fit in the cycle of judicial longevity, given that justices are more likely to retire when the president is one they are comfortable with. Hence, one-term president Jimmy Carter did not get a chance to nominate a justice to the Court, while one-term president George H. W. Bush got to place two members on the Court.

Yet, while nominating justices to the Supreme Court is one of the acts taken by presidents that can leave a legacy well beyond their time in office, the evidence suggests that this is not always the legacy that they intended. One of George H. W. Bush's nominees was David Souter, who turned into a reliable liberal vote and, importantly, retired from office to let a Democrat replace him. Even President Reagan's nominees did not all turn into conservative stalwarts. Sandra Day O'Connor proved to be a genuine "swing justice" and Anthony Kennedy, while mostly siding with the Court's conservatives, was a decisive liberal vote on same-sex rights as well as reproductive rights. The example of Kennedy's role on the Court and his standing as part of the Reagan legacy is especially illustrative of why it is important to pay attention to individual cases as well as broad data points. Before Kennedy took his place on the Court, Reagan had nominated Robert Bork to the vacant seat. Bork, who was (in)famously rejected by the Senate, later helped draft a proposed constitutional amendment that would have prevented same-sex marriage. The difference between the judicial philosophies of Bork and Kennedy and the fact that the latter rather than the former served as a justice leaves a distinct imprint on the legacy of the Reagan presidency.[64]

As it is, the more recent evidence, from President Clinton onwards, suggests that administrations have become more adept at choosing justices who will be consistently sympathetic to the preferences of the president who nominated them. It may be that the vetting applied by outside groups to check a president's choice means that the chances of further Earl Warren or David Souter type "mistakes" are much diminished.

Second, there is the question of how to weigh the decisions that occur during a particular presidency. If the Court rules in a case directly related to an action taken by the administration, be that the ACA or DAPA, then clearly that decision will weigh directly upon a presidential legacy. Yet the judiciary can make decisions that carry significant public policy implications, which the White House may support or oppose, but which arise from challenges to pre-existing federal or state law. Hence, the Court's capacity to reinforce or disrupt the status quo remains in place. Sometimes a president may welcome a Court's decision and so effectively adopt the outcome as part of the administration's legacy. For example, the Obama White House celebrated the Supreme Court decision that effectively granted a constitutional right to same-sex marriage and the administration certainly made wider efforts to promote LGBT+ rights.[65] This included the Department of Justice filing an amicus brief in the *Obergefell* case, as it had also done two years earlier when asking the Court to strike down California's Proposition 8, with reporting that Obama personally helped craft that brief.[66] So, in the *Obergefell* case, the White House very credibly chose to own the Court's decision, even though the new right was not a direct result of presidential action and was conferred by a 5–4 decision with Chief Justice John Roberts vocal in his displeasure.[67] On the other hand, the Obama administration would hardly claim the undoing of campaign finance reform as part of its legacy, but that was the consequence of the 2010 *Citizens United* decision of the Supreme Court; nor would it want the elimination of part of the Voting Rights Act that occurred in the *Shelby County* ruling to be counted as part of its record.[68]

Things undone and unintended

Heclo's category of things "left undone" can be further divided into things undone as a result of a president's failed efforts, or because a president shied away from a major political challenge despite being aware of the core unresolved problem, or potentially through a conscious decision not to address a particular issue.

Furthermore, the evidence can sometimes be contradictory. President Obama became only the third president not to sign into law an increase in the value of the minimum wage, despite repeated efforts during his second term in office to persuade Congress to lift the level from $7.25 to $10.10.[69] Hence, one legacy of the Obama presidency was a decline in the real value of the federally mandated minimum wage of 9.6 percent.[70] Clearly, advocates for the Obama White House would push back against such a categorization, noting that he did aggressively push for an increase but was thwarted by a recalcitrant Republican Congress and that he took executive action where he could. Moreover, the Obama White House did celebrate the fact that from 2013, when the President started to press for an increase in the federal level of the minimum wage, through to the end of his time in office, eighteen states plus Washington, DC did increase their minimums, with a further flurry of activity at city and county level.[71] The example of the minimum wage also illustrates the importance of issue framing when assessing legacy. One of the other presidents not to sign into law an increase in the minimum level was Ronald Reagan. The nominal minimum stayed at $3.35 an hour from 1981 through 1989, which was the equivalent of a decrease, in constant 2015 dollars, from $8.71 to $6.38.[72] Yet, for Reagan this represented a positive legacy, as by ideological inclination he was skeptical of the whole notion of a mandated minimum.[73]

The question of how to account for the unintended consequences of presidential decisions when assessing legacy provides a further layer of uncertainty. This is particularly the case as these consequences are likely to emerge after the passage of time and only come into focus with the benefit of hindsight: For example, while there were plenty of contemporaries who criticized US actions during the 1980s that provided support for authoritarian regimes in Latin American and Africa, there was less understanding of how Reagan's fixation on seeing the world as either communist or non-communist led him to support actions in the name of anti-communism, particularly in Lebanon, that reinforced an image of the US as an imperialist, anti-Islamic power, which "did much to aid the growing cause of radical jihadists in the Middle East."[74] Oddly, it can also be argued that the Reagan administration's decision to decline to cooperate with a plan by Soviet Premier Mikhail Gorbachev to begin to move Soviet forces out of

Afghanistan in 1987 helped create the conditions for the continued rise of Islamic radicalism in that country.[75]

In turn, this brings into focus the problem of deciding when it is appropriate to judge a legacy. In reality, few commentators have the patience to wait any decent length of time, but as the case of Harry S. Truman illustrates, snap judgments based on low approval ratings and difficult circumstances at the time a president leaves office can lead to a premature negative verdict. In addition, a successor can make a predecessor's missteps look less damning. As Rockman, if a little cruelly, concludes in his assessment of George W. Bush, one of his most significant legacies was "the rehabilitation of his father's presidential reputation."[76] Our purpose, however, is less to judge where Obama's legacy should place him in the pantheon of presidential greatness, but to investigate what he was able to achieve and how those "achievements" survived when under intense fire after he left office.

Rollback

As the discussion above illustrates, defining legacy is problematic, but we also need to explain what we mean by "rollback." The term implies that some action has been deliberately taken in order to reverse direction. It is possible to conceive of accidental rollback, where a policy is undone as an unintended consequence of other actions, but in the context of Trump's treatment of the Obama legacy what might be described as "blue on blue" rollback is not the issue. The Trump administration was often happy to be very public in its effort at legacy reversal. In fact, as we shall see, Trump himself was eager to announce the end of Obama-era initiatives when it was far from clear that this was the case.

More generally, given the nature of presidential power, the tools afforded a president for rolling back a predecessor's legacy and the strengths and weaknesses of those tools are much the same as for legacy creation, as is the likelihood of sources of effective resistance to presidential action. Whether rollback efforts are successful will likely depend on the institutional balance of partisan power across federal and state governments. Further, the extent to which a legacy in a specific policy field has embedded itself and established positive feedback effects impacts the capacity to undo what has been done.[77] If a policy has generated strong supportive constituencies amongst the public and/or influential elite or economic actors, this can generate stiff resistance to reversing that policy. As discussed in Chapter 2, the Affordable Care Act proved to be more resilient than might have been anticipated given the constant promises from candidate Trump and congressional Republicans to "repeal Obamacare." Part of the reason for this resilience was that it turned out that the law had higher levels of public support than indicated by polling since the law's enactment in 2010 and it had also benefited key health care providers, who therefore wished to preserve its central aspects.[78]

On the other hand, negative feedback can lead to reversal of policy even when this has been enacted in a bipartisan fashion. This reversal can be prompt, as witnessed in the case of the Medicare Catastrophic Care Act (MCCA). The MCCA, which added a catastrophic coverage package to Medicare for beneficiaries who had used up their Medicare entitlements, was enacted in summer of 1988 only to be almost entirely repealed just over a year later.[79] This was not a law that would seem a natural fit for the Reagan administration, but it was advocated by the administration's Secretary of Health and Human Services, Otis Bowen, and appealed to congressional Democrats. It was enacted with large majorities in both chambers, with the administration happy to engage in credit claiming. The expectation on all sides was that this would be a popular measure, and Vice President Bush, running for the presidency in the election later that year, reportedly urged Reagan to back the measure. Yet the law drew a sharp backlash due its funding mechanism that relied on increased contributions from seniors and as Congress hurriedly backtracked so too did President Bush.[80]

If the MCCA was an odd example of uncoordinated rollback of an unlikely legacy, the slow death of the No Child Left Behind law (NCLB) suggests a type of political suffocation of a law that was also passed with bipartisan congressional majorities, and which, in this case, was very much embraced by the president who signed it. The NCLB, which imposed new federal testing standards on schools, was not popular with all conservatives, but it was one of President Bush's top priorities when he took office in January 2001. As the NCLB was rolled out, however, it aggravated state and local educational administrators as well as drawing the ire of the teacher unions and became a target for both left and right of the political spectrum. In 2008 candidate Obama was critical of some central aspects, but did not demand a simple repeal.[81] As it was, the law was supplanted rather than directly rebuked in December 2015 when Obama signed into law the Every Student Succeeds Act.[82] This case might best be described as legacy rollback with a soft landing.

Importantly, rollback can take other forms than highly visible legislative repeal or direct revocation of an executive action. As the Obama administration had illustrated, executive actions can take the form of interpreting and implementing existing rules differently.[83] Furthermore, as we will discuss in Chapter 2 with respect to the Consumer Finance Protection Bureau, executive agencies can be led in ways that undermine the original intent of the agency's role and so effectively hollow out its mission.

A similar example would be the shift in behavior by the Department of Justice with regard to investigating alleged malpractice and discrimination by local police departments. For Attorneys General Eric Holder and Loretta Lynch, conducting these investigations and publishing the results had been an important part of an effort to increase transparency and potentially improve relations between the police and local communities, especially minorities, where these had become strained. In the aftermath of the rioting that followed the death of Michael Brown in August 2014 in Ferguson, Missouri, the Justice Department looked at the wider role of the police in the city. The report did clear the officer involved in Brown's death of all federal charges, but Holder spoke of how the police regularly "blatantly cross the line" in their use of force, particularly against African Americans. Holder also noted how the police acted as a "collection agency for the municipal court rather than a law enforcement entity" and added that while the problems in Ferguson may have been "particularly acute," they raised "questions about fairness and trust that are truly national in scope."[84] President Trump's first Attorney General, Jeff Sessions, on the other hand, announced that these types of study would be scaled back and resources prioritized elsewhere in order to "fulfill my commitment to respect local control and accountability, while still delivering important tailored resources to local law enforcement to fight violent crime."[85]

Assessing legacy reversal in foreign policy is perhaps even more difficult than in domestic affairs. Ending (or starting) a war, withdrawing troops from (or introducing them to) a combat zone, or pulling the US out of (or entering into) an international treaty contrary to the policies pursued by a predecessor would all constitute tangible measures of legacy reversal. For Obama and Trump the clear-cut cases would be the latter's withdrawal from the Iran nuclear deal and, taking a broad definition of international affairs, the Trans Pacific Partnership trade deal and the Paris climate agreement. Yet much of foreign affairs is less categorical than is apparent in these types of instance. And this is further complicated by the somewhat ambiguous nature of Obama's foreign policy as we discuss in Chapter 4, and also the emerging evidence in Trump's opening 30 months in office that his willingness to back up a loud rhetorical bark with a sharp-toothed bite was sometimes questionable. Yet the distinct overarching approach on offer from the two presidents was clear and is captured in the following commentary from summer 2018 by Jeffrey Goldberg, editor of *The Atlantic*:

> The administration officials, and friends of Trump, I've spoken with in recent days believe . . . that Trump is rebuilding American power after an eight-year period of willful dissipation. "People criticize [Trump] for being opposed to everything Obama did, but we're justified in canceling out his policies," one friend of Trump's told me. This friend described the Trump Doctrine in the simplest way possible. "There's the Obama Doctrine, and the 'Fuck Obama' Doctrine," he said. "We're the 'Fuck Obama' Doctrine.'"[86]

This quotation also explains the importance of thinking about the different ways in which a president can try to exercise their powers and communicate with the public. Leadership is a less tangible resource than policy accomplishments, but the effectiveness of the executive branch's internal processes and its capacity to work with its political allies to achieve what might be regarded as achievable objectives can significantly impact presidential legacy. One area, for example, where presidents leave a legacy that extends well beyond their time in office is in the choice of judges to the federal bench including, but also beyond, the Supreme Court. In addition, there are legacies that a president would rather avoid—most notably scandal, be that all-consuming, as in Watergate, or a stain on a presidency, as witnessed through the Lewinsky-related impeachment proceedings. As it turned out, the Obama White House was certainly not free from scandal, but it did avoid the indignity of being investigated by a special prosecutor. The Trump White House, on the other hand, was quickly engulfed in scandal.

Structure of the book

It is not our purpose to provide an exhaustive account of the Obama and Trump presidencies. Rather than offer a comprehensive account of all aspects of either presidency, we are looking at areas where the Obama administration worked toward cementing strands of legacy, which were later challenged or overturned by President Trump. The work attempts to set up a framework for examining the Obama legacy, which will provide context to readers who are curious to know to what extent the Trump administration is genuinely fulfilling its promise to reverse the direction taken by the Obama White House. Looking beyond the noise and hyperbole, the book will examine how robust the Obama legacy proves to be in the face of Trump's challenge. Others before Trump have promised to tear up the rule book, but Washington's institutional obstacles and constitutional safeguards have often proved to be more resilient than anticipated.

The next section of the book will contain examples of Obama's policy implementation, and his successor's aims and efforts of rollback. In Chapters 2 and 3 we discuss aspects of what we describe as Obama's "hard" and "soft" legacies and the Trump administration's attempts to repeal these. The distinction between hard and soft is not a scientific one. In what might be thought of as "material" policy domains it does reflect a division between legacies arrived at through legislative action (hard) and those relying on executive action (soft). Hence much of the focus of discussion with respect to hard legacy is on the Affordable Care Act (ACA) and the creation of the Consumer Financial Protection Bureau (CFPB) as part of the Dodd-Frank Wall Street Reform and Consumer Protection Act. With regard to soft legacy, we concentrate on the Obama administration's executive actions on immigration policy and environmental regulation after its efforts to bring about policy change in those areas through the legislative process largely failed. Yet, we also consider LGBT+ issues as part of hard legacy. This did include some legislative measures and executive actions, but the landmark moment came from the judicial branch. Finally, we look at trade policy as an aspect of soft legacy. Here Obama followed a familiar trajectory of being a free trade skeptic as a candidate before switching to broadly endorse the expansion of free trade agreements when in office. As it was, he left a potentially significant but very thinly embedded legacy in the shape of the Trans Pacific Partnership, which was negotiated but bereft of congressional ratification as he left office. As we shall see, aspects of both types of legacy proved perhaps surprisingly resilient, others susceptible to what might be thought of as hidden rollback, and others still predictably vulnerable to effective repeal.

Next we turn to international affairs. To what extent did Obama turn the ship of foreign policy state around from George W. Bush's tumultuous presidency and establish an identifiable and distinctive trajectory? And how did the "Fuck Obama" doctrine materialize in practice? The final section of the book will consider the significance of the exercise of presidential powers of appointment, particularly to positions of influence that last beyond the lifetime of a presidency, as well as matters of presidential communication, interaction, public perception, use of the media and engagement with other actors.

The content of the book will look at key areas of domestic policy, including health care, immigration, financial regulation, racial justice and reproductive rights. On the foreign policy front, relations with Iran and Russia will be considered, along with how a president prioritizes a range of international commitments and challenges including, for example, climate change. Both domestic and foreign policy case studies will be considered in the context of the president's relations with other actors, and his ability or desire to implement his campaign promises.

Conclusion

Clearly, writing before the end of the first term of the Trump presidency, it is too early to make a judgment on how historians will treat Obama's legacy. And while even Trump was already included in at least one presidential ranking less than two years after his inauguration, it is too soon to say how Obama's time in office will look in the round in a generation's time, when specific policy initiatives have matured or withered and when there is a better sense of how the causes he embraced have stood the test of time.[87] For example, his efforts at promoting LGBT+ rights were of some immediate consequence, but were not completely fulfilled during his time in office: In the future, however, Obama's leadership on LGBT+ issues, or at least his willingness to offer presidential approval to the wider movement, may look like a significant turning point that clearly established a direction of travel, if with some diversions along the way, toward a full equalization of rights. Or, more particularly, the change in relationship with Cuba might come to be seen as a pivotal moment that helped foster a change in the nature of the regime in that country in the long term; or it might be seen as a moment when the US helped keep in place an unrelenting dictatorship; or it might merit no more than a footnote in history books. Fortunately, the aim here is not to make premature judgments about how the Obama legacy will be perceived in 2040, but to assess how far he was able to turn his central policy goals into some sort of legacy and then to look at how much of that survived the immediate hostility of his successor. In turn, this will help inform us not just about Obama and Trump—riveting though that story is—but also about the manner in which presidents try to exercise their institutional authority in order to imprint their vision and how easily their efforts can be overturned by a legatee with an inimical vision.

This book is an early assessment of an ongoing experiment, testing the resilience of a president's legacy in the context of a successor dedicated to unraveling that legacy. At the time of writing, we are only 36 months into that experiment. There have been signs that explicitly undoing things might prove to be more frustrating for Trump than he may have imagined, just as doing things in the first place proved so aggravating for the Obama administration. Trump's ability to act to further de-Obamafication and perhaps even to contemplate a legacy of his own will depend on the partisan balance in Washington, DC. The November 2018 midterm results suggest further legislative rollback of Obama's legacy, at least the intended legacy, is unlikely. Yet, as presidential scholar Andy Rudalevige has charted, the Obama administration stretched the scope of the administrative presidency in its effort to bypass the legislative process, providing a precedent and template for Trump. In this context, the Trump White House has shown it has the capacity to at least halt the direction of travel with regard to LGBT+ rights and, even though Congress has not repealed and replaced the ACA, the administration has undermined its effective functioning and legal challenges persist. And here it is necessary to understand the importance of the executive branch beyond the confines of the Oval Office and the stream-of-consciousness Twitter feed. For example, in terms of LGBT+ rights, look closely at the actions of the Justice Department and former Attorney General Sessions. What instructions were being given out about how rigorously to apply Obama-era regulations? With regard to health care, how much more flexibility will Health and Human Services (HHS) allow states in terms of the waivers it grants? For example, the Obama Health and Human Services refused states permission to include work requirements for people newly eligible for Medicaid through the ACA. Or consider how much effort HHS is putting into enrolling people into the health care marketplaces. On the other hand, the Medicaid expansion is proving popular at the ballot box, as evidenced by the results of statewide referenda. It is more necessary now than ever to look beyond shiny distractions and consider the substance.

Notes

1. Theda Skocpol and Vanessa Williamson, *The Tea Party and the Remaking of Republican Conservatism* (New York: Oxford University Press, 2012).
2. See for example Charles Jones, *The Presidency in a Separated System* (Washington, DC: Brookings Institution, 1994); Richard Neustadt, *Presidential Power: The Politics of Leadership* (New York: John Wiley, 1960); Mark Peterson, *Legislating Together: The White House and Capitol Hill from Eisenhower to Reagan* (Cambridge, MA: Harvard University Press, 1990).
3. On the increased nature of partisan polarization see Barbara Sinclair, *Party Wars: Polarization and the Politics of National Policy Making* (Norman, OK: University of Oklahoma Press, 2006); Thomas Mann and Norm Ornstein, *It's Even Worse than it Looks: How the American Constitutional System Collided with the New Politics of Extremism* (New York: Basic Books, 2012); James E. Campbell, *Polarized: Making Sense of a Divided America* (Princeton, NJ: Princeton University Press, 2017).
4. "When did McConnell say he wanted to make Obama a 'one-term president'?" *The Washington Post*, September 25, 2012, <https://www.washingtonpost.com/blogs/fact-checker/post/when-did-mcconnell-say-he-wanted-to-make-obama-a-one-term-president/2012/09/24/79fd5cd8-0696-11e2-afff-d6c7f20a83bf_blog.html> (last accessed May 5, 2020).
5. Andy Barr, "The GOP's No-Compromise Pledge," Politico, October 28, 2010, <https://www.politico.com/story/2010/10/the-gops-no-compromise-pledge-044311> (last accessed December 11, 2019).
6. For the election eve forecasts, see for example Maya Rhodan and David Johnson, "Here Are 7 Electoral College Predictions for Tuesday," *Time*, November 8, 2016, <https://time.com/4561625/electoral-college-predictions/> (last accessed December 11, 2019).
7. Peter Baker, "Trump's Ascendance Upends Obama's Vision for America," *The New York Times*, November 13, 2016, A1; Juliet Eilperin and Darla Cameron, "How Trump is Rolling Back Obama's Legacy," *The Washington Post*, January 20, 2018, <https://www.washingtonpost.com/graphics/politics/trump-rolling-back-obama-rules/?utm_term=.ae870386d4d7>; David Smith, "The

Anti-Obama: Trump's Drive to Destroy His Predecessor's Legacy," *The Guardian*, May 11, 2018, <https://www.theguardian.com/us-news/2018/may/11/donald-trump-barack-obama-legacy>; Adam Taylor, "The Stark Contrast Between Trump's Trip to Iraq and Obama's 2009 Visit," *The Washington Post*, December 27, 2018, <https://www.washingtonpost.com/world/2018/12/27/stark-contrast-between-trumps-trip-iraq-obamas-visit/?utm_term=.d9c4fae6cae6> (last accessed December 11, 2019).

8. Chuck Todd, Mark Murray and Carrie Dann, "Trump Shows He Remains Fixated on Obama," *NBC News*, June 24, 2019, <https://www.nbcnews.com/politics/meet-the-press/trump-shows-he-remains-fixated-obama-n1020916> (last accessed December 11, 2019).

9. Jill Lawless, "Leaked UK Memo Says Trump Axed Iran Deal to Spite Obama," *The Washington Post*, July 14, 2019, <https://www.washingtonpost.com/world/europe/leaked-uk-memo-says-trump-axed-iran-deal-to-spite-obama/2019/07/14/> (last accessed December 11, 2019).

10. Fueled by some speculative reporting, it became something of a meme that the jokes aimed at Trump by Obama and the comedian Seth Meyers were a key reason why Trump launched his presidential bid, but the actual evidence for this is thin. For the original report, see Adam Gopnik, "Trump and Obama: A Night to Remember," The New Yorker, September 12, 2015, <https://www.newyorker.com/news/daily-comment/trump-and-obama-a-night-to-remember>. For a more skeptical analysis see Roxanne Roberts, "I Sat Next to Donald Trump at the Infamous 2011 White House Correspondents' Dinner," *The Washington Post*, April 28, 2016, <https://www.washingtonpost.com/lifestyle/style/i-sat-next-to-donald-trump-at-the-infamous-2011-white-house-correspondents-dinner/2016/04/27/5cf46b74-0bea-11e6-8ab8-9ad050f76d7d_story.html?utm_term=.765a9f59fb65> (last accessed 3 January, 2020).

11. Paul Saunders, "Obama's Reckless Overseas Attack on Trump," *National Interest*, May 26, 2016, <https://nationalinterest.org/feature/obamas-reckless-overseas-attack-trump-16366> (last accessed December 11, 2019).

12. Barney Henderson, "Barack Obama Ruthlessly Mocks Donald Trump on Jimmy Kimmel Saying he Laughs at him 'Most of the Time,'" The Telegraph, October 25, 2016, <https://www.telegraph.co.uk/tv/2016/10/25/barack-obama-ruthlessly-mocks-donald-trump-on-jimmy-kimmel-sayin/> (last accessed December 11, 2019).

13. It should be acknowledged that, if for quite different reasons, Gore and McCain were happy to pass on having Bill Clinton and George W. Bush as active surrogates. The political symbiosis that had marked the early relationship between Clinton and Gore had disintegrated in the aftermath of the Lewinsky scandal, despite Clinton's continuing high approval ratings. Bush, more straightforwardly, was deeply unpopular by the fall of 2008.
14. Julie Hirschfield Davis and Gardiner Harris, "An Energized Obama Stumps for Clinton, and His Own Legacy," *The New York Times*, November 8, 2016, A1, <https://www.nytimes.com/2016/11/08/us/politics/obama-donald-trump.html> (last accessed January 3, 2020).
15. Peter Baker, "Trump's Ascendance Upends Obama's Vision for America," *The New York Times*, November 13, 2016, <https://www.nytimes.com/2016/11/13/us/politics/obama-legacy-donald-trump.html> (last accessed January 3, 2020).
16. David Remnick, "Obama Reckons with a Trump Presidency," *The New Yorker*, November 28, 2016, <https://www.newyorker.com/magazine/2016/11/28/obama-reckons-with-a-trump-presidency> (last accessed December 12, 2019).
17. Michael Tesler, "Monkey Cage: Birtherism Was Why So Many Republicans Liked Trump in the First Place," *The Washington Post*, September 19, 2016, <https://www.washingtonpost.com/news/monkey-cage/wp/2016/09/19/birtherism-was-why-so-many-republicans-liked-trump-in-the-first-place/?utm_term=.1f31d07da069> (last accessed December 12, 2019).
18. Michelle Obama, *Becoming* (New York: Viking, 2018).
19. Donald Trump, "The Inaugural Address," The White House, January 20, 2017, <https://www.whitehouse.gov/briefings-statements/the-inaugural-address/> (last accessed December 11, 2019).
20. Brad Plumer, "Full Transcript of Donald Trump's Acceptance Speech at the RNC," *Vox* (July 22, 2016), <https://www.vox.com/2016/7/21/12253426/donald-trump-acceptance-speech-transcript-republican-nomination-transcript> (last accessed December 11, 2019).
21. "Donald Trump Would 'Cancel' Paris Climate Deal," *BBC News*, May 27, 2016, <https://www.bbc.co.uk/news/election-us-2016-36401174> (last accessed January 3, 2020).
22. "Full Text: Donald Trump Immigration Speech in Arizona," *Politico*, August 31, 2016, <https://www.politico.com/story/2016/08/

donald-trump-immigration-address-transcript-227614> (last accessed December 11 2019)
23. Brandon Rottinghaus and Justin Vaughn, "Measuring Obama Against the Great Presidents," *Brookings*, February 13, 2015, <https://www.brookings.edu/blog/fixgov/2015/02/13/measuring-obama-against-the-great-presidents/> (last accessed January 4, 2020); Arthur Schlesinger, "Rating the Presidents: Washington to Clinton," *Political Science Quarterly*, 112.2 (1997): 179–90.
24. George Edwards and William Howell, *The Oxford Handbook of the American Presidency* (Oxford: Oxford University Press, 2009).
25. See for example Colin Campbell, Bert Rockman, and Andrew Rudalevige, *The George W. Bush Legacy* (Washington, DC: CQ Press, 2008); Bert Rockman and Andrew Rudalevige, *The Obama Legacy* (Lawrence: University Press of Kansas, 2019); Steven Schier, *The Postmodern Presidency: Bill Clinton's Legacy in US Politics* (Pittsburgh, PA: University of Pittsburgh Press, 2000).
26. George Edwards III, *Overreach: Leadership in the Obama Presidency* (Princeton, NJ: Princeton University Press, 2012).
27. Jeremi Suri, *The Impossible Presidency: The Rise and Fall of America's Highest Office* (New York: Basic Books, 2017); William Howell and Terry Moe, *Relic: How Our Constitution Undermines Effective Government and Why We Need a More Powerful Presidency* (New York: Basic Books, 2016).
28. Howell and Moe, *Relic*, 107.
29. Ibid. 108.
30. Lyndon Johnson, *Vantage Point: Perspectives of the Presidency* (Worthing: Littlehampton Books, 1971).
31. For Nixon revisionism see Joan Hoff, *Nixon Reconsidered* (New York: Basic Books, 1995). For a weighty analysis, with Watergate as a part rather than the whole of the story see Melvin Small, *The Presidency of Richard Nixon* (Lawrence: University of Kansas Press, 1999).
32. Bert Rockman, "The Legacy of the George W. Bush Presidency—A Revolutionary Presidency," in Campbell et al., *The George W. Bush Legacy*.
33. Hugh Heclo, "The Mixed Legacies of Ronald Reagan," *Presidential Studies Quarterly*, 38.4 (2008): 555.
34. Stephen Skowronek, *The Politics Presidents Make: Leadership from John Adams to George Bush* (Cambridge, MA: Harvard University Press, 1993).

35. Andrew Rudalevige, "The Obama Administrative Presidency: Some Long-Term Patterns," *Presidential Studies Quarterly*, 46.4 (2016): 868–90.
36. Skowronek, *The Politics Presidents Make.*
37. Fred Greenstein, *The Presidential Difference: Leadership Style from FDR to Barack Obama* (Princeton, NJ: Princeton University Press, 2009).
38. Jacob Hacker, *The Divided Welfare State: The Battle Over Public and Private Social Benefits in the United States* (New York: Cambridge University Press, 2002).
39. See Gareth Davies and Martha Derthick, "Race and Social Welfare Policy: The Social Security Act of 1935," *Political Science Quarterly*, 112.2 (1997): 217–35; Larry DeWitt, "The Decision to Exclude Agricultural and Domestic Workers from the 1935 Social Security Act," *Social Security Bulletin*, 70.4 (2010): 49–68; Linda Gordon, *Pitied But Not Entitled: Single Mothers and the History of Welfare, 1890–1935* (New York: Free Press, 1994); Robert Lieberman, *Shifting the Color Line: Race and the American Welfare State* (Cambridge, MA: Harvard University Press, 1998).
40. Sean Wilentz, *The Age of Reagan: A History, 1974–2008* (New York: Harper Collins, 2008).
41. Andrew Rudalevige, *Managing the President's Program: Presidential Leadership and Legislative Policy Formulation* (Princeton, NJ: Princeton University Press, 2002).
42. Barack Obama, "United States Health Care Reform: Progress to Date and Next Steps," *JAMA* 316.5 (2016): 525–32.
43. George W. Bush, "Remarks by the President at Tax Cut Bill Signing Ceremony," The White House, Office of the Press Secretary, June 7, 2011, <https://georgewbush-whitehouse.archives.gov/news/releases/2001/06/20010607.html> (last accessed January 4, 2020).
44. Clay Risen, *The Bill of the Century: The Epic Battle for the Civil Rights Act* (New York: Bloomsbury Press, 2014).
45. Robert Caro, *The Passage of Power: The Years of Lyndon Johnson* (London: The Bodley Head, 2012). See also Todd Purdum, *An Idea whose Time Has Come: Two Presidents, Two Parties, And the Battle for the Civil Rights Act of 1964* (New York: Henry Holt and Co., 2014).
46. See for example Mary Jo Bane, "Welfare as We Might Know It," *The American Prospect*, 30 (1997): 47–55; David Ellwood, November 19, 2001, "Welfare Reform as I Knew It: When Bad Things Happen to Good Policies," *The American Prospect*, <https://prospect.

org/economy/welfare-reform-knew-it-bad-things-happen-good-policies/> (last accessed January 4, 2020).
47. George Stephanopoulos, *All Too Human: A Political Education* (Boston: Little Brown and Company, 1999).
48. Bill Clinton, "How We Ended Welfare Together," *The New York Times*, August 21, 2006, <https://www.nytimes.com/2006/08/22/opinion/22clinton.html?mtrref=www.google.com&gwh=F6AFB494077AFD9924438C8BBEC5E669&gwt=pay&assetType=REGIWALL> (last accessed January 4, 2020).
49. For a detailed history of PRWORA see R. Kent Weaver, *Ending Welfare As We Know It: Context and Choice in Policy Towards Low-Income Families* (Washington, DC: Brookings Institute, 2000).
50. R. Draper, Dead Certain: The Presidency of George W. Bush (New York: Free Press, 2007); Joel Aberbach, "The Political Significance of the George W. Bush Administration," Social Policy and Administration, 39.2 (2005): 130–49.
51. Douglas Jaenicke and Alex Waddan, "President Bush and Social Policy: The Strange Case of the Medicare Prescription Drug Benefit," *Political Science Quarterly*, 121.2 (2006): 217–40.
52. Jim Morris, "How Politics Gutted Workplace Safety," Slate, July 7, 2015, <http://www.slate.com/articles/business/moneybox/2015/07/osha_safety_standards_how_politics_have_undermined_the_agency_s_ability.html> (last accessed January 4, 2020).
53. Jerry Gray, "House Passes Bar to US Sanction of Gay Marriage," *The New York Times*, July 13, 1996, <http://www.nytimes.com/1996/07/13/us/house-passes-bar-to-us-sanction-of-gay-marriage.html> (last accessed January 4, 2020).
54. Howard Kurtz, "Ad on Christian Radio Touts Clinton's Stands," *The Washington Post*, October 15, 1996, <https://www.washingtonpost.com/archive/politics/1996/10/15/ad-on-christian-radio-touts-clintons-stands/3e2bb15d-555e-44d7-b8c7-a3f87127063f/?utm_term=.80105ce91f8c>; Richard Socarides, "Why Bill Clinton Signed the Defense of Marriage Act," *The New Yorker*, March 8, 2013, <https://www.newyorker.com/news/news-desk/why-bill-clinton-signed-the-defense-of-marriage-act> (last accessed January 4, 2020).
55. Bill Clinton, "It's Time to Overturn DOMA," *The Washington Post*, March 7, 2013, <https://www.washingtonpost.com/opinions/bill-clinton-its-time-to-overturn-doma/2013/03/07/fc184408-8747-11e2-98a3-b3db6b9ac586_story.html?utm_term=.6c4671a723cc> (last accessed January 4, 2020).

56. Louis Fisher, *Presidential War Power* (Lawrence: University of Kansas Press, 2004); William Howell, *Power Without Persuasion: The Politics of Direct Presidential Action* (Princeton, NJ: Princeton University Press, 2003); William Howell, "Unilateral Powers: A Brief Overview," *Presidential Studies Quarterly*, 35.3 (2005): 417–39; Kenneth Mayer, *With the Stroke of a Pen: Executive Orders and Presidential Power* (Princeton, NJ: Princeton University Press, 2001); Mark Rozell, *Executive Privilege: Presidential Power, Secrecy, and Accountability* (Lawrence: University of Kansas Press, 2002); Andrew Rudalevige, The New Imperial Presidency: Renewing Presidential Power after Watergate (Ann Arbor: University of Michigan Press, 2005); Rudalevige, "The Obama Administrative Presidency."
57. Matthew Dickinson and Jesse Gubb, "The Limits to Power Without Persuasion," *Presidential Studies Quarterly*, 46.1 (2016): 48–72.
58. Howell, *Power Without Persuasion*.
59. Rudalevige, "The Obama Administrative Presidency."
60. "Republican Town Hall: CNN's Reality Check Team Inspects the Claims," *CNN Politics*, February 19, 2016, <https://edition.cnn.com/2016/02/18/politics/republican-town-hall-fact-check/> (last accessed December 11, 2019).
61. Andrew Rudalevige, "Monkey Cage: As a Candidate, Trump Criticized Obama's Use of Executive Power. So Guess What Powers President Trump Has Been Leaning On?" *The Washington Post*, January 20, 2018, <https://www.washingtonpost.com/news/monkey-cage/wp/2018/01/20/as-a-candidate-trump-criticized-obamas-use-of-executive-power-so-guess-what-powers-president-trump-has-been-leaning-on/?utm_term=.94b06b152971> (last accessed December 11, 2019).
62. Andrew Rudalevige, "Monkey Cage: Trump May Have the 'Most Executive Orders' Since Truman. But What Did They Accomplish?" *The Washington Post*, April 28, 2017, <https://www.washingtonpost.com/news/monkey-cage/wp/2017/04/28/trump-may-have-the-most-executive-orders-since-truman-but-what-did-they-accomplish/?utm_term=.887f22b6a679> (last accessed December 11, 2019).
63. Howell, *Unilateral Powers*, 422 fn. 4.
64. Joel Dodge, "Why We Live in Anthony Kennedy's America, Not Robert Bork's," *The Hill*, July 2, 2018, <https://thehill.com/opinion/healthcare/395178-why-we-live-in-anthony-kennedys-america-not-robert-borks> (last accessed December 11, 2019).

INTRODUCTION

65. Barack Obama, "Remarks by the President on the Supreme Court Decision on Marriage Equality," The White House, Office of the Press Secretary, June 26, 2015, <https://obamawhitehouse.archives.gov/the-press-office/2015/06/26/remarks-president-supreme-court-decision-marriage-equality> (last accessed December 12, 2019).
66. Kendall Breitman, "Dems, Obama Administration Press SCOTUS on Gay Marriage," *Politico*, March 6, 2015, <https://www.politico.com/story/2015/03/president-obama-amicus-brief-same-sex-marriage-115844>; Richard Socarides, "Obama's Brief Against Proposition 8 Goes Far," *The New Yorker*, February 28, 2013, <https://www.newyorker.com/news/news-desk/obamas-brief-against-proposition-8-goes-far> (last accessed January 4, 2020).
67. Arriane De Vogue, "Roberts Issues Stern Dissent in Same-Sex Marriage Case," *CNN Politics*, June 26, 2015, <http://edition.cnn.com/2015/06/26/politics/john-roberts-gay-marriage-dissent/index.html> (last accessed January 4, 2020).
68. *Shelby County, Alabama, v. Holder, Attorney General*, <https://www.supremecourt.gov/opinions/12pdf/12-96_6k47.pdf> (last accessed January 4, 2020).
69. Jana Kasperkevic, "Republicans at Fault if Obama Can't Raise Minimum Wage, US Labor Secretary Says," *The Guardian*, September 5, 2016, <https://www.theguardian.com/business/2016/sep/05/barack-obama-us-minimum-wage-republicans-tom-perez> (last accessed January 4, 2020).
70. Drew Desliver, "5 Facts About the Minimum Wage," *Pew Research Center*, January 4, 2017, <http://www.pewresearch.org/fact-tank/2017/01/04/5-facts-about-the-minimum-wage/> (last accessed January 4, 2020).
71. "Raising the Minimum Wage: A Progress Update," Executive Office of the President, October 2016, <https://obamawhitehouse.archives.gov/sites/default/files/minimum_wage/6_october_2016_min_wage_report-final.pdf> (last accessed January 4, 2020).
72. Analyn Kurtz and Tal Yellin, "The Minimum Wage Since 1938," *CNN Money*, 2015, <http://money.cnn.com/interactive/economy/minimum-wage-since-1938/index.html> (last accessed January 4, 2020).
73. Francis Clines, "Reagan's Wish is No Minimum Wage for Youths," *The New York Times*, February 10, 1983, <http://www.nytimes.com/1983/02/10/us/reagan-s-wish-is-no-minimum-wage-for-youths.html> (last accessed January 4, 2020).
74. Heclo, "The Mixed Legacies of Ronald Reagan."

75. Steve Coll, *Ghost Wars: The Secret History of the CIA, Afghanistan, and Bin Laden, from the Soviet Invasion to September 10, 2001* (New York: Penguin Press, 2004); Fred Kaplan, "Reagan's Osama Connection," *Slate*, June 10, 2004, <http://www.slate.com/articles/news_and_politics/war_stories/2004/06/reagans_osama_connection.html> (last accessed December 11, 2019).
76. Rockman, *The Legacy of the George W. Bush Presidency*, 375.
77. On policy feedback, see Daniel Béland, "Reconsidering Policy Feedback: How Policies Affect Politics," *Administration & Society*, 42.5 (2010): 568–90.
78. Daniel Béland, Phil Rocco, and Alex Waddan, *Obamacare Wars: Federalism, State Politics, and the Affordable Care Act* (Lawrence: University Press of Kansas, 2016).
79. Richard Himmelfarb, *Catastrophic Politics: The Rise and Fall of the Medicare Catastrophic Coverage Act of 1988* (University Park: Pennsylvania State University Press, 1999).
80. Daniel Béland and Alex Waddan, *The Politics of Policy Change: Welfare, Medicare, and Social Security Reform in the United States* (Washington, DC: Georgetown University Press, 2012).
81. Jon Herbert, "The Struggles of an 'Orthodox Innovator': George W. Bush, the Conservative Movement, and Domestic Policy," in Joel Aberbach and Gillian Peele (eds.), *Crisis of Conservatism? The Republican Party, the Conservative Movement and American Politics after Bush* (Oxford: Oxford University Press, 2011), 151–77.
82. Julie Hirschfield Davis, "Revamping of No Child School Act is Signed," *The New York Times*, December 11, 2015, A22.
83. Rudalevige, *The Obama Administrative Presidency*.
84. Adam Lerner, "Holder Slams Ferguson Police Force: 'Collection Agency,'" *Politico*, March 4, 2015, <https://www.politico.com/story/2015/03/eric-holder-slams-ferguson-police-force-collection-agency-115772> (last accessed December 11, 2019).
85. Mary Kay Mallonee and Eli Watkins, "DOJ Scaling Back Program to Reform Police Departments," *CNN*, September 15, 2017, <https://edition.cnn.com/2017/09/15/politics/doj-police-program/index.html> (last accessed December 11, 2019).
86. Jeffrey Goldberg, "A Senior White House Official Defines the Trump Doctrine: 'We're America, Bitch,'" The Atlantic, June 11, 2018, <https://www.theatlantic.com/politics/archive/2018/06/a-senior-white-house-official-defines-the-trump-doctrine-were-america-bitch/562511/> (last accessed January 2, 2020).

INTRODUCTION

87. Brandon Rottinghaus and Justin Vaughn, "How Does Trump Stack Up Against the Best—and Worst—Presidents?" *The New York Times*, February 19, 2018, <https://www.nytimes.com/interactive/2018/02/19/opinion/how-does-trump-stack-up-against-the-best-and-worst-presidents.html?smid=tw-share> (last accessed December 11, 2019).

2
A "hard" legacy, under pressure

The first two years of the Obama presidency were ones that saw substantive legislative action. The American Recovery and Reinvestment Act created a stimulus package that contained some long-term legacy-building elements such as the expansion of the Earned Income Tax Credit, but the most singular aspect of the Obama legacy was the Affordable Care Act (ACA). In addition to questions about health care coverage and cost, the ACA became a flashpoint for those concerned with "moral values." Issues such as reproductive rights came to the fore and went beyond the socioeconomic concerns regarding health care provision. While repeal of "Obamacare" had been central to wider Republican attacks on Obama well before Trump arrived on the political scene, as a candidate he eagerly adopted language about the "disastrous" ACA. Hence this chapter will examine the aims and achievements of the Trump administration, working with congressional Republicans, in relation to further reform of the US health care system. Furthermore, in the context of "values" issues the chapter will examine the Obama legacy on LGBT+ rights and the extent to which the Trump administration was able and willing to pursue an agenda promoted by more religious conservative groups to undo that legacy. The chapter will also consider the creation and subsequent hollowing out of the Consumer Financial Protection Bureau (CFPB).

We have termed these three elements as Obama's "hard legacy," as they went a long way toward (or even beyond, in the case of same-sex marriage) fulfilling the administration's original goals. Moreover, in the case of the ACA and CFPB, these were accomplishments that came through the legislative process rather then relying on the blunter instruments of executive action. Yet, the substantive nature of these achievements did not mean that they were invulnerable to future rebuke. As we will explain, the ACA was damaged but still very much the law of the land when Democrats took control of the House in January 2019. On the other hand, the CFPB had survived in appearance but less so in substance. The story of LGBT+ rights is somewhat different inasmuch as the most dramatic move in the Obama era came as a result of court action. Still, the administration did consistently try to expand the realm of LGBT+ rights and history has already deemed Obama a champion of the cause, but this aspect of his progressive legacy would be tested by the election of a successor increasingly indebted to socially conservative supporters.

The Affordable Care Act

There can be little question that the stand-out domestic policy legacy of the Obama era was the Affordable Care Act (ACA). This was the biggest reform of the American health care system since the mid-1960s, when President Lyndon Johnson signed into law a bill bringing the Medicare and Medicaid programs to life. A comprehensive health care reform package had been the "holy grail" for Democratic administrations dating back to Harry Truman's presidency. In addition to the intense efforts of presidents Truman and Clinton and the rather more tepid foray into health care politics by Carter, the Nixon administration had also tried but failed to find a way through the legislative maze that was effectively made into a series of dead ends. The purpose here is not to re-litigate whether those efforts failed primarily due to the institutional fragmentation of US government, the mobilization of interest group opposition, the deep-seated cultural fear of collective social provision or the legacy of racism that was embedded into key features of the early American welfare state. These are fundamental issues when thinking about the evolution and development of US social welfare arrangements, but the focus here is on what the ACA did and did not accomplish and the extent to which the Trump administration managed to roll the law back after years of Republican calls to "repeal Obamacare."

The answers to the different parts of these questions are complicated and involve accommodating and reconciling potentially contrary perspectives. Firstly, on the one hand, as Vice President Joe Biden was caught saying on microphone at the ACA's signing ceremony, this was a "big fucking deal."[1] On the other hand, the ACA did contain many compromises to placate potentially hostile stakeholders in the health care system and its policy design provided political opponents with important venues through which to continue their opposition in ways that materially limited the implementation and hence impact of the law. Second, on the one hand, when the Democrats took control of the House of Representatives in January 2019, the ACA was still the law of the land after two years of unified Republican government, led by the Trump administration, had failed to fulfill the repeated pledge to "repeal and replace" the law; and, with health care playing as a winning issue for the Democrats in the 2018 midterm elections, that shift in partisan control of the House all but guaranteed an end to legislative efforts to repeal the ACA through Trump's first term. Yet, on the other hand, Trump's Health and Human Services had used various administrative means to chip away at the functioning of the law.

The story of the enactment of the ACA has been well told already, but it is worth remembering some key features of the legislative process when judging the actual impact of the law and hence the ACA's true worth as a signature legacy of the Obama administration. Firstly, although the White House delegated much of the responsibility for drawing up the ACA to congressional Democrats, the decision to press ahead with health care reform from the very start of the presidency was very much Obama's own. When he arrived in office, faced with an expanding economic crisis, there were important voices, including his chief of staff Rahm Emmanuel and Vice President Biden, who worried that tackling the recession and reforming health care together might prove overwhelming. They urged that the economy should be the priority.[2] Obama, however, insisted that the administration and Congress could deal with two major tasks simultaneously.

Secondly, at key points during the process Obama stepped in to reinforce the reform effort, including holding a televised "health care summit" in February 2010 at a point when it looked like the legislative train had been derailed by the loss of the Democrats' 60 to 40 vote majority in the Senate after the surprise election of Republican Scott Brown in a special Senate election in Massachusetts in January 2010. Brown's election came after both House and Senate had passed their own version of reform, but before a Conference Committee had worked on bringing the two bills together for a final up or down vote in each chamber. Suddenly, with Republicans now having the numbers for a veto in the Senate, a means had to be found that bypassed the Conference Committee stage. Through his public performance at that "summit," Obama "gave Democrats in Congress the cover they needed" to move ahead with a controversial legislative endgame.[3] This involved the House passing the Senate version of reform, which could then be signed into law, before a series of "fixes" were enacted to iron out some of the more obvious wrinkles in the Senate bill. In order to get these "fixes" through Senate, Democrats controversially turned to the reconciliation process that did not allow for a filibuster.[4]

Third, even though these manoeuvres did mean that Obama had a major bill that he could sign into law, the need to bring the legislative process to a close in this way was unsatisfactory from both a political and policy perspective. In political terms, it allowed Republicans to cry foul over the use of reconciliation while simultaneously setting a precedent that Republicans could turn to should they get a chance to repeal the law; and from a policy viewpoint, it meant that some of the more radical elements of the House bill were written out of the equation. The House bill, for example, had included a small so-called public option whereby a government-run insurance package would compete with private insurers. This proposal might well not have made it through the final Conference Committee stage, but its absence from the Senate bill was indicative of the more moderate and more fundamentally piecemeal approach taken by the Senate through 2009, due to the need to keep all wavering Democrats and the Independent senator Joe Lieberman of Connecticut on board.

Furthermore, the manner in which the ACA folded together a vast range of changes, from creating new institutions designed to offer health insurance to low- to middle-income households, to expanding the existing Medicaid program, to imposing new regulations on insurers, to putting in place the "individual mandate," meant that there were a variety of grounds on which opponents could continue to challenge the law as it was implemented and also turn to the courts. And turning to the judicial branch to challenge the law is what opponents immediately did, as twenty-six states and various business interests came together to ask that the law be declared unconstitutional. These challenges came together in a case known as *National Federation of Independent Businesses (NFIB) v. Sebelius*. The primary focus throughout the case had been on the so-called "individual mandate," which required people to buy health insurance if they could afford it. This was designed to add an element of collectivism to the private insurance market by making sure that healthier people could not choose to opt out. In the end, that part of the ACA was ruled constitutional by the Court in the summer of 2012, if only by a 5–4 majority, crucially allowing the law to stand.

Less attention had been paid to the accompanying challenge to the manner in which the ACA effectively compelled states to expand their Medicaid programs to cover everyone with an income below 138 percent of the poverty line. Medicaid, as a program jointly administered and funded by the federal and state governments, had an array of different rules and eligibility criteria with variations from state to state such that no two states had the same regulations prior to the ACA. Moreover, very few states allowed able-bodied childless adults access to Medicaid, however poor they might be. In fact, despite the shorthand description of Medicaid as a program providing health insurance for poor Americans, fewer than half of the working non-aged poor population were covered by Medicaid in 2012.[5] The ACA proposed to introduce rules that would establish a new income floor of 138 percent of the federal poverty level for access to Medicaid for everyone regardless of their perceived "moral worthiness." This was to be put in place through a mix of financial carrots and sticks offered and waved by the federal government to the states. Firstly, the federal government would pay all the costs for new enrolees to the program as a result of the expansion for the opening three years and then 90 percent of costs afterwards, which was a much more generous rate of federal disbursement than for regular Medicaid. Secondly, any state that did not sign up for the expansion would lose all its existing Medicaid funding. The Supreme Court, however, found that this second aspect equated to unjustified financial pressure.[6] Hence the carrot remained, but the stick was gone and some Republican-run states made clear that they were allergic to carrots.[7]

Nevertheless, despite the setback over Medicaid and the refusal of Republican-controlled states to cooperate with other aspects of the ACA, the various measures that made up the ACA were gradually implemented over the remaining years of the Obama presidency.[8] By the time Obama left office the percentage of Americans who lacked health insurance coverage stood at 8.7, having been 15.5 percent in 2010.[9] Some of that decline was due to the improved economy, but much was a direct result of the efforts in the ACA to significantly reduce the numbers of uninsured. Furthermore, people with pre-existing conditions could no longer be denied insurance or offered only prohibitively expensive packages. It is important to understand that the newly insured not only benefited from their improved access to medical care but also, on an everyday basis, enjoyed the economic security of not being constantly haunted by the prospect of an unaffordable medical expense. In short, despite the fact that as Obama left office nineteen states had not joined the Medicaid expansion, the ACA was a legacy of deep real-world consequence.

The law also, however, left a legacy in political terms that was much less appealing to Obama and Democrats, as Republicans continued to agitate against "Obamacare" through to the end of Obama's time in office. As Obama signed the ACA, Senator Max Baucus of Montana, who as chair of the Senate Finance Committee had played a key role in steering the law through the Senate, told his Republican colleagues that it was time to move on and accept what had happened: "Now it is fact. Now it is law. Now it is history."[10] From the perspective of the Obama administration and the wider Democratic Party, that statement proved to be hopelessly optimistic. As noted above, legal challenges to the ACA started immediately it was signed and Republicans launched political attacks on "Obamacare" through the next four political cycles. These were not always successful, but brought real dividends in 2010, contributing to the GOP's success in federal- and state-level elections.[11] In fact, despite the evidence of a decline in the uninsured rate, the ACA remained underwater in public opinion throughout Obama's terms in office. The partisan differences in perception of the law were stark, but Independents sided with the "unfavorable" opinion column, particularly through 2013 and 2014 as central aspects of the law were rolled out.[12]

The clearest manifestations of Republican hostility to the ACA were repeated votes in the House to repeal all or significant parts of the law. These votes were symbolic inasmuch as they were never going to actually result in repeal while Obama remained in office,[13] but they did serve to stoke the conservative political base and maintain the impression that the ACA was somehow still illegitimate. And that was certainly the mantra of candidate Trump as he emerged into the political spotlight during the fall of 2015. In July 2015, in typically bombastic but unspecific terms, he said of the ACA: "It's gotta go. . . . Repeal and replace with something terrific."[14] In the final stages of the campaign he again attacked the ACA and promised that he would be the one to correct the problems with the country's health care system:

> Together we're going to deliver real change that once again puts Americans first. That begins with immediately repealing and replacing the disaster known as Obamacare. My first day in office, I'm going to ask Congress to put a bill on my desk getting rid of this disastrous law and replacing it with reforms that expand choice, freedom, affordability. You're going to have such great health care, at a tiny fraction of the cost—and it's going to be so easy.[15]

The early stages of his presidency saw similar brash promises and a neglect of the evidence. Speaking at the Conservative Political Action Conference in Washington, DC in February 2017, he declared that "Obamacare covers very few people,"[16] despite the fact that over 20 million people were covered by either the Medicaid expansion or the market insurance exchanges that provided subsidies for people with household incomes between 100 and

400 percent of the poverty level. A few weeks after taking office, President Trump met with senior executives from the health insurance industry, telling them that he would soon put forward a "fantastic plan" that would "be a great plan for the patients, for the people, and hopefully for the companies."[17] At almost the same time he insisted to a meeting of the country's governors, "We have come up with a solution that's really, really I think very good," before acknowledging "I have to tell you, it's an unbelievably complex subject. . . . Nobody knew health care could be so complicated."[18] Beyond the point that everyone involved in, or even simply an informed observer to, previous efforts at health care reform was very aware of how "complicated" a subject it was, it also turned out that the administration and congressional Republicans had not come up with "a solution." In fact, far from it, as Republican efforts to "repeal and replace" the ACA floundered in Congress over the summer of 2017.

The House did pass a bill, the American Health Care Act, which the President greeted by holding a celebration in the Rose Garden in the manner typically accompanying an actual signing ceremony.[19] That proper climax to the legislative process did not materialize, however, as the Senate could not manage to agree on its own version of reform despite multiple iterations of a bill being put to a vote. The GOP's 52–48 majority in the Senate did not suffice even though the votes were conducted through the reconciliation process, thus bypassing a filibuster and effectively needing only a 50–50 tie that would have allowed Vice President Pence to cast the decisive vote. In fact, the process not only bypassed a possible filibuster but also disregarded so-called "regular order," through which each prospective bill would have been subjected to lengthy committee hearings.

The closest vote was over a motion referred to as "skinny repeal." This bill made little effort to fulfill the "replace" part of the "repeal and replace" equation, but if passed it would have paved the way for a fuller bill to be constructed in a Conference Committee. Yet, even this proposal was defeated 51–49 in the Senate. Most of the focus after this vote was on Arizona Senator John McCain, who cast his vote, to gasps in the chamber, with a thumbs-down movement. This generated considerable conversation, especially given President Trump's antagonistic relationship with the GOP's

2008 presidential nominee, who had just been diagnosed with terminal cancer. That drama somewhat obscured the fact that the two most consistent opponents of their party's efforts in the Senate were Senators Lisa Murkowski of Alaska and Susan Collins of Maine, who were amongst the very diminished ranks that could properly be regarded as "moderate" within the GOP's Senate caucus.[20]

One problem for Republicans in trying to craft a legislative package was that the Congressional Budget Office consistently scored the emerging proposals as likely to add over 20 million to the ranks of uninsured.[21] They also struggled to find ways to keep in place the very popular aspects of the ACA, most notably the protection for Americans with pre-existing conditions, while dismantling the other parts of the law due to the manner in which the less well-liked aspects effectively sustained the popular elements. Furthermore, the concerted attacks on the ACA helped turn around its fortunes in terms of its public approval. The switch should not be exaggerated, but polls moved from showing consistent majorities expressing "disapproval" to consistent majorities offering "approval" of the ACA.[22]

Hence, by January 2019 it was clear that any chance of a legislative repeal of the ACA during President Trump's first mandate was gone. In this sense perhaps the most important domestic legacy of the Obama presidency was intact. Yet, the story was not quite that simple. The ACA remained the law of the land, but the Trump administration, primarily through a series of executive actions, undermined its effectiveness and also chipped away at some of the principles underlying the law. One legislative act came in December 2017 as part of the Tax Cut and Jobs Act (TCJA). The TCJA was mostly focused on cutting corporate and individual income taxes, but it also reduced the penalty that could be applied to people refusing to buy health insurance and thus running foul of the "individual mandate" to zero. This was widely described as a "repeal" of the mandate, though this was technically not the case.[23] This move did prompt President Trump to claim,

> The individual mandate is being repealed . . . that means Obamacare is repealed. Because they get their money from the individual mandate. . . . So in this bill . . . we have essentially repealed Obamacare

and will come up with something that will be much better, whether it's block grants or whether it's taking what we have and doing something terrific.[24]

In reality the TCJA did not repeal the ACA and there was no movement toward "something terrific," but the move did potentially undermine the stability of insurance markets. This was also a potential outcome of the administration's actions to make it easier for individuals to buy cheaper, less comprehensive, short-term insurance packages that did not contain the array of benefits mandated by the ACA. This type of change may sound innocuous, but in allowing people willing to gamble on their health status the chance to opt out of broader insurance packages, it potentially undercut the stability of the insurance risk pools covering less healthy individuals.[25]

Other moves potentially reduced the numbers of people signing up for insurance via the market insurance exchanges and allowed states to toughen access to the Medicaid expansion. In the former case, there was a downscaling of the outreach to encourage individuals to sign up for the marketplace insurance exchanges.[26] With regard to Medicaid, the Trump administration encouraged states to request waivers that would demand work requirements of Medicaid beneficiaries. This meant that states could apply a degree of conditionality to eligibility to the Medicaid expansion in a manner that the Obama administration had explicitly prevented. Nevertheless, despite these efforts the ACA did remain the law of the land through the opening years of the Trump presidency.

The Consumer Financial Protection Bureau

Had it not been for the political battle and policy controversies over health care, the arguments over financial reform through 2009 and 2010 would likely have attracted more notice than they did. When President Obama signed the Wall Street Reform and Consumer Protection Act, better known as Dodd-Frank after its chief congressional sponsors Senator Christopher Dodd of Connecticut and Representative Barney Frank from Massachusetts, he finalized the "most sweeping overhaul of financial regulations in the United States since the New Deal."[27] Reflecting its controversial nature, Dodd-Frank passed Congress very largely along partisan lines, although three Senate Republicans including the near nemesis of health care reform, Scott Brown, did support the act.

There were many aspects to the law, which included new regulation of banks and a range of other financial and corporate institutions. Through the legislative process the bill was watered down from its original intent,[28] but rather than covering all the bill's features we concentrate on the creation of a new, potentially powerful government agency that became known as the Consumer Financial Protection Bureau (CFPB). As he signed the Dodd-Frank bill Obama spoke of how the CFPB would help Americans who were vulnerable to misleading sales pitches from financial institutions:

> Now, for all those Americans who are wondering what Wall Street Reform means for you, here's what you can expect. If you've ever applied for a credit card, a student loan, or a mortgage, you know the feeling of signing your name to pages of barely understandable fine print.
>
> But what often happens as a result, is that many Americans are caught by hidden fees and penalties, or saddled with loans they can't afford.

Obama continued that these sharp practices would be checked with "protections . . . enforced by a new consumer watchdog with just one job: looking out for people."[29] The idea behind the CFPB could in fact be traced back to work done by Elizabeth Warren and her colleagues in the mid-2000s, when she was a professor at Harvard. Warren argued that people should have similar protections when buying financial products as they would when buying faulty homeware.[30] As manifested by the CFPB, this notion looked as if it was to be implemented in a robust fashion by an agency with considerable autonomy and a strong remit.

Three aspects of its institutional configuration reinforced the potential powers given to this new agency. Firstly, the CFPB was to be funded by the Federal Reserve. This was perhaps problematic given the Fed's sometime complicity in looking past dubious financial activities, but it did mean that the new agency was not dependent on congressional funding. Secondly, it was to be headed by a director who, once confirmed for a five-year term, was effectively only responsible to the president rather than to the legislative branch. Third, its rules were not subject to scrutiny by the Office of Information and Regulatory Affairs or the Office of Management and Budget.[31] These features drew fire from Republican opponents, who protested at the concentration of power in the hands of the director, comparing this unfavorably to the broader, board-like organization of existing financial regulatory bodies, the Securities Exchange Commission and the Federal Deposit Insurance Commission.[32] Hence, in protest, they successfully filibustered the nomination of Richard Cordray to the post of director. Cordray, a former Attorney General from Ohio, was Obama's pick after speculation that he might choose Warren to be the first head of the agency sparked controversy. The filibuster and what followed was indicative of the fraught relationship between the Obama White House and congressional Republicans and the ill will that could emerge on both sides.

When justifying the filibuster in December 2011 Senator Lindsay Graham likened the CFPB's powers to "something out of the Stalinist era" and protested the role of the director as "there's no oversight under this person; he gets a check from the Federal Reserve. We want him under the Congress so we can oversee the overseer."[33] In response, at the start of January 2012, Obama appointed Cordray to his post under the guise of it being a recess appointment, which could last for two years. This was particularly provocative to Republicans who had used technical measures, previously employed by Democrats to thwart George W. Bush from making recess appointments, to prevent the Senate falling into recess over the holiday period. House Speaker Boehner called Obama's action an "extraordinary and entirely unprecedented power grab."[34] In June 2014, these Republican complaints were backed up by the Supreme Court, which ruled in a unanimous verdict that Senate had not been in recess and the appointment was void.[35] By that point, however, the two sides had managed to come to a compromise. In an effort to prevent a stand-off over whether to end the filibuster for a range of presidential appointments it was agreed that Cordray would be subject to a straight up or down Senate confirmation vote. As it was, that stand-off over the filibuster for presidential nominations was postponed rather than cancelled, but Cordray was confirmed to take up the position of director of the CFPB in July 2013. Elizabeth Warren, by now a senator from Massachusetts, celebrated that her plan was firmly in place: "There is now no doubt that the American people will have a watchdog that's … holding financial institutions accountable when they break the rules."[36]

While the wider Dodd-Frank regulations did come under some criticism from liberals for not being aggressive enough in the regulation of the financial sector, the CFPB proved to be a robust and assertive new agency under Cordray's leadership throughout the remainder of the Obama presidency. It quickly established a reputation as an agency that interpreted its remit broadly and was prepared to exercise its powers. By the summer of 2014, *US News and World Report* offered the following summary of its early actions:

> Getting credit card companies to cough up more than $1.8 billion in refunds to consumers they had cheated. Directing mortgage lenders to limit charges and stop making loans that borrowers can't afford. Cracking down on "last dollar" scams that collect up-front fees from financially desperate people for help that is never actually delivered. Establishing a consumer complaint database to track financial market trends and help consumers get individual problems addressed.[37]

Under Cordray's leadership the CFPB returned nearly $12 billion to 29 million consumers found to have been exploited by unscrupulous financial organizations.[38] When Cordray announced his resignation in late 2017 a *Politico Magazine* profile of the CFPB described it as having "quietly established itself as the most powerful and consequential new federal agency since the Environmental Protection Agency opened its doors nearly half a century ago."[39] Hence the CFPB was a substantive legacy. It was a new executive branch agency, structured in a manner that empowered rather than constrained its leadership.

It turned out, however, that much depended on the ambition and nature of that leadership and Cordray's resignation proved a turning point. Republicans had never reconciled themselves to the CFPB's powers. In September 2014, then congressman Mick Mulvaney from South Carolina said in an interview with the Credit Union Times that the agency was "a wonderful example of how a bureaucracy will function if it has no accountability to anybody . . . It turns up being a joke, and that's what the CFPB really has been, in a sick, sad kind of way."[40] The party's 2016 platform described the CFPB as "the worst" part of Dodd-Frank and alleged that it was "deliberately designed to be a rogue agency." The platform continued, "Its Director has dictatorial powers unique in the American Republic."[41] Given this background, it was ominous for the continued effectiveness of the CFPB that the person who took over these "powers" from Cordray was Mick Mulvaney. Cordray did protest that his chief of staff, Leandra English, be acting director until a replacement was confirmed by the Senate, but President Trump nominated Mulvaney, then the director of the Office of Management and Budget, to that role and it was the President's wishes that prevailed.

Yet, the Trump administration did not move to abolish the CFPB, rather under Mulvaney its activities were significantly curtailed. One example of this came when the Bureau dropped an ongoing legal case known as *Golden Valley*. The biggest single source of the complaints that CFPB received were in fact about debt collectors, but some of its most high-profile work under Cordray had been its pursuit of payday loan companies. Golden Valley, along with three other lenders, claimed to be incorporated on an Indian reservation in California, even though their operations were run online with a base in a call center in Kansas. The claim to be based on a reservation was important as it meant the company was not bound by state rules, allowing Golden Valley to charge extremely high interest rates that were banned in some states. The case, which was opened in spring 2017 after many months of investigation, was dropped with minimal explanation shortly after Mulvaney took over running the CFPB.[42] A study by the *Washington Post* found that in the year after Mulvaney assumed control of the agency: "Publicly announced enforcement actions by the bureau have dropped about 75 percent from average in recent years, while consumer complaints have risen to new highs."[43]

As he staffed the senior positions of the CFPB with appointees whose previous experience was in working and advocating for the financial sector, Mulvaney explained the changed philosophy from the Obama–Cordray regime in an email to the agency's staff: "We don't just work for the government, we work for the people. . . . And that means everyone: those who use credit cards, and those who provide those cards; those who take loans, and those who make them."[44] Mulvaney's argument was that the CFPB had over-reached its authority under Cordray and it was the case that courts had blocked some of the bureau's investigations. Cordray himself explained that he encouraged a mentality amongst the agency's staff that they should push the boundaries of their authority: "I've never had any qualms about telling our people, if we have a case involving things people really shouldn't have been doing, bring the case, right the wrong, and if a judge tells us we can't, fine."[45] In another message to the Bureau's staff Mulvaney made clear that this strategy was no longer going to prevail: "I intend to execute the statutory mandate of the bureau to protect consumers. . . . But we will no longer go beyond that mandate."[46] The approach taken under Mulvaney did see some open rebellion from CFPB staff who had worked under the Cordray regime. Most notably, Seth Frotman, the student loan ombudsman, resigned from his post. His resignation letter maintained that the CFPB had "abandoned its duty to fairly and robustly enforce the law." Moreover, he explicitly condemned Mulvaney's role in diminishing the agency: "Unfortunately, under your leadership, the Bureau has abandoned the very consumers it is tasked by Congress with protecting," it read. "Instead, you have used the Bureau to serve the wishes of the most powerful financial companies in America."[47]

In December 2018 Kathy Kraninger, who had worked under Mulvaney at the OMB, was confirmed by the Senate, over the protests of Democrats and consumder advocacy organizations, in a 50–49 vote to take over the role of CFPB director.[48] In her first public speech in her new role Kraninger indicated that she would be following Mulvaney's model of governance as director rather than Cordray's. She emphasized that the CFPB should not be judged according to its enforcement actions: "All too often, agencies tend to judge themselves on their outputs. For example, how many complaints did they handle, how many cases did they bring, how much money did they recover?" Rather, she reflected, it was better to encourage a culture of good behavior amongst financial institutions before the event than to challenge them afterwards for poor behavior.[49] Critics, however, might note that there was little previous evidence of such a culture of self-improvement emerging amongst those financial institutions accused of exploiting the needs of economically vulnerable households.[50]

Overall, therefore, the story of the creation and institutional growth of the CFBP as what we have labeled as "hard legacy" during the Obama presidency and the subsequent effort to roll it back during the Trump era is an important and interesting one. When Obama left office, the CFBP was an agency with both a bark and a bite. By the time that Mick Mulvaney moved on to become President Trump's chief of staff after a year as director of the agency, its voice was quiet and its fang teeth blunted. Yet, this was done through an administrative putsch rather than a legislative reversal of Dodd-Frank. So while Mulvaney and Kraninger diminished the mission of the CFBP as compared to that envisioned by Cordray and Warren, the agency will continue to operate. In this context this Obama legacy might be temporarily rather than permanently moribund, with a future change in leadership possibly reinvigorating its appetite for chasing financial rodents. Ironically, however, a future Democrat administration and Congress may come to regret the safeguards put in place to protect the director's position should a Trump appointee remain in place, as Kraninger is scheduled to do until the end of 2023.

LGBT+ rights

The evolution of gay rights in the US is one of many strands of the nation's wider civil rights struggle. If certain periods are defined by particular moments of social progress, as the 1960s were by African American and women's rights, then the second decade of the twenty-first century was the time when LGBT+ rights flourished, even if that was not apparent in the opening decade of the millennium. Throughout the Bush presidency, the conventional wisdom held that the issue of same-sex marriage in particular was a wedge issue that played to the political benefit of the GOP. Two data points were deemed to provide illustration of this. Firstly, Republicans were largely united in their opposition to same-sex marriage, while the Democratic Party was deeply divided over the issue. Secondly, polls showed majorities of the public opposed to same-sex marriage. In 2004, polling by the Pew Research Center found Americans expressing disapproval of same-sex marriage by very nearly a two to one margin.[51]

Moreover, the notion that same-sex marriage was a winning issue for Republicans was strongly reinforced by the events of the 2004 presidential election cycle. Conservative activists had managed to place initiatives or referendum questions, which effectively banned same-sex marriage, on the ballot in eleven states to be decided on the same day as the presidential election. In all those states the measures were passed and much breathless reporting in the days after the election suggested that the issue had boosted conservative turnout, helping push Bush over the winning line. The Democrat candidate, Massachusetts senator John Kerry, had not explicitly supported same-sex marriage but he had been one of only fourteen senators to vote against the Defense of Marriage Act (DOMA) in 1996. In the immediate aftermath of the election former President Bill Clinton, who had signed DOMA in an election year despite reservations about doing so, claimed, "the gay-marriage issue . . . was an overwhelming factor in the defeat of John Kerry."[52] Later analysis questioned just how important gay marriage really had been in terms of influencing votes in the presidential election, but the results of the ballots certainly suggested that promoting same-sex marriage was not a politically winning path.[53]

Yet, by the end of the Obama presidency, that conventional wisdom had been turned on its head as same-sex marriage had become a constitutional right across the whole country with opinion polls showing majority support for that right. In 2015, reflecting a dramatic shift from only ten years earlier, Pew reported support for same-sex marriage at 55 percent, compared to 39 percent of the population who remained opposed.[54] In this context, it is perhaps difficult to discern whether Obama should be credited with being a leader of events or more a follower. The most decisive move came via the Supreme Court in 2015 in the case of *Obergefell v. Hodges*, rather than through legislation or executive action, but by that point the President had "evolved" to a position of explicit public support for same-sex marriage. Moreover, the administration had pushed for legislative action to repeal the notorious "Don't Ask, Don't Tell" policy with regard to gays serving in the US military, which had been a completely unsatisfactory legacy of the Clinton administration. In addition, the administration did push for an extension of rights for transgender individuals.

Initially, there was little evidence to suggest how dramatically opinions and practice were to change under Obama. During the 2008 campaign, the BarackObama.com website did not make explicit reference to supporting gay rights, apart from reference to the Employment Non-Discrimination Act and the expansion of some hate crime statutes. Whilst these were commendable aims from a progressive perspective in themselves, the website did not mention the word "gay."[55] A June 2008 CNN/Opinion Research Corporation poll taken on issue importance for voters put gay and lesbian issues at the bottom of the fifteen-item list. Only 36 percent of those polled considered this topic to be extremely or very important. This sat in contrast to, for example, the importance of health care or education, which 83 percent of those polled considered extremely or very important.[56] Of those who cited gay rights as an issue of importance for them, a majority were McCain supporters. In other words, voters who were more likely opposed to the prospect of gay marriage tended to prioritize it more highly as a voting item than those who were in favor of it.[57]

Doubtless, Barack Obama had to balance his own views, hopes and desires for social change with the demographic and political realities that he faced. In the 2008 election, of the 4 percent of voters who identified (in exit polls) as gay, 70 percent voted for the Democrat candidate.[58] Hence, there was a balance to be struck between having some appeal to moderately conservative voters on the broader question of same-sex rights (for example, those who were supportive of gay rights in terms of issues such as employment or social discrimination, but not ready to embrace same-sex marriage) while retaining the loyalty of this usually reliable, but relatively small, Democratic constituency. Interestingly, the Roper Center notes that Obama received less of the gay vote in 2008 than the 77 percent that John Kerry had in 2004, though the lower profile of the issue of same-sex marriage in the latter election may help explain this difference.[59]

Obama's track record on publicly supporting gay marriage itself is somewhat patchy, the result, in part at least, of trying to toe the line on pushing for progress without moving too far ahead of the average Democrat voter. In 2008, 20 percent of those who self-identified as conservative in exit polls voted for Obama. This was a 4 percent increase on Kerry in 2004 and so there was something of a balancing act needed to keep this wider constituency on board. Even as late as spring 2008, Obama was publicly drawing a distinction between his support for civil partnerships and federal rights for LGBT+ individuals. Both Obama and Biden made it clear on the campaign trail the first time around that support for gay marriage was not on their to-do list.[60] This wasn't particularly surprising, as both men spoke publicly about their Christian faith and were up against a popular religious Republican opponent and his out-and-proud Evangelical running mate. At this time, only a small proportion of states had gay marriage legislation in place and it was just a few years since *Lawrence v. Texas* (2003) had struck down the same-sex sodomy law in Texas and elsewhere as unconstitutional.[61]

Yet, during his first term President Obama did edge toward a more supportive stance over same-sex marriage and his administration took a number of steps to promote same-sex rights more broadly. There were a number of key moments, particularly in 2010–11, when the President spoke publicly about the evolution of his own reflections on gay marriage. He declared that it was "something that I think a lot about."[62] Then in May 2012, only six months before the 2012 election, he said in interview, "I've just concluded that—for me personally, it is important for me to go ahead and affirm that—I think same-sex couples should be able to get married."[63] At that particular point Obama's hand had been somewhat forced by the manner in which Vice President Biden had publicly stated his support for gay marriage on an episode of *Meet the Press*. After Biden's announcement there was little chance for Obama to continue to obfuscate, though there was reporting that some White House aides were frustrated that Biden had so unequivocally pushed the matter to the top of the news agenda. For his part, Obama commented that Biden's actions had led him to fast-forward his own public statement, but that it did reflect his changed view. He added that the election-year timing was hardly opportunistic, since it would "be hard to argue that somehow this is something that I'd be doing for political advantage. Because frankly, you know, the politics—it's not clear how they cut."[64]

If his "evolution" on gay marriage specifically had been somewhat delayed, and perhaps conveniently timed to coincide with shifts in public opinion, during his second term President Obama did take a more decisive leadership role on LGBT+ issues. More broadly, the legacy of his time in office on LGBT+ rights can quite literally be described as monumental. Even in its first term the administration pushed through a series of important initiatives. Most visibly it had revisited the legacy of the last Democrat in the White House. Firstly, Clinton's pledge to allow gay and lesbian individuals to serve openly in the US military was finally fulfilled as "Don't Ask, Don't Tell" was repealed via legislation in the lame duck session of Congress in December 2010. This was passed largely on a party line vote, but with a handful of Republican votes giving it an appearance of bipartisanship.[65] Secondly, the Obama administration argued that the 1996 DOMA, signed by President Clinton after passage by hefty majorities in both chambers of Congress, violated the equal protection clause of the 14th Amendment and, in February 2011, Attorney General Eric Holder announced that the Justice Department would no longer uphold the constitutionality of Section 3 in the *Windsor* case. This decision should be understood not just in terms of its political ramifications, but also its legal ones. The failure of the executive to defend a statute passed by Congress in the courts was not unprecedented, but it was highly unusual.[66] Subsequently, in the landmark *US v. Windsor* (2013) case, the Supreme Court reached a 5–4 decision that section 3 of DOMA was unconstitutional under the due process clause of the Fifth Amendment.[67]

Prior to those actions, in October 2009 Obama had signed the Matthew Shepard and James Byrd Jr. Hate Crimes Prevention Act into law. This bill, which made crimes motivated by animus toward people according to their gender, gender identity, sexual orientation or disability a federal hate crime, had been stymied in Congress a number of times during the Bush years, with the Bush administration threatening a potential veto should it reach his desk. In contrast, Obama and his attorney general, Eric Holder, made clear their desire to see the bill become law. Further, Section 1557 of the ACA prohibited any health provider or health plan or related entity that was in receipt of federal funding from discriminating on the basis of race, age, national origin, disability or gender. The administration was clear that gender included protections against discrimination on the basis of an individual's gender identity or on the basis of sexual stereotypes. This was codified by a final rule in 2016 that protected gay, lesbian and transgender individuals from discrimination in health insurance and care and did not offer a religious exemption.[68] In 2012 the Department of Housing and Urban Development (HUD) issued the Equal Access Rule, forbidding discrimination on the grounds of sexual orientation or gender identity across HUD's housing programs. In 2016 this was amended to clarify that the rule applied to multi-occupancy emergency shelters with shared living space.[69]

Continuing this pattern of incrementally extending LGBT+ rights through executive action, in July 2014 President Obama issued Executive Order 13672, which implemented safeguards to ensure that federal contractors have guarantees against discrimination on the basis of their sexual orientation or gender identity. Here Obama built on and extended the actions of his predecessors, specifically President Johnson's 1965 Order 11246, which punished discrimination on the basis of race, color, religion, sex or national origin.[70] It also chimed with later Order 11478 from Richard Nixon in 1969, which added disability and age, and Bill Clinton's 1998 Order 13087, which included sexual orientation.[71] Unsurprisingly, a request was made to the President from 160 faith group representatives who asked for religious organizations to be exempt from the EO provision.[72] In June 2016 Obama designated the creation of the Stonewall National Monument to gay rights, the first of its kind in the country.[73]

As noted, however, the most dramatic expansion of same-sex rights came as a result of judicial action in the summer of 2015 when the Supreme Court, by a 5–4 majority, effectively ruled that there was a constitutional right to gay marriage. Clearly, therefore, this cannot be seen as a legacy reflecting the use of presidential power, beyond the fact that Obama's two nominees to the court were part of that majority opinion, but the administration had filed a supportive amicus brief in the case, just as had been the case in 2013 when it had supported the move to roll back California's Proposition 8.[74] In welcoming the Court's decision, Obama explicitly linked this "victory for America" to the various moves that the administration had previously made to expand same-sex rights:

> This decision affirms what millions of Americans already believe in their hearts: When all Americans are treated as equal we are all more free.
>
> My administration has been guided by that idea. It's why we stopped defending the so-called Defense of Marriage Act, and why we were pleased when the Court finally struck down a central provision of that discriminatory law. It's why we ended "Don't Ask, Don't Tell." From extending full marital benefits to federal employees and their spouses, to expanding hospital visitation rights for LGBT patients and their loved ones, we've made real progress in advancing equality for LGBT Americans in ways that were unimaginable not too long ago.[75]

In October 2015, in response to *Obergefell v. Hodges*, the Treasury Department moved to ensure that same-sex spouses would be treated the same by law for tax purposes.[76] In addition, the Social Security Administration took steps to bring entitlement for same-sex spouses into line with those for heterosexual marriages. This included health benefits.[77]

It is clear that the prioritization of LGBT+ rights grew exponentially during the Obama years, and not only via the message emanating from the White House. Like many other "culture wars" issues it gained traction over time, and change came via legislative, judicial and executive avenues. In addition, the issue demonstrated how civil rights progress can come from below, at a local and state level, and influence the federal agenda.[78]

President Trump on LGBT+ issues

Early on the 2016 campaign trail, anyone trying to second-guess the approach candidate Trump would take toward LGBT+ issues would have drawn a blank. Historically, the New York billionaire did not present as a social conservative. No bastion of progressive thinking in his business and entertainment life, nonetheless comments that he made over time as a private individual were captured that suggested that he was, at least, not on the same page as his more religious GOP rivals. In a 2016 campaign documentary, *The Choice*, creator Michael Kirk argued that in his pre-political life Trump had divided the world into "winners and losers," based on their capacity to perform and succeed. Their sexual orientation, in Kirk's view, was irrelevant to him.[79] When running against deeply conservative Republican opponents in the primaries, candidate Trump appeared at the very least neutral on issues pertaining to gay rights. The *New York Times* reminded readers that not only was Mar-a-Lago the first private club in the US to admit openly gay members, but the president of the pro-gay-rights Log Cabin Republicans stated that Trump would be "the most gay-friendly Republican nominee for president ever."[80] That was a low bar, but the daylight on this issue between the former reality television star and, for example, Ted Cruz or Rick Santorum, was clear.

Asked in 2011 about his thoughts on gay marriage, Trump responded that his opinion on the matter "was not fully formed."[81] This was clearly not in line with the traditional GOP position, which states that marriage should be between one man and one woman.[82] Nor did he line up with his fellow GOP candidates for the 2016 nomination. Ted Cruz, for example, spoke repeatedly about his opposition to gay marriage and his desire to respond to the Supreme Court ruling on the matter with a constitutional amendment.[83]

Trump may not have overtly supported marriage equality but repeatedly stated that in his opinion, the matter was "already settled." As president-elect, he told *NBC News*, "I'm fine with that."[84] However, gay rights campaigners were more concerned about the position of Vice President Pence. Whilst gay marriage itself may not have been directly under threat, individual states, including Pence's Indiana, implemented religious freedom bills. Barney Frank and others feared that such legislation could be used to undermine LGBT+ rights. In the case of Indiana, the 2015 Religious Freedom Restoration Act signed by Pence was met, predictably, with conservative evangelical support and liberal protest.[85] The latter included high-profile organizations and individuals such as the (Republican) mayor of Indianapolis and Apple CEO Tim Cook. One week later, a subsequent RFRA bill was signed, with the intention of offering protection to LGBT+ citizens.[86] Pence's Christian Evangelical supporters were deeply unimpressed at the move, with one conservative radio host declaring that "it was the worst we've ever been stabbed in the back by a Republican."[87]

On the campaign trails, the hot-button issue of public bathroom use became, momentarily at least, as much of a yardstick of voter political affiliation as abortion rights. In April 2016, Trump caused surprise by stating in an NBC interview that students should use the bathroom they felt most comfortable with, including those using the facilities at Trump Tower.[88] Again, this was far from the GOP party line, and in direct contradiction to the ruling in North Carolina on the matter by a Republican governor.[89] It was clear that Trump's area of passion and interest were far removed from issues around gender and toilets. It is reasonable to assume that he did not care. Trump's attitude was grist for the in-party opposition mill, with Ted Cruz accusing him of embracing political correctness and sounding like Obama and Clinton.[90] Even the *New York Times* was producing articles on Trump as the could-be-worse candidate on gay rights.[91] Notably, in his acceptance speech at the GOP convention, Trump explicitly spoke of the terrorist attack at a nightclub in Orlando a few weeks earlier as an attack on the LGBT+ community and insisted that he would do all he could to protect "our LGBTQ citizens" from similar violence. When the convention crowd applauded he added, if somewhat incongruously given the subject matter,

"I have to say as a Republican it is so nice to hear you cheering for what I just said."[92]

Nevertheless, on election day in 2016, as was the case in 2004, 77 percent of the gay vote went to the Democrat candidate. On taking office, Trump did not immediately change his agenda or rhetoric on LGBT+ issues, yet he won with a majority of the Protestant and Catholic vote (56 percent and 50 percent respectively) and his appeal to more conservative religious voters was doubtless strengthened by the overt religiosity of his vice president.[93]

As it is, the Obama-era legacy on same-sex rights has largely been maintained, at least in law if not in its progressive spirit. Counter-factual speculation has limited value, but a President Ted Cruz might have been more explicit in supporting efforts to find ways around the *Obergefell* decision. The administration did, however, side with Colorado baker Jack Phillips, who had refused to bake a same-sex couple a wedding cake. The Colorado Civil Rights Commission had found against Phillips, but the Supreme Court ruled in his favor. White House Press Secretary Sarah Sanders announced that the administration was "pleased" with the decision after Solicitor General Neal Francisco had argued on Phillips' behalf before the Court.[94] Importantly, however, the Court in fact issued a limited ruling based on the actions of Colorado officials that created only limited precedent for future similar confrontations.

The Obama legacy with regard to transgender rights came under more direct attack from the Trump administration. In February 2017, the Justice Department dropped its support for Obama-era protection of transgender students. The ruling had been instigated during the Obama years in an effort to prevent bullying of transgender children. In May 2016, the Departments of Justice and Education moved to allow students to use bathrooms that corresponded with their gender identity. Officials in twelve states had vowed to sue the Obama administration in relation to the bathroom issue. A federal judge in Texas ruled to initiate a nationwide injunction on the Obama initiative. The day that Jeff Sessions was sworn in, the Justice Department withdrew its Obama-era appeal, so as it could "best decide" how to proceed with the lawsuit. A few weeks later, the

Trump administration withdrew the guidelines entirely. This is not a wholesale reversal of Obama's policy, but clearly a departure from the path and intention of his predecessor.[95] President Trump signed an executive action re bathrooms and stated that in his opinion, the bathroom issue, like many others, "should be decided at state level." The move met with predictable responses from progressives and conservatives. The issue directly affected approximately 0.6 percent of the population.[96] Despite its narrow reach, it had exponential political significance. LGBT+ advocates saw the order as a threat to civil rights, whilst conservatives applauded it as a move away from what they perceived as Barack Obama's radical social agenda.

In other moves, mostly below the public radar, the administration sought to reverse protections for the most vulnerable transgender individuals put in place by the Obama administration. For example, in spring of 2019, HUD Secretary Ben Carson proposed a rule that would undo some of the intent of the 2012 Equal Access Rule. The proposed change would allow homeless shelters to turn individuals away on religious grounds and to force transgender women to sleep in male quarters.[97] Similarly, in May 2019, HHS proposed a rule to diminish the protections for transgender people under Section 1557 of the ACA. Arguing that the Obama-era rule imposed unnecessary regulatory costs, Trump's HHS sought to water down language prohibiting discrimination on the grounds of gender identity.[98]

Conclusion

In this chapter we have looked at what might be thought of as some of the most embedded aspects of the Obama legacy. This does not refer so much to the amount of time they had been in place—by definition they were all recent in a historical context—as to the means by which they had been put in place. The ACA and CFPB were the result of legislative action and built on existing institutions or established new ones to implement their intent and by 2017, despite many frustrations in the case of the ACA, the consequences of those intentions were evident in both cases. Yet, as Patashnik and Zelizer note, new reforms remain at risk in the early stages of their development—especially if they were legislated in a highly partisan fashion as were both the ACA and the Dodd-Frank financial reform, which incorporated the creation of the CFPB.[99]

Hence, ACA advocates had reason to be fearful when President Trump entered office accompanied by Republican majorities in Congress. Furthermore, even without a filibuster-proof majority in the Senate, Republicans could use the "reconciliation" process to bring about the end of the ACA. As events unfolded, however, it turned out that the complexity of the ACA, which had made so many of its benefits opaque even to beneficiaries, helped save the law. The White House and congressional Republican efforts to repeal the law were stymied as the law proved impossible to pull apart without leaving some very clear losers in the process. Hence the ACA did remain a substantive legacy of the Obama era in a manner that its advocates must have feared would not be the case in January 2017, even as the politics and policy surrounding the law remained contested. The continuing conflict was illustrated by ongoing legal actions in mid-2019. One case, *Texas v. Azar*, supported by eighteen state attorneys general and the Trump administration, would effectively declare the ACA to be unconstitutional because of the way the 2017 TCJA had reduced the penalty for failing to comply with the individual mandate to $0. Though initially regarded as a weak legal argument, this challenge to the ACA gained momentum after a ruling in its favor by a district court judge allowed it to move further up the judicial system.[100] In other cases, ACA advocates themselves turned to the courts to challenge the legitimacy of waivers granted by the Trump administration that allowed states to apply work requirements to the Medicaid expansion.[101]

The CFPB also remained alive, but compared to the aggressive and interventionist agency that had evolved under the leadership of Richard Cordray, by the end of 2018 it had a more zombie-like existence. In his analysis of Mick Mulvaney's reign at the CFPB, *New York Times* journalist Nick Confessore wrote:

> Mulvaney's careful campaign of deconstruction offers a case study in the Trump administration's approach to transforming

Washington, one in which strategic neglect and bureaucratic self-sabotage create versions of agencies that seem to run contrary to their basic premises.[102]

In this context, a future Democratic administration might revivify the CFPB and give life to its fangs. Thus this is not a legacy lost but one placed on hold, its future fate to be decided.

The Trump administration did not directly try to roll back the major expansion of same-sex rights extended by the Supreme Court in summer of 2015, but it clearly reversed the direction of travel with regard to LGBT+ rights more widely. The manner in which the Trump White House had come to rely on the evangelical wing of the conservative movement and the manner in which that appreciation was reciprocated was illustrated as early as May 2017 when Johnnie Moore, former vice president of private evangelical Liberty University, tweeted: "evangelicals feel right at home in the @White House." This came after Trump had signed the Religious Liberty Executive Order.[103] It begins by mapping out the constitutional legitimacy for the order, and some detail (in six sections) of how and why it will occur. There are two key aspects to the Order: It instructs the Internal Revenue Service to "not take any adverse action against any individual, house of worship, or other religious organization" that endorses or opposes candidates from the pulpit. Prior to the Order, churches were forbidden from directly supporting or opposing a political candidate, and doing so would threaten their tax-exempt status. In addition, it instructs the Departments of Treasury, Labor, and Health and Human Services to consider amending regulations in the Affordable Care Act that require most employers to cover contraception in employee insurance plans.[104] On the day of the signing, Trump declared, "We are giving churches their voices back."[105]

Notes

1. Sheryl Gay Stolberg and Robert Pear, "Obama Signs Health Care Overhaul Bill, with a Flourish," *The New York Times*, March 23, 2010, <https://www.nytimes.com/2010/03/24/health/policy/24health.html> (last accessed December 12, 2019).

2. Ezekial Emmanuel, *Reinventing Health Care: How the Affordable Care Act will Improve Our Terribly Complex, Blatantly Unjust, Outrageously Expensive, Grossly Ineffective, Error-Prone System* (New York: Public Affairs, 2014.)
3. Lawrence Jacobs and Theda Skocpol, "Hard Fought Legacy: Obama, Congressional Democrats and the Struggle for Comprehensive Health Care Reform," in Theda Skocpol and Lawrence Jacobs (eds.), *Reaching for a New Deal: Ambitious Governance, Economic Meltdown, and Polarized Politics in Obama's First Two Years* (New York: Russell Sage Foundation, 2011), 53–104, at 74.
4. For a fuller narrative of how the ACA became law, see: Tom Daschle with David Nather, *Getting It Done: How Obama and Congress Finally Broke the Stalemate to Make Way for Health Care Reform* (New York: Thomas Dunne Books, 2010); Lawrence Jacobs and Theda Skocpol, *Health Care Reform and American Politics: What Everyone Needs to Know* (New York: Oxford University Press, 2010); Washington Post Staff, *Landmark: The Inside Story of America's Health Care Law and What it Means for All of US* (New York: Public Affairs, 2010).
5. *Medicaid: A Primer*, Kaiser Commission on Medicaid and the Uninsured, March 2013, <https://www.kff.org/medicaid/issue-brief/medicaid-a-primer/> (last accessed July 14, 2019).
6. Alex Waddan, "Health Care Reform after the Supreme Court: Even More Known Unknowns," *Health, Economics, Politics and Law*, 8.1 (2013): 139–43.
7. Lawrence Jacobs and Timothy Callaghan, "Why States Expand Medicaid: Party, Resource, and History," *Journal of Politics, Policy and Law*, 38.5 (2013).
8. Daniel Beland, Phil Rocco, and Alex Waddan, *Obamacare Wars: Federalism, State Politics and the Affordable Care Act* (Lawrence: University Press of Kansas, 2016).
9. *Health Insurance Coverage in the United States, 2017*, United States Census Bureau, Report No. 60-264, <https://www.census.gov/library/publications/2018/demo/p60-264.html> (last accessed December 12, 2019).
10. Stolberg and Pear, "Obama Signs Health Care Overhaul Bill, with a Flourish."
11. Robert Saldin, "Healthcare Reform: A Prescription for the 2010 Republican Landslide," *Forum* 8.4 (2010).

12. *KFF Tracking Poll: The Public's Views on the ACA*, Kaiser Family Foundation, 2019, <https://www.kff.org/interactive/kff-health-tracking-poll-the-publics-views-on-the-aca/> (last accessed December 12, 2019).
13. Gardiner Harris, "Obama Vetoes Bill to Repeal Health Law and End Planned Parenthood Funding," *The New York Times*, January 8, 2016, <https://www.nytimes.com/2016/01/09/us/politics/obama-vetoes-bill-to-repeal-health-law-and-end-planned-parenthood-funding.html> (last accessed December 12, 2019).
14. Sarah Ferris, "Trump: 'I'll replace Obamacare with something terrific,'" *The Hill*, July 29, 2015, <http://thehill.com/policy/healthcare/249697-trump-replace-obamacare-with-something-terrific> (last accessed December 12, 2019).
15. "How the Obamacare Lie is an Opportunity for Trump; Trump Family Talks Importance of Millennial Vote," transcript of *Hannity*, Fox News, October 25, 2016, <http://www.foxnews.com/transcript/2016/10/25/how-obamacare-lie-is-opportunity-for-trump-trump-family-talks-importance.html> (last accessed December 12, 2019).
16. Alicia A. Caldwell and Ricardo Alonso-Zaldivar, "Fact Check: Obamacare Covers More than 20 Million People, Not 'Very Few,'" February 24, 2017, <https://www.bostonglobe.com/news/nation/2017/02/24/fact-check-obamacare-covers-more-than-million-people-not-very-few/htGxOsLeOOaWGuOGMNUvCO/story.html> (last accessed December 12, 2019).
17. Tami Luhby, "Trump Promises Health Insurance Ceos Will Like His 'Fantastic Plan' For Obamacare," *CNN Money*, February 27, 2017, <http://money.cnn.com/2017/02/26/news/economy/health-insurers-trump-obamacare/index.html> (last accessed December 12, 2019).
18. Kevin Liptak, "Trump: 'Nobody knew health care could be so complicated,'" *CNN*, February 28, 2017 <https://edition.cnn.com/2017/02/27/politics/trump-health-care-complicated/index.html> (last accessed December 12, 2019).
19. Ed O'Keefe, Paige Winfield Cunningham, and Amy Goldstein, "House Republicans Claim a Major Victory with Passage of Health-Care Overhaul," *The Washington Post*, May 4, 2017, <https://www.washingtonpost.com/powerpost/republicans-plan-health-care-vote-on-thursday-capping-weeks-of-fits-and-starts/2017/05/03/e7dd7c28-306d-11e7-9dec-764dc781686f_story.html> (last accessed December 12, 2019).

20. Tom McCarthy, "Susan Collins and Lisa Murkowski: The GOP Senate Duo Keeping Trump in Check," *The Guardian*, July 27, 2017, <https://www.theguardian.com/us-news/2017/jul/27/susan-collins-lisa-murkowski-senate-republicans-healthcare> (last accessed December 12, 2019); Robert Pear, Thomas Kaplan, and Emily Cochrane, "Health Care Debate: Obamacare Repeal Fails as McCain Casts Decisive No Vote," *The New York Times*, July 27, 2017, <https://www.nytimes.com/2017/07/27/us/politics/senate-health-care-vote.html> (last accessed December 12, 2019).
21. Thomas Kaplan and Robert Pear, "Senate Health Bill in Peril as C.B.O. Predicts 22 Million More Uninsured," *The New York Times*, June 26, 2017, <https://www.nytimes.com/2017/06/26/us/politics/senate-health-care-bill-republican.html> (last accessed December 12, 2019).
22. *KFF Tracking Poll*.
23. Timothy Jost, "The Tax Bill and the Individual Mandate: What Happened, and What Does It Mean?" *Health Affairs* blog, December 20, 2017, <https://www.healthaffairs.org/do/10.1377/hblog20171220.323429/full/> (last accessed December 12, 2019).
24. Byron Wolf, "Donald Trump Thinks He Just Quietly Repealed Obamacare," *CNN*, December 21, 2017, <https://edition.cnn.com/2017/12/20/politics/donald-trump-thinks-he-tricked-everyone-into-repealing-obamacare/index.html> (last accessed December 12, 2019).
25. Katie Keith, "Final Rule Rapidly Eases Restrictions On Non-ACA-Compliant Association Health Plans," *Health Affairs* blog, June 21, 2018, <https://www.healthaffairs.org/do/10.1377/hblog20180621.671483/full/> (last accessed December 12, 2019).
26. Shannor Seervai, "Cuts to the ACA's Outreach Budget Will Make It Harder for People to Enroll," *The Commonwealth Fund*, October 11, 2017, <http://www.commonwealthfund.org/publications/features/2017/slashing-aca-funding> (last accessed December 12, 2019).
27. Daniel Carpenter, "The Contest of Lobbies and Disciplines: Financial Politics and Regulatory Reform," in Skocpol and Jacobs, *Reaching for a New Deal*, 139–88, at 139.
28. Lawrence Jacobs and Desmond King, *Fed Power: How Finance Wins* (New York: Oxford University Press, 2016).
29. Barack Obama, "President Obama signs Wall Street Reform: 'No Easy Task,'" The White House, July 21, 2010, <https://obamawhitehouse.

archives.gov/blog/2010/07/21/president-obama-signs-wall-street-reform-no-easy-task> (last accessed December 12, 2019).
30. Elizabeth Warren, "Unsafe at Any Rate," *Democracy: A Journal of Ideas*, Summer 2007, No.5, <https://democracyjournal.org/magazine/5/unsafe-at-any-rate/> (last accessed December 12, 2019).
31. Carpenter, "The Contest of Lobbies and Disciplines," 169.
32. Richard Shelby, "The Danger of an Unaccountable 'Consumer Protection' Czar," *Wall Street Journal*, July 21, 2011, <https://www.wsj.com/articles/SB10001424053111903554904576457931310 81446> (last accessed December 12, 2019).
33. Robin Bravender, "Graham Calls CFPB 'Stalinist,'" *Politico*, December 11, 2011, <https://www.politico.com/story/2011/12/graham-calls-cfpb-stalinist-070269> (last accessed December 12, 2019).
34. Helen Cooper and Jennifer Steinhauer, "Bucking Senate, Obama Appoints Consumer Chief," *The New York Times*, January 5, 2012, A1.
35. *National Labor Relations Board v. Noel Canning, SCOTUSblog*, 2014, <https://www.scotusblog.com/case-files/cases/national-labor-relations-board-v-noel-canning/> (last accessed December 12, 2019).
36. Danielle Douglas, "Senate Confirms Cordray to head Consumer Financial Protection Bureau," *The Washington Post*, July 16, 2013, <https://www.washingtonpost.com/business/economy/senate-confirms-consumer-watchdog-nominee-richard-cordray/2013/07/16/965d82c2-ee2b-11e2-a1f9-ea873b7e0424_story.html> (last accessed December 12, 2019).
37. Rebecca Thiess, "Paying Off for Consumers: How the Consumer Financial Protection Bureau is Getting the Job Done," *US News and World Report*, July 24, 2014, <https://www.usnews.com/opinion/economic-intelligence/2014/07/24/four-years-after-dodd-frank-the-cfpb-is-paying-off> (last accessed December 12, 2019).
38. Sarah O'Brien, "The Consumer Financial Protection Bureau Has Been Under Siege For Years. Here's Why," CNBC, November 27, 2017, <https://www.cnbc.com/2017/11/27/the-consumer-protection-financial-bureau-has-been-under-siege-for-years-heres-why.html> (last accessed December 12, 2019).
39. Michael Grunwald, "Trump Wants to Dismantle Elizabeth Warren's Agency: Good Luck With That," *Politico Magazine*, December 3, 2017, <https://www.politico.com/magazine/story/2017/12/03/trump-cfpb-elizabeth-warren-215997> (last accessed December 12, 2019).

40. Interview with Mick Mulvaney, *Credit Union Times*, September 10, 2014, <https://www.youtube.com/watch?v=RaVeNafdyVA> (last accessed December 12, 2019).
41. "2016 Republican Party Platform," available at Gerhard Peters and John T. Woolley, *The American Presidency Project*, Republican Party Platforms, July 18, 2016, <https://www.presidency.ucsb.edu/node/318311> (last accessed December 12, 2019).
42. Nicholas Confessore, "Mick Mulvaney's Master Class in Destroying the Government from Within," *The New York Times Magazine*, April 16, 2019, <https://www.nytimes.com/2019/04/16/magazine/consumer-financial-protection-bureau-trump.html> (last accessed December 12, 2019).
43. Robert O'Harrow, Jr., Shawn Boburg, and Renae Merle, "How Trump Appointees Curbed a Consumer Protection Agency Loathed by the GOP," *The Washington Post*, December 4, 2018, <https://www.washingtonpost.com/investigations/how-trump-appointees-curbed-a-consumer-protection-agency-loathed-by-the-gop/2018/12/04/3cb6cd56-de20-11e8-aa33-53bad9a881e8_story.html> (last accessed December 12, 2019).
44. Ibid.
45. Grunwald, "Trump Wants to Dismantle Elizabeth Warren's Agency."
46. Confessore, "Mick Mulvaney's Master Class."
47. Cory Turner, "Student Loan Watchdog Quits, Says Trump Administration 'Turned Its Back' on Borrowers," *NPR*, August 27, 2018, <https://www.npr.org/2018/08/27/642199524/student-loan-watchdog-quits-blames-trump-administration> (last accessed December 12, 2019).
48. Emily Sullivan, "Senate Confirms Kathy Kraninger as CFPB Director," *NPR*, December 6, 2018, <https://www.npr.org/2018/12/06/673222706/senate-confirms-kathy-kraninger-as-cfpb-director> (last accessed December 12, 2019).
49. Jim Saska, "CFPB to Focus on Protecting Consumers, Not Enforcing Laws on Financial Institutions," *Roll Call*, April 17, 2019, <https://www.rollcall.com/news/congress/kraninger-signals-pro-market-cfpb-de-emphasizes-enforcement> (last accessed December 12, 2019).
50. David Lazarus, "CFPB Head, Charged With Protecting Consumers, Says People Need 'to Help Themselves,'" *Los Angeles Times*, April 19, 2019, <https://www.latimes.com/business/lazarus/la-fi-lazarus-cfpb-kraninger-takes-consumers-to-school-20190419-story.html> (last accessed December 12, 2019).

51. "Attitudes on Same Sex Marriage," Pew Research Center Factsheet, May 14, 2019, <https://www.pewforum.org/fact-sheet/changing-attitudes-on-gay-marriage/> (last accessed December 12, 2019).
52. William Schneider, "On This, Clinton and Rove Agree," *National Journal*, November 20, 2004, <https://www.aei.org/articles/on-this-clinton-and-rove-agree/> (last accessed December 12, 2019).
53. See for example Sunshine Hillygus and Tod Shields, "Moral Issues and Voter Decision Making in the 2004 Presidential Election," *PS Political Science and Politics*, 38.2 (May 10, 2009): 201–9; Gary Segura, "A Symposium on the Politics of Same-Sex Marriage: Introduction and Commentary," *PS Political Science and Politics* 38.2: 189–93; Miriam Smith, "Explaining Human Rights Protections: Institutionalist Analysis in the Lesbian and Gay Rights Case," paper presented at the Annual Meeting of the Canadian Political Science Association, University of Western Ontario, 2–4 June 2005, <https://www.cpsa-acsp.ca/papers-2005/Smith,%20Miriam.pdf> (last accessed December 12, 2019).
54. "Attitudes on Same Sex Marriage," Pew Research Center Factsheet.
55. Nate Silver, "On Transition Website, Obama Promises More to Gay Community," *FiveThirtyEight*, December 26, 2008, <https://fivethirtyeight.com/features/on-transition-website-obama-promises/> (last accessed December 12, 2019).
56. Morris P. Fiorina, "Culture War? The Road to and From 2008," in George Edwards, *Obama: Year One* (New York: Longman, 2010).
57. "Issues and the 2008 Election: Top Issues for 2008," *Pew Research Center*, August 21, 2008, <http://www.people-press.org/2008/08/21/section-3-issues-and-the-2008-election/> (last accessed December 12, 2019).
58. "How Groups Voted in 2008," Roper Center, 2008, <https://ropercenter.cornell.edu/how-groups-voted-2008> (last accessed December 12, 2019).
59. Ibid.
60. CNN Election Center, 2008, <http://edition.cnn.com/ELECTION/2008/issues/issues.samesexmarriage.html> (last accessed December 12, 2019).
61. *Lawrence v. Texas*, 539 US 558 (2003), Docket No. 02-102, <https://www.oyez.org/cases/2002/02-102> (last accessed December 12, 2019).
62. Zack Ford, "Timeline: Tracking Barack Obama's Position on Marriage Equality," *Think Progress*, June 22, 2011, <https://thinkprogress.org/timeline-tracking-barack-obamas-position-

on-marriage-equality-3168f2d8ae60/> (last accessed December 12, 2019).

63. Katy Steinmetz, "See Obama's 20 Year Evolution on LGBT Rights," *Time Magazine*, April 10, 2015, <https://time.com/3816952/obama-gay-lesbian-transgender-lgbt-rights/> (last accessed December 12, 2019).

64. Jessica Yellin, "Biden Apologizes to Obama for Marriage Controversy," *CNN*, May 11, 2012, <https://edition.cnn.com/2012/05/10/politics/obama-same-sex-marriage/index.html> (last accessed December 12, 2019).

65. HR 2965—Don't Ask, Don't Tell Repeal Act of 2010, Sponsor Rep. Jason Altmire (D-PA), December 18, 2010, <https://www.congress.gov/bill/111th-congress/house-bill/2965> (last accessed December 12, 2019).

66. Charlie Savage and Sheryl Gay Stolberg, "In Turnabout, US Says Marriage Act Blocks Gay Rights," *The New York Times*, February 23, 2011, A1.

67. *United States v. Windsor* 570 US_(2013), Docket No. 12-307, <https://www.oyez.org/cases/2012/12-307> (last accessed December 12, 2019).

68. Kellan Baker, "LGBT Protections in Affordable Care Act Section 1557," *Health Affairs* blog, June 6, 2016, <https://www.healthaffairs.org/do/10.1377/hblog20160606.055155/full/> (last accessed December 12, 2019).

69. Federal Register, 81 (183), September 21, 2016, 64763, <https://transequality.org/sites/default/files/docs/resources/Equal-Access-Final-Rule-2016.pdf> (last accessed December 12, 2019).

70. David Hudson, "President Obama Signs a New Executive Order to Protect LGBT Workers," White House blog, July 21, 2014, <https://obamawhitehouse.archives.gov/blog/2014/07/21/president-obama-signs-new-executive-order-protect-lgbt-workers> (last accessed December 12, 2019).

71. Cindi Love, "President Obama Signs Executive Order on LGBTQ Workplace Equality," *ACPA*, July 21, 2014, <http://www.myacpa.org/blogs/dr-cindi-love-executive-director/president-obama-signs-executive-order-lgbt-workplace-equality> (last accessed December 12, 2019).

72. Peter Sprigg and Travis Weber, "Obama Executive Order on 'Sexual Orientation' and 'Gender Identity,'" *Family Research Council*, n.d., <https://downloads.frc.org/EF/EF14I27.pdf> (last accessed December 12, 2019).

73. Erin Blakemore, "President Obama Just Created the First National Monument to Gay Rights," *Smithsonian Magazine*, June 24, 2016, <https://www.smithsonianmag.com/smart-news/president-obama-just-created-first-national-monument-gay-rights-180959562/> (last accessed December 12, 2019).
74. Kendall Breitman, "Dems, Obama Administration Press SCOTUS on Gay Marriage," *Politico*, March 6, 2015, <https://www.politico.com/story/2015/03/president-obama-amicus-brief-same-sex-marriage-115844> (last accessed December 12, 2019); Richard Socarides, "Obama's Brief Against Proposition 8 Goes Far," *The New Yorker*, February 28, 2013, <https://www.newyorker.com/news/news-desk/obamas-brief-against-proposition-8-goes-far> (last accessed December 12, 2019).
75. Barack Obama, "Remarks by the President on the Supreme Court Decision on Marriage Equality," The White House, Office of the Press Secretary, June 26, 2015, <https://obamawhitehouse.archives.gov/the-press-office/2015/06/26/remarks-president-supreme-court-decision-marriage-equality> (last accessed December 12, 2019).
76. "All Legal Same-Sex Marriages Will Be Recognized for Federal Tax Purposes," US Department of the Treasury press release, August 29, 2013, <https://www.treasury.gov/press-center/press-releases/pages/jl2153.aspx> (last accessed December 12, 2019).
77. "Fact Sheet: Obama Administration's Record and the LGBTQ Community," The White House, Office of the Press Secretary, June 9, 2016, <https://obamawhitehouse.archives.gov/the-press-office/2016/06/09/fact-sheet-obama-administrations-record-and-lgbt-community> (last accessed December 12, 2019).
78. Emma Margolin, "The Best and Worst States for LGBT Equality," MSNBC, December 18, 2014, <http://www.msnbc.com/msnbc/the-best-and-worst-states-lgbt-equality> (last accessed December 12, 2019).
79. Michael Kirk, "US Elections Unspun," British Library event, October 2016; Michael Kirk, "The Choice," *Frontline*, 2016, <https://www.pbs.org/wgbh/frontline/film/the-choice-2016/> (last accessed 12 December 5, 2019).
80. Maggie Haberman, "Donald Trump's More Accepting Views on Gay Issues Set Him Apart in GOP," *The New York Times*, April 22, 2016, <https://www.nytimes.com/2016/04/23/us/politics/donald-trump-gay-rights.html> (last accessed December 12, 2019).

81. "Donald Trump, Attitude to Gay Marriage," March 7, 2011, <http://www.ontheissues.org/News_Gay_Rights.htm> (last accessed December 12, 2019).
82. Republican Party Platform, at Gerhard Peters and John T. Woolley, *The American Presidency Project*, <https://www.presidency.ucsb.edu/documents/2016-republican-party-platform> (last accessed December 12, 2019).
83. "Ted Cruz on Civil Rights" (various dates), <http://www.ontheissues.org/2016/Ted_Cruz_Civil_Rights.htm> (last accessed December 12, 2019).
84. Noel Gutierrez-Morfin, "Trump Says He's 'Fine' With Gay Marriage in *60 Minutes* Interview," *NBC News*, November 14, 2016, <https://www.nbcnews.com/feature/nbc-out/trump-says-he-s-fine-gay-marriage-60-minutes-interview-n683606> (last accessed December 12, 2019).
85. SEA 101 Religious Freedom Restoration Act (RFRA) Resource Page, Indiana House of Republicans, <https://www.indianahouserepublicans.com/sea-101-religious-freedom-restoration-act-rfra-resource-page/> (last accessed December 12, 2019).
86. Tony Cook, Tom LoBianco, and Brian Eason, "Gov. Mike Pence Signs RFRA Fix," *Indystar*, April 2, 2015, <https://eu.indystar.com/story/news/politics/2015/04/01/indiana-rfra-deal-sets-limited-protections-for-lgbt/70766920/> (last accessed December 12, 2019).
87. Kate Glueck, "Evangelicals Still Peeved Over Pence's Religious Freedom Act Flip," *Politico*, July 15, 2016, <https://www.politico.com/story/2016/07/trump-vp-pick-mike-pence-evangelicals-225623> (last accessed December 12, 2019).
88. Ashley Parker, "Trump Breaks From Many Republicans on Transgender Restroom Issue," *The New York Times*, April 21, 2016, A17.
89. North Carolina General Assembly Vote History, March 23, 2016, <https://www.ncleg.gov/Legislation/Votes/2019> (last accessed December 12, 2019).
90. Trip Gabriel, "Ted Cruz, Attacking Donald Trump, Uses Transgender Bathroom Access as Cudgel," April 29, 2016, <https://www.nytimes.com/2016/04/30/us/politics/indiana-republican-transgender-rights-bathroom.html> (last accessed December 12, 2019).
91. Haberman, "Donald Trump's More Accepting Views on Gay Issues Set Him Apart."
92. "Full Text: Donald Trump's 2016 Republican National Convention Speech," *ABC News*, July 22, 2016, <https://abcnews.go.com/Politics/full-text-donald-trumps-2016-republican-national-convention/story?id=40786529> (last accessed December 12, 2019).

93. CNN Election Exit Polls, 2016, <https://edition.cnn.com/election/2016/results/exit-polls> (last accessed December 12, 2019).
94. Chris Johnson, "White House Hails Masterpiece Cakeshop Ruling as Religious Liberty Win," *The Washington Blade*, June 5, 2018, <https://www.washingtonblade.com/2018/06/05/white-house-hails-masterpiece-cakeshop-ruling-as-religious-liberty-win/> (last accessed December 12, 2019).
95. Emanuella Grinberg, "The First 100 Days in LGBT Rights," *CNN Politics*, April 29, 2017, <https://edition.cnn.com/2017/04/28/politics/first-100-days-lgbt-rights-trnd/index.html> (last accessed 12 December 10, 2019).
96. Andrew Flores, Jody Herman, Gary Gates, and Taylor Brown, "How Many Adults Identify as Transgender in the United States," *The Williams Institute*, June 2016, <https://williamsinstitute.law.ucla.edu/wp-content/uploads/How-Many-Adults-Identify-as-Transgender-in-the-United-States.pdf> (last accessed December 12, 2019).
97. Tracy Jan, "Proposed HUD rule Would Strip Transgender Protections at Homeless Shelters," *The Washington Post*, May 22, 2019, <https://www.washingtonpost.com/business/2019/05/22/proposed-hud-rule-would-strip-transgender-protections-homeless-shelters> (last accessed December 12, 2019).
98. Katie Keith, "HHS Proposes To Strip Gender Identity, Language Access Protections from ACA Anti-Discrimination Rule," *Health Affairs* blog, May 25, 2019, <https://www.healthaffairs.org/do/10.1377/hblog20190525.831858/full/> (last accessed December 12, 2019).
99. Eric Patashnik and Julian Zelizer, "The Struggle to Remake Politics: Liberal Reform and the Limits of Policy Feedback in the Contemporary American State," *Perspectives on Politics* 11.4 (2013): 1071–87.
100. Li Zhou, "The Latest Legal Challenge to the Affordable Care Act, Explained," *Vox*, July 10, 2019, <https://www.vox.com/policy-and-politics/2019/7/9/20686224/affordable-care-act-constitutional-lawsuit-fifth-circuit-court-texas-district-court> (last accessed December 12, 2019).
101. Andy Schneider, "Judge Blocks Arkansas and Kentucky Medicaid Work Requirement Waivers: What Does This Decision Mean for Other States?" *Say Ahh!* blog, Georgetown University Health Policy Institute, March 28, 2019, <https://ccf.georgetown.edu/2019/03/28/judge-blocks-arkansas-and-kentucky-medicaid-work-requirement-waivers/> (last accessed December 12, 2019).

102. Confessore, "Mick Mulvaney's Master Class."
103. Johnnie Moore (@JohnnieM) on Twitter, May 4, 2017, <https://twitter.com/johnniem/status/859974122880872449> (last accessed December 13, 2019).
104. Donald Trump, "Presidential Executive Order Promoting Free Speech and Religious Liberty," White House, May 4, 2017, <https://www.whitehouse.gov/presidential-actions/presidential-executive-order-promoting-free-speech-religious-liberty/> (last accessed December 12, 2019).
105. "President Trump National Prayer Event," *C-Span*, May 4, 2017, <https://www.c-span.org/video/?428059-1/president-trump-signs-religious-liberty-executive-order> (last accessed 12 December 4, 2019).

3

An uncertain "soft" legacy, under fire

There were areas where the Obama administration's legacy fell short of its bold aims, most notably in relation to the climate crisis and immigration. In addition, ambitions to promote free trade were only partially fulfilled. Importantly in the cases of the climate crisis and immigration the administration's attempts to push legislative efforts failed even when Democrats controlled both chambers of Congress. Immigration reform did later see a successful bipartisan, and comprehensive, measure in the Senate that gathered 68 votes, but the feeling that there was also a majority in the House to support reform was never put to the test. Speaker John Boehner was not going to let his caucus divide so publicly on such a high-profile issue. The chance of a serious legislative effort on climate change effectively ended when the GOP took control of the House. Hence, Obama's attempts at legacy-building in these two areas primarily relied on executive actions. While falling short of the ambitions expressed in the legislative efforts, these moves, notably the Clean Power Plan (CPP), Deferred Action on Childhood Arrivals (DACA), and Deferred Action for Parents of Americans (DAPA), were of real potential significance. That potential, however, was never fully realized as the courts stepped in to prevent and delay the implementation of the CPP and DAPA even before the Trump administration got its chance to reverse them.

The politics surrounding trade policy was even more confusing, partially because it was one area where the prevailing high levels of partisan polarization broke down somewhat. In particular, as, toward the end of his time in office, Obama worked to negotiate the Trans Pacific Partnership trade agreement—which was a major multilateral deal involving twelve countries—it looked to congressional Republicans as much as to Democrats for support in Congress. In the end, the administration did manage to get Congress to renew Trade Promotion Authority (TPA) that would have given the TPP the chance of an up or down vote in Congress, but the deal itself was never put before Congress for that vote while Obama was in office. To further confuse the picture, the new Republican president rebuked his party's positioning as the pro-free-trade faction in American politics and promptly withdrew the US from the TPP. Hence this chapter will focus on Obama's limited achievements in the areas of climate, immigration, and trade, looking at the institutional obstacles that blocked more radical change and the extent of Trump's fierce repudiation of the diminished legacy that was put in place.

Climate change policy

The conservation movement in fact dates back over a century in US history, but its modern form emerged and gained notable traction from the 1960s onwards, specifically in relation to air, water, soil, and concerns relating to the nation's nuclear capacity. In recent decades, the topic has gone through a number of labeling incarnations: discussion of "conservation" and "the environment" evolved more recently to focus specifically on global warming and then climate change as the science increasingly pointed toward a man-made crisis.

On the campaign trail, Barack Obama shared his plans for the promotion of a "green economy." This framing of climate change in direct connection with the nation's wealth clearly demonstrated his awareness that if these issues were presented as mutually exclusive, enthusiasm for his plans would be limited to certain sections of the voting population. Relying on support only from environmentalists and organic food advocates was not a guaranteed path to the Oval Office. Hence, his message was a twofold one, promoting the urgency of the green agenda and its benefit to the economy. In October 2008, Obama told *Time* magazine's Joe Klein that an "Apollo project" for a new energy economy was his "top priority."[1] This was a relief to those climate activists who had watched with concern throughout the Bush years as that administration failed to prioritize climate change. The 43rd president had nailed his environmental colors to the mast weeks after he took office in 2001, by announcing his refusal to adhere to the Kyoto Protocol.[2] Instead, Bush had presented an alternative emissions reduction plan, which would tie greenhouse gas and economic output together. Critics rejected the plans as a "do nothing" solution to a serious and growing problem, and the administration faced claims of allowing its friends in business to get away with little or no regulation.[3]

As the decade progressed, climate change became an increasingly partisan issue, with many conservatives firmly and publicly rejecting any connection between changing world temperature and weather patterns, and human activity. In addition, the percentage of Americans polled who stated that they would prioritize environmental considerations over economic growth dropped noticeably during the Bush years, after reaching highs of more than 70 percent in the 1990s. Around the time that Obama was on the campaign trail promoting a green economy for the future, public opinion polling showed support for prioritizing the environment was little more than 50 percent.[4] Nevertheless, during the 2008 campaign the Obama-Biden Energy Plan for America laid out a series of ambitious objectives, including creating "five million new jobs by strategically investing $150 billion over the next ten years to catalyze private efforts to build a clean energy future" and introducing "an economy-wide cap-and-trade program to reduce greenhouse gas emissions by 80 percent by 2050."[5]

Whilst the Energy Plan was well received in expected quarters, and Obama was welcomed as the first green president, Team Obama had to contend with an American economy in cardiac arrest just at a time when they were envisaging health care reform and green economy promotion among their expenditure priorities. Subsequently, finding $150 billion for long-term clean energy plans seemed a low priority to taxpayers facing bank bailouts and emergency economic recovery plans. The American Recovery and Reinvestment Act did contain an "Energy Efficiency and Renewable Energy Research and Investment" section with a price tag of $27 billion. Nonetheless, the public swiftly re-prioritized the economy over the environment, and the administration was obliged to consider a recalibration of its concerns accordingly.[6]

Despite this, the new administration maintained its promotion of green-collar jobs as a key component of economic recovery. This message was crafted to offer a double appeal both to blue-collar and green voters. President Obama touched on the issue in his 2009 inaugural address, and more forcefully in his Earth Day speech three months later. In this, he called on American government, business and citizens to take a progressive approach, to move toward clean energy and increase efficiency.[7]

As ever, however, making this happen was more problematic than expressing the hope that it would happen. Writing in 2012, John Berg mapped out three institutional channels for action on climate change faced by the Obama administration. Firstly, there was a binding international agreement option through the United Nations Framework Convention on Climate Change (UNFCCC), which the US was still a part of despite having not ratified the Kyoto Protocol. Secondly, the President could reach out to Congress with a view to passing greenhouse-gas-reducing legislation. The third option was via the Environmental Protection Agency (EPA), which could regulate carbon emissions as pollutants.[8] Before long it was apparent that options one and two were problematic. The 2009 United Nations UNFCCC meeting in Copenhagen generated a lot of pre-summit excitement but brought about only a rather toothless accord, whereby nations signed up to reducing emissions as they saw fit.[9]

The legislative route did show some initial promise. The American Clean Energy and Security Act of 2009 got off to a hopeful start in the House of Representatives, with that chamber approving the bill by a majority of 219 to 212 in June 2009.[10] The bill did not satisfy all activists, particularly as it relied on market-based mechanisms to control the cost of carbon and the distribution of future emissions. Although it received strong support from some environmental groups, other high-profile NGOs such as Greenpeace and Friends of the Earth criticized the 2009 Act for not going far enough. That narrative was reflected in the House of Representatives, with more conservative-minded Democrats unwilling to sign up to it and those with a strong green agenda disappointed by the watering down that came in the form of 400 amendments. Yet with Speaker Nancy Pelosi aggressively whipping to get the bill through and the White House pitching in to convince wavering members, the "vote marked the first time either chamber had passed a bill to address climate change."[11]

At this point it looked as if the administration might have found a formula for "capitalizing on conservative ideas to achieve liberal policy goals."[12] Still, it was ominous for the bill's supporters that forty-four House Democrats had voted against passage (with eight Republicans in support); and the legislative route through the Senate was always likely to be even more difficult to navigate, with Democrats from states heavily reliant on coal for their electricity production, such as Evan Bayh from Indiana, very wary. Initial signs that a bipartisan deal might be struck with figures such as senators John McCain from Arizona and Lindsay Graham of South Carolina proved to be misleading as conservative climate change skepticism hardened. McCain quickly dropped out of negotiations as he came under threat of a primary challenge in his bid for re-election in 2010, but Graham did work with Senator John Kerry of Massachusetts through to April 2010 before the effort at compromise fell apart. In June 2010 President Obama acknowledged that the Senate process had stalled: "the votes may not be there right now, but I intend to find them in the coming months." In his detailed account of these events the journalist Ryan Lizza commented, "He never found them, and he didn't appear to be looking very hard."[13] In the end, Capitol Hill offered a legislative cul-de-sac. Even though aspects of Obama's climate change agenda progressed in the early "honeymoon" period of his administration, using his party's majority in Congress, his plans were largely foiled. The "shellacking" that the Democrats took in the 2010 midterm elections ensured that congressional progress on this complex and thorny issue ground to a standstill.

Nevertheless, Obama did remain committed to pushing climate issues onto the political agenda, though this was mostly delayed until after he had won re-election as the Obama campaign agenda for 2012 was clearly focused on jobs and economic growth. There was little mention of his green agenda the second time round. Clearly voters had other priorities, with the percentage listing the environment as "very important" actually declining in the course of Obama's first term.¹⁴

Newly liberated from re-election constraints, Obama was in a position to move forward with his mandate. In his 2013 inaugural address he declared, "our obligations as Americans are not just to ourselves, but to all posterity. We will respond to the threat of climate change, knowing that the failure to do so would betray our children and future generations."¹⁵ In his 2015 State of the Union address, he insisted "no challenge—no challenge—poses a greater threat to future generations than climate change."¹⁶ Yet, that speech came shortly after Republicans had gained a Senate majority. As Meg Jacobs notes, this meant that James Inhofe from Oklahoma would become chair of the Senate Energy and Environment Committee only two years after he had published a book titled *The Greatest Hoax: How the Global Warming Conspiracy Threatens Your Future*.¹⁷ In the circumstances, it was not surprising that Obama's second-term efforts focused more on executive action and empowering the EPA than on pushing legislation through Congress.

The administration did follow up on the rhetoric of the inaugural by putting forward the 2013 Climate Action Plan. By now the focus was very much on the third of Berg's channels, as the administration turned to the EPA and its authority to regulate carbon emissions as a pollutant in the same way as toxins like mercury and arsenic.¹⁸ Once again, the President's launch speech was full of eloquent vision. As before, some environmental groups applauded loudly, but others rued what they perceived as a too-little-too-late approach.¹⁹

In retrospect, Obama's climate change efforts grew as the administration years rolled by. Rather than achieving big and fast in those heady "new New Deal" days, the 44th president appeared to gather environmental steam, particularly during his second term. One attempt to establish a signature aspect of Obama's green legacy was the 2015 Clean Power Plan (CPP), aimed at lowering the carbon dioxide emissions from power generators by 32 percent over twenty-five years, bringing levels back to those of 2005. After two years of preparation, Obama referred to the plan as the "single most important step that America has ever made in the fight against global climate change."[20] It remained to be seen how durable this step actually was. Immediately upon its release, the CPP was challenged by twenty-four states' attorneys general, who maintained that it went beyond the EPA's remit: "The final rule is in excess of the agency's statutory authority, goes beyond the bounds set by the United States Constitution, and otherwise is arbitrary, capricious, an abuse of discretion and not in accordance with law."[21] In February 2016, by which point twenty-nine states along with various industry groups were challenging the legitimacy of the CPP, the Supreme Court stepped in to issue a stay on the implementation of the CPP, pending a decision by the US Court of Appeals for District of Columbia Circuit, where the case was being heard. The *New York Times* reported that the decision "was unprecedented—the Supreme Court had never before granted a request to halt a regulation before review by a federal appeals court."[22]

Another attempt by the administration to leave a signature green legacy was America's commitment to the Paris Climate Change Accord. It was clear before the November 2015 event took place that the President intended to circumvent Senate scrutiny of the agreement. When asked by a reporter if Congress should have access to the protocol, White House spokesman Josh Earnest replied, "I think it's hard to take seriously from some Members of Congress who deny the fact that climate change exists, that they should have some opportunity to render judgment about a climate change agreement."[23]

Inevitably, such an admission by the administration brought howls of derision from opposing quarters, along with accusations of imperial behavior. It was not entirely unusual for a president to suggest bypassing the legislature when signing up to a major international agreement. Obama was clearly mindful of history repeating itself, as the president bringing home a grand international vision only for it to be foiled by domestic opposition.[24] The Paris Agreement targets were significant, yet modest when considered in the context of the scientific evidence underpinning the extent of anthropomorphic climate change. Nonetheless, without the US on board, there was no doubt that its significance would be undermined and the impetus for other big polluters to get on board would inevitably be diminished. The Obama administration submitted its plan to the UNFCCC in March 2015, outlining its emissions target reduction. The goal was to reduce greenhouse gas output by 26 percent to 28 percent by 2015.[25] A 2015 *New York Times/CBS* poll showed that two-thirds of the US public supported their country signing up to a binding agreement. Unsurprisingly, opinions were divided along partisan lines.[26]

Since the rapid growth of the environmental movement in the 1960s, the Democrats have always appeared to be the major party most capable of handling the climate change issue and offering appropriate solutions. Research by *Forbes* magazine have found this to be the case since 1971, and especially so in the 2016 election, with Hillary Clinton leading in polls on the issue and many GOP voters not simply downplaying climate change as an issue, but positively hostile to the policy direction of Obama's green economy initiatives.[27] It seemed fitting, then, that only a few weeks into his presidency Donald Trump signed Executive Order 13787 to undo his predecessor's Clean Power Plan.[28]

This was one reflection of Trump's embrace of climate change denialism. His own personal twist, expressed in 2012, was to blame the Chinese for perpetuating the "global warming" hoax.[29] In 2016, his campaign trail rhetoric was fiery and uncompromising. Trump spoke to and for those who did not believe that climate change was a priority, or that it was human-made. Two key promises of his stump speech were to withdraw America from the Paris Climate Accords, and to cancel the nation's spending to the UN for climate-related matters.[30]

This chimed well with Trump's "America First" mantra, which promoted the needs and priorities of the nation above those of the international community. However, climate change progress needs collective action in order to succeed, and Trump's position was a major blow to international climate finance. Rhetorically channeling—consciously or not—a Republican predecessor, his "Contract with the American Voter" included seven action plans to protect the nation's workers. He pledged to act within 100 days to "cancel billions in payments to UN climate change programs and use the money to fix America's water and environmental infrastructure."[31]

The US coal industry has been in serious decline for decades, and the job losses and social dysfunction that have accompanied this have brought profound challenges to communities that historically depended on mining and associated employment. More than two-thirds of industry jobs have disappeared since the 1980s.[32] After eight years of perceiving a liberal president's "War on Coal," seeing the GOP candidate brandishing placards claiming "Trump Digs Coal" meant that some voters were attracted to Trump on the basis of his promises to bring back coal and reinvigorate the sector. Trump spoke directly to coal miners, telling them to "get ready, because you're going to be working your asses off."[33] The day after the election, coal stock prices soared as their green energy counterpart tanked.[34]

President Trump also promptly withdrew the US from the 2015 Paris Agreement, joining Syria and Nicaragua as non-participants.[35] His quip, "I was elected to represent the citizens of Pittsburgh, not Paris," was catnip to blue-collar voters concerned about their jobs and the wider economy.[36] A *Forbes* magazine headline captured the mainstream media mood in response to President Trump's decision to withdraw the US from the agreement. Stating that "America is Officially the Only Nation on Earth to Reject the Paris Agreement," it pointed out that even North Korea, not known for its adherence to international norms, had signed up.[37] The respective mayors of Pittsburgh and Paris, meanwhile, co-authored an op-ed piece in the *New York Times*, which noted among other commitments that "Pittsburgh is one of nearly 250 cities in the United States, representing 56 million Americans, whose mayors have committed to honor and uphold the goals of the Paris Agreement."[38]

This defiance, however, ran into the hard reality that the President set the national agenda and his cabinet picks for the key posts related to climate change issues were clear evidence that even the incremental moves made by the previous administration were to be reversed where possible and at least halted from making further progress. Trump's choice for secretary of energy was former Texas governor Rick Perry, a man who had proposed in his aborted bid for the 2012 GOP nomination that the department should be abolished. *Newsweek* offered some insight into Trump's selection, describing Texas as "the sort of unregulated, small government, tort-reformed, low-tax state that provides a model for what the United States would look like at the end of a Trump presidency."[39]

Meanwhile, over at Woodrow Wilson Plaza, Scott Pruitt was appointed as head of the Environmental Protection Agency, despite having no formal scientific or environmental training. As attorney general of Oklahoma, Pruitt had (unsuccessfully) sued the EPA fourteen times; with ties to the oil and gas industries, he was known as a vocal critic of Obama's climate change agenda. Even as the World Health Organization warned that global warming is "among the greatest health risks of the twenty-first century," Pruitt told CNBC that he did not think that carbon dioxide was a primary contributor to global warming.[40] In July 2018, when Pruitt was forced to step down following numerous allegations of unethical behavior, he was replaced by Andrew Wheeler, a former lobbyist for the coal industry. Trump's climate change plans and relevant staffing choices demonstrate that the US has taken a significant step away from its previous, if halting, direction during the Obama years.

In the summer of 2019 the *New York Times* reported that the Trump administration had, or was in the process of, rolling back eighty-three federal environmental protections.[41] On the other hand, just as the Obama administration found itself stymied by the courts, so legal challenges slowed the pace of deregulatory change. While acknowledging that the rollback of environmental protections was real, the Sabin Center for Climate Change Law, based at Columbia University, reported in summer 2019: "The Trump Administration is losing on climate in the courts. More than two and a half years into the Trump Administration, no climate change-related regulatory rollback brought before the courts has yet survived legal challenge."[42] In the early days at least, some of these setbacks for the Trump team resulted from sloppy legal preparation in the rush to get things done.[43]

It is also worth noting how liberal states and cities such as Pittsburgh could try to exert their power in ways that disrupted the deregulatory agenda, bringing opposition to the Trump administration from unexpected quarters. Most significant was California with its huge economic clout. An illustration of the state's determination to use that leverage came with efforts to improve fuel efficiency in the auto industry. The Obama administration had issued a rule saying that cars and trucks needed to average 43 miles per gallon by 2025. In an illustration of the difficulty in actually drawing up these regulations, the EPA had announced its intent to apply such a rule in 2012, but it was not finalized until the final week of Obama's time in office in a scramble to get it done before Trump's arrival in the White House. Automakers did not like that proposal, but then they did not cheer when the Trump administration removed the imperative for an annual improvement in fuel efficiency standards. This concern for increased efficiency may not have been purely altruistic: Car makers were concerned by the possibility of a segmented US market, as California promised to continue to unilaterally enforce the Obama-era standard. The likely lengthy legal battle between the federal government and California over the latter's right to enforce its own rules threatened disruption to an industry that was also concerned about its image with respect to climate change. Hence in April 2018 the Auto Alliance urged the EPA to reconsider and lay out new rules, if less stringent than those set in January 2017, for demanding continued improvements in fuel efficiency.[44]

Furthermore, whilst a climate skeptic in the Oval Office was clearly significant, some of America's most influential tech giants, Apple, Facebook, Google, IBM, Microsoft, and Amazon, stated that they planned to make efforts to meet the Paris Accord requirements even without a steer from the federal government.[45] By June 2017, eleven states along with Washington, DC and Puerto Rico had joined the United States Climate Alliance (USCA). The USCA is one of a number of groups set up in order to ensure that areas, cities, and groups within the US maintain adherence to the Paris deal.[46] So just as Obama had found it difficult to engage all the forward gears in his administration's efforts to act on climate change, so also the actions taken by President Trump's administration did not mean that all the ongoing initiatives to pursue a green agenda were slammed into reverse.

Immigration policy

Throughout the Obama era and the opening years of the Trump presidency, the tension between the notion of America as a country built on an ideology of immigration and the fear of the prevailing culture being under threat by alien people and their values was on clear display. This tension took its most crystalized form in the debate about how to handle illegal immigration, which remained at the forefront of America's political conversation. In a nation of immigrants, the issue of what to do about the estimated 11 million individuals residing illegally is a perennial bugbear for politicians and voters.[47] Most agree that the system is defective and something must be done, but there the consensus ends. On one side, pro-immigrant advocates call for a path to citizenship for "undocumented aliens," while those opposed to them demand rigorous enforcement of the law and deportation of "illegal immigrants." Furthermore, the disagreement is not only about what policy should be, but extends to the question of which branch of government should set that policy.

In 2016 immigration ranked highly as a key voter issue, along with the economy and terrorism.[48] Candidate Trump was highly adept at honing his campaign message to address those with border security concerns, reflecting that the issue was far from resolved despite the Obama administration's actions. As Obama left office, neither the immigrants' rights groups nor the restrictionists were satisfied. In fact, Obama's efforts at immigration policy reform had followed a similar trajectory to the administration's moves on climate regulation. As legislative moves proved largely unproductive and pressure from outside groups for action grew, Obama turned increasingly to executive action to achieve his objectives, with those actions getting a mixed reception in the courts. In the end, Obama's legacy with regard to immigration was an uncertain one both in terms of its message and its lasting effect. Trump's message, by contrast, was unambiguous, although translating it into policy would not prove to be so simple.

On August 25, 2008, addressing the Democrat Party Convention, Barack Obama declared that America's current immigration system "has been broken for too long." When addressing the topic his rhetoric was constructive, including terms such as "humane," "welcoming," "generous," and "fair," though he also spoke about the need for the US to be tough and practical in relation to rolling out comprehensive reform.[49] Like his Republican opponent, Obama supported the need for improved border security. On a number of immigration-related issues, the candidates did not differ significantly, but John McCain's position hardened as the campaign progressed, culminating in him distancing himself from a bill that he had helped to draft only a year earlier. That bill—the 2007 Comprehensive Immigration Reform Act, which would have granted amnesty in some form to millions who resided illegally in the US—made little progress despite clear support from President Bush.[50] This was a manifestation of how Republicans, whatever the party leadership might wish, were taking a more clearly restrictionist approach, and this was their stance in the 2008 campaign. As it was, on election day 2008, Obama fared well with the 9 percent of the voting population that was Latino: He took 67 percent of the vote, to McCain's 31 percent. The youth vote more overtly favored the Democrat, with 71 percent support. Even in Florida, with its Cuban-American population more likely to tilt Republican, Latinos turned out to support the Democratic nominee.[51]

During the campaign Obama had promised that he would introduce a comprehensive immigration plan during his first year in office. He specifically stated: "I cannot guarantee that it's going to be in the first 100 days. But what I can guarantee is that we will have in the first year an immigration bill that I strongly support and that I'm promoting and that I want to move that forward as quickly as possible."[52] Yet the first year passed with no sign of an immigration bill. This was partially due to the need to recalibrate his policy priorities in order to manage the Great Recession. There was some consensus, even among Latinos, that the economy and health care reform were higher priorities for the administration than immigration reform.

However, if the pressures of the recession could be used to explain the delay in a push at comprehensive immigration reform including a path to legalization, the early emphasis on enforcement and the levels of deportation were unexpected. Immigration advocates dubbed Obama the "Deporter in Chief" as more than 2.5 million illegal immigrants were forced via immigration orders to leave the US during his time in office.[53] It was the case, however, that Immigration and Customs Enforcement (ICE) personnel were directed by Obama to focus more sharply on "felons, not families," and on average, approximately 90 percent of those deported in any given year had a criminal record. Specifically, gang members and lawbreakers were prioritized. Overall, the deportation figure is higher than the combined number of those deported from the US in the twentieth century. For comparison, two million illegal immigrants were deported during George W. Bush's time in office.[54] But if this record of deportation seems an odd legacy for the administration, it is important to recognize, as John Skrentny explains, that "an enforcement first strategy" was a means to "gain credibility for legalization."[55]

As things turned out, however, that strategy paid no legislative dividends. There were two points at which it looked as if important steps might be taken, but in both cases congressional institutional fragmentation proved insurmountable. Firstly, in the lame duck session of Congress at the end of 2010, the House passed the Development, Relief, and Education for Alien Minors Act (DREAM Act), giving legal status to some undocumented immigrants who had arrived in the US as children, by a vote of 216 to 198.[56] The measure failed in the Senate, however, when it only gained fifty-five votes in an effort to beat a filibuster. That number did include three Republicans, so if the Democrats had stuck together they could have carried the day, but five Democrats voted against the wishes of President Obama and the congressional leadership. Republican Senator Jeff Sessions from Alabama, well known for his hawkish views on immigration, commented: "This bill is a law that at its fundamental core is a reward for illegal activity."[57] Few would have predicted it at the time, but Sessions was to become President Trump's first attorney general and hence a key figure in driving immigration policy.

Secondly, in 2013, a bipartisan group of eight senators drafted a document with the intention of transforming US immigration law.[58] Two months later, in June 2013, the Senate voted 68–32 in favor of what was described at the time as "the most monumental overhaul of US immigration laws in a generation." The vote included the support of fourteen Republicans.[59] The bill proposed a path to citizenship for many living illegally in the US that would take thirteen years, as well as stronger border enforcement and measures to deter employers from hiring illegal immigrants as workers. At that point there was some optimism that something similar could be delivered in the House despite it being under Republican control, as it seemed likely that there was an overall majority in the chamber to proceed with a reform bill. That was not to be the case, however. Speaker Boehner was willing to contemplate a deal, but he did not want the legislation to pass on the basis of a minority of Republicans allying with nearly all Democrats to form a majority in a manner that would violate the so-called "Hastert rule." According to this principle, a majority of the Republican majority needed to support a bill before leadership would move it to the floor.[60]

The diminishing chance that the Republican majority would take up a bill to follow up on Senate action was dealt a severe blow in June 2014, when House Majority Leader Eric Cantor lost in a primary in his Virginia district to a little-known challenger, Dave Brat. If not entirely accurately, "in the post-mortems, the role of immigration reform quickly hardened into conventional wisdom," as Cantor had been open to some smaller-scale reforms.[61] Speaking shortly after Cantor's defeat, President Obama railed against what he saw as the GOP's intransigence and partisan game-playing:

> Our country and our economy would be stronger today if House Republicans had allowed a simple yes-or-no vote on this bill or, for that matter, any bill. They'd be following the will of the majority of the American people who support reform. Instead, they've proven again and again that they're unwilling to stand up to the Tea Party in order to do what's best for the country. And the worst part about it is a bunch of them know better.[62]

These words, however, carried no weight and the Senate bill came to nought.

Obama had in fact turned to executive action prior to the failure of the 2013–14 legislative package to get through Congress when he pushed through a version of the DREAM Act in 2012. The Deferred Action on Childhood Arrivals program (DACA) granted a two-year renewable legal status for undocumented immigrants currently under the age of thirty-one, who had lived in the US for at least five years, having arrived in the US while they were younger than sixteen. They also needed to have graduated from high school or served in the military, and be free from a criminal record. At the time it was estimated that 1.5 million might benefit from DACA.[63] Obama's actions were commonly referred to as an "executive order," but this is misleading, as DACA took the form of a direction to the Department of Homeland Security about which groups to prioritize for deportation—in short, Obama claimed to be using existing powers rather than creating new ones. He also acknowledged: "It's not a permanent fix. This is a temporary stopgap measure that lets us focus our resources wisely while giving a degree of relief and hope to talented, driven, patriotic young people."[64] For critics, this claim carried little weight; they insisted that the President had done an unconstitutional end run around Congress.[65]

Conservative anger over DACA, however, was overshadowed two years later in November 2014 (shortly after the midterm elections), when Obama, frustrated by developments in Congress and under increasing pressure from immigrants' rights activists, used executive authority to announce a package labeled Deferred Action for Parents of Americans (DAPA). This was a significantly more expansive move than DACA, affecting an estimated 5.5 million people. The Department of Homeland Security described how "within the confines of the law" the administration had identified measures it could implement "to increase border security, focus enforcement resources, and ensure accountability in our immigration system."[66] In reality it was the second of these clauses that was at the heart of the policy, as DAPA declared that people who were not priorities for removal—identified as those who had entered the US prior to 2014, with no criminal record, and had children who were now either citizens or lawful residents—would be allowed to apply for effective temporary legal status, including the capacity to work. When laying out his reasons for proceeding with DAPA, Obama again lamented how the House had stymied reform.

> I worked with Congress on a comprehensive fix, and last year, sixty-eight Democrats, Republicans, and independents came together to pass a bipartisan bill in the Senate. It wasn't perfect. It was a compromise. But it reflected common sense. . . .
>
> Had the House of Representatives allowed that kind of bill a simple yes-or-no vote, it would have passed with support from both parties, and today it would be the law. But for a year and a half now, Republican leaders in the House have refused to allow that simple vote.

Obama acknowledged that some people had a genuine concern about what high levels of immigration might mean for American society, but he went on to make what might be described as the "moral" case for his actions: "Are we a nation that accepts the cruelty of ripping children from their parents' arms? Or are we a nation that values families, and works together to keep them together?"[67]

These words did not assuage his critics and twenty-six states, led by Texas, promptly launched legal action to challenge Obama's authority to act in this manner. House Speaker Boehner had outlined likely Republican opposition in the summer of 2014 when he insisted that any further executive action on immigration after DACA would reinforce Obama's "legacy of lawlessness."[68] Furthermore, Republican opponents pointed to the many times that President Obama had himself referred to his limited powers to reform the immigration system through executive action. For example, when asked in February 2013 what he could do to prevent families being split apart, Obama explained:

> [T]his is something I've struggled with throughout my presidency. The problem is that I'm the president of the United States. I'm not the emperor of the United States. My job is to execute laws that are passed, and Congress, right now, has not changed what I consider

to be a broken immigration system, and what that means is we have certain obligations to enforce the laws that are in place, even if we think in many cases the results may be tragic.[69]

Later that year, in September, he rationalized the DACA package, but added, "if we start broadening that, then essentially I would be ignoring the law in a way that I feel would be very difficult to defend legally."[70] As it was, the administration maintained that DAPA structured deportation priorities and did not offer a permanent path to legalization for illegal immigrants, hence staying within the boundaries of presidential authority. Crucially, however, the courts agreed more with Obama's earlier statements about the limits of his authority than with the later attempt to rationalize the administration's actions. First a US District judge in Texas imposed an injunction against the implementation of DAPA, with that decision upheld by in November 2015 by the Fifth Circuit Court of Appeals. Next, the administration appealed to the Supreme Court. After an expedited hearing in the case, known as *Texas v. United States*, the Supreme Court effectively sided with Texas after a 4–4 decision, issued with no explanation of its rationale. President Obama bemoaned the outcome: "I think it is heartbreaking for the millions of immigrants who made their lives here, who've raised families here, who hope for the opportunity to work, pay taxes, serve in our military, and fully contribute to this country we all love in an open way."[71]

In the end, Obama's legacy on immigration was mixed. The record rate of forced removals from the country did not persuade immigration skeptics that his administration could be trusted to enforce border protection as part of a comprehensive reform package, and in this context internal Republican Party dynamics prevented the House from taking up the Senate's 2013 bill. The turn to executive action did mean that about 750,000 people got temporary legal status through DACA; but DAPA, which would have benefited many more, never came into force. As it was, immigration did take center stage in the 2016 election, but not in the manner that immigrants' rights activists would have hoped for.

AN UNCERTAIN "SOFT" LEGACY, UNDER FIRE

Of all the colorful campaign rhetoric employed by candidate Trump, he sounded more authentic on some topics than others—and immigration was one area in which his rhetoric seemed real. His message on the issue was clear: too many immigrants were detrimental to the country, and in order to Make America Great Again, dramatic steps should be taken to tighten the nation's porous borders. This was a key plank of his candidacy from the very moment he announced his bid for the presidency. His startling announcement speech, with its vilification of Mexican immigrants, contained a statement of what was to become his campaign rallying cry: "I would build a great wall, and nobody builds walls better than me, believe me, and I'll build them very inexpensively. I will build a great great wall on our southern border and I'll have Mexico pay for that wall."[72] His supporters did not seem to mind when he played fast and loose with the numbers—for example, claiming in 2016 that there were over 30 million illegal immigrants in the country. In fact, estimates showed that number had reduced by about one million since the economic collapse, which had dissuaded many from entering the US.[73]

Once in office, President Trump moved to implement his agenda. It did become quickly evident that Mexico was not going to pay for the wall, and the administration then struggled to find the funds. Despite his party having a congressional majority, Trump lost the first round of the funding battle. The White House request for a starting amount of $1 billion, the estimated cost of building one mile of wall, was rejected. Nonetheless, the Department of Homeland Security began soliciting proposals with the intention to carry out a series of pilot cases on the border before proceeding more widely. By 2019, the wall had become a major political football between the Democrat-led House of Representatives and a president determined not to lose face. The resulting conflict led to the longest government shutdown in the nation's history.[74]

In the aftermath of that stand-off, President Trump declared a national emergency and claimed the authority to use other federal funds to pay for the wall. Unsurprisingly, Democrats immediately responded with accusations that Trump was acting beyond his authority. House Speaker Nancy Pelosi of California and Senate Minority Leader Chuck Schumer from New York issued a statement saying: "The president's actions clearly violate the Congress's exclusive power of the purse, which our Founders enshrined in the Constitution."[75] Furthermore, Congress responded with a resolution rebuking this declaration in votes in both chambers that included twelve Senate Republicans. In turn, this saw Trump issue the first veto of his presidency.[76] The battle then moved to the courts.

During his opening thirty months in office President Trump developed a meme whereby he talked of the Democrats as being in favor of "open borders," tweeting, for example, in June 2016: "Too bad the Dems in Congress won't do anything at all about Border Security. They want Open Borders, which means crime. But we are getting it done, including building the Wall!" The same week he said, "Democrats want Open Borders, which equals violent crime, drugs and human trafficking."[77] For all this fiery language, however, Trump did seem initially uncertain about whether to overturn DACA, which was Obama's most significant legacy with regard to providing legal status to undocumented immigrants. As Trump entered office, around 700,000 people had taken advantage of the temporary protections offered by DACA. This number was not as high as the original predictions, but it still meant that for many individuals who had come forward to the authorities to acknowledge their undocumented status, the stakes with regard to the longevity of the program were extremely high. Reflecting his hesitancy, in September 2017 Trump tweeted: "Does anybody really want to throw out good, educated and accomplished young people who have jobs, some serving in the military? Really!"[78] Yet, that month the administration moved to end the program when pressured by Republican state attorneys general to do so.

At this point, though, what should have been a relatively straightforward process was undermined by administrative incompetence. When revoking the Obama administration's actions, the Department of Homeland Security provided minimal rationale for doing so beyond asserting that the original decision to introduce DACA had been unlawful. This left open the possibility that a court might find that DACA had been lawful, and therefore the revocation was not lawful. Crucially, if the revocation had been accompanied by a policy explanation, the grounds for challenging the move would have been considerably reduced. Led by, amongst others, the University of California (whose president was former Obama Secretary of Homeland Security Janet Napolitano), a range of plaintiffs argued that the Trump Department of Homeland Security action was not based on proper reasoning and would cause undue harm. The United States Court of Appeals for the Ninth Circuit agreed with the plaintiffs. It acknowledged that a proper reasoning would have left the Trump administration on much firmer ground, while questioning "the cruelty and wastefulness of deporting productive young people to countries with which they have no ties."[79] Thus DACA lived, or perhaps limped, on—at least until the Supreme Court heard the case as part of its 2019–20 docket.

Trade policy

Prior, at least, to the presidency of Donald Trump, trade policy in recent decades had become notable for the difference between the rhetoric embraced by "out" party presidential candidates and the practice of those candidates once they became White House incumbents. That is, campaign expressions of skepticism about the benefits of trade and declarations about how American workers should be protected against unfair competition from abroad gave way to executive branch efforts to promote free trade agreements and secure congressional authorization for those agreements. Further, and again prior to Trump, the tension between campaign protectionism and pro-trade agreement in governance was most evident in the Democratic Party, as it was the Democratic base, with labor unions to the fore, that most protested new trade deals. For example, the fact that NAFTA had been negotiated largely by a Republican administration before being assertively pushed toward congressional ratification by Bill Clinton confused partisan loyalties; but it was notable that Clinton ended up with more Republican votes supporting his position in both chambers of Congress, despite their then Democratic majorities.[80]

Certainly, if with important caveats, Obama's 2008 campaign and his subsequent presidency fit both the patterns outlined above. Firstly, his initial criticism of existing trade pacts gave way to the promotion of trade agreements from the Oval Office. Secondly, even in the highly partisan atmosphere that prevailed throughout his presidency, on trade it was a case of a Democratic president looking to secure Republican congressional votes as much as those from his own party. As we will see, Trump undid both of these patterns as he carried his campaign skepticism into the White House and upended the Republican Party through his decisions, even if his actions in office did not match the extraordinary bombast of his campaign promises. Crucially, in the context of our study, he rapidly pulled the US out of the embryonic Trans Pacific Partnership, which had been a significant last-gasp, but unconsummated, legacy from the Obama administration.

Throughout his presidential campaigining in 2008, Obama's negative narrative on trade was at its sharpest in the Democratic nomination battle with Hillary Clinton. Just prior to the Democratic primary in Ohio, Obama attacked Clinton for her previous support for the NAFTA deal signed by President Bill Clinton.

> One million jobs have been lost because of NAFTA, including nearly 50,000 jobs here in Ohio. And yet, 10 years after NAFTA passed, Senator Clinton said it was good for America. Well, I don't think NAFTA has been good for America—and I never have.[81]

Furthermore, both Obama and Clinton attacked proposed agreements with South Korea and Colombia. Yet, candidate Obama, when he thought he was off camera, also expressed his frustration at the manner in which free trade policies had become an easy target for those Americans disappointed by the loss of manufacturing jobs, and at the failure of elites to match their rhetoric about restoring well-paid work to those communities with effective action. Speaking to an audience at a fund-raising event in San Francisco just prior to the Pennsylvania primary, he reflected on how working-class Americans had reacted to their economic woes: "[I]t's not surprising then they get bitter, they cling to guns or religion or antipathy to people who aren't like them or anti-immigrant sentiment or anti-trade sentiment as a way to explain their frustrations."[82] When these comments were reported, most of the commentary focused on the disparaging tone in which Obama talked of "guns" and "religion," but the reference to understandable, but by implication misguided, anti-trade sentiment suggested that the attacks on Clinton over NAFTA were more about public theater as a role in the Democratic primary battle than about how he viewed the merits of a free trade agenda. And that interpretation was borne out by Obama's time in office.

The administration's record was not unambiguous. For example, "in early September 2009, the administration imposed a 35 percent import fee on certain Chinese low-cost tyres."[83] Leo Gerard, President of the United Steelworkers enthusiastically welcomed that decision:

> The International Trade Commission recommended sanctions under "Section 421" four times before Obama took office. Nothing was done. The result was closed American factories, lost American manufacturing jobs, diminished American dreams. Not this time though. Not this president. Obama showed he's made of tougher stuff. By placing tariffs on imported Chinese tires, President Obama put himself in the line of fire for the jobs of US workers, for the preservation of US manufacturing and, ultimately, for the stabilization of the US economy.[84]

Furthermore, the administration was aggressive in defending US interests before the World Trade Organization, presenting twenty-five cases for arbitration. Overall, however, it is fair to summarize the Obama administration as pursuing a free trade agenda, while trying to persuade skeptics within Democratic ranks that trade liberalization could be compatible with maintaining labor protections and improving environmental regulation.

In December 2010 the administration agreed changes to the free trade agreement with South Korea that had originally been negotiated by the Bush administration. Similarly, there were tweaks to the previously negotiated bilateral agreement with Colombia, with both agreements duly ratified by Congress. The White House marked these deals with little fanfare, reflecting the fact that a majority of Democrats had voted against their passage.[85]

It was the TPP, though, which came to define Obama-era trade policy. The administration's efforts need to be understood in the context of the rather fuzzy nature of the balance of power between the executive and legislative branches over which of them has the higher authority in determining trade policy. The Constitution affords the president "the authority to negotiate international agreements, including free trade agreements (FTAs), but the Constitution gives Congress sole authority over the regulation of foreign commerce and tariffs."[86] Through to the 1930s Congress set tariffs, but in the post-war world the executive branch became increasingly involved in the negotiation of major trade deals, which would then go to Congress for ratification. If this relationship was going to work, it became evident that Congress would need to vote on any deal in its entirety rather than debating and casting votes on any negotiated agreement on a line-by-line basis. Hence, one critical feature of getting Congress to ratify free trade agreements was the need for an up or down vote on any package—rather than letting Congress pick apart a deal, approving some parts but not others in a way that would make negotiations with other countries impossible for the executive branch. Since 1974, Congress has periodically granted the executive authority to negotiate on the basis that any agreement would be subject to a straight vote. This so-called fast track or trade promotion authority was renewed in 1979, 1988, and 2002. Obama's first battle with regard to TPP was to renew that authority once again. Here the normal partisan battle lines were redrawn and Obama worked with the congressional Republican leadership to secure that authority as most Democrats sought ways to block the maneuver.

In fact, in early June 2015 it looked as if the opposition to granting TPA had won the day. In a bizarre move, House Democrats voted against extending Trade Adjustment Assistance (TAA), a program designed to help workers displaced by new trade patterns, which liberals and their union allies had come to accept as a "consolation prize" that came alongside TPA.[87] This vote against TAA was a parliamentary tactic to prevent a bill passing through Congress that Obama could sign. By the end of the month, however, as it became clear that the White

House and Republican leaders would go ahead with a stand-alone TPA bill, enough Democrats relented, so allowing TPA and TAA to go through. Notably, it was Republicans who provided the strongest endorsement of this legislation. For example, the chair of the Senate Finance Committee, Senator Orrin Hatch of Utah, talked of a "critical day for our country" as TPA was "the most important bill we'll do this year." In contrast, Sander Levin, the ranking Democrat member on the House Ways and Means Committee, protested the outcome and promised that he would "work harder than ever to bring about a real confrontation" on trade agreements.[88] And, if organized labor had praised Obama for his earlier action against China, union leaders were furious about the TPP negotiations. At one point, in an effort to stop the granting of TPA, the AFL-CIO PAC froze its donations to Democratic members of Congress.[89] The opposition to TPA did gain some concessions; for example, to allow for full transparency, any trade deals could not be considered by Congress for two months after they had been negotiated. As the *New York Times* reported at the time, such a "delay will most likely push any consideration of the Pacific accord well into the presidential election season," which was likely to be a "difficult political environment" for debating a major trade package.[90] That description turned out to be a considerable understatement.

As the negotiations over TPP neared their end in late fall 2015, Obama tried hard to sell the agreement. He asserted that it reflected "America's values," and that it would encourage trade while maintaining protections for American workers and the environment:

> This partnership levels the playing field for our farmers, ranchers, and manufacturers by eliminating more than 18,000 taxes that various countries put on our products. It includes the strongest commitments on labor and the environment of any trade agreement in history, and those commitments are enforceable, unlike in past agreements. It promotes a free and open Internet. It strengthens our strategic relationships with our partners and allies in a region that will be vital to the 21st century. It's an agreement that puts American workers first and will help middle-class families get ahead.[91]

These arguments, however, were very much running against the tide in the electoral sea of 2016. On the Democratic side, as Hillary Clinton found herself under challenge from Senator Bernie Sanders of Vermont, the pressure grew on her to renounce the deal she had previously described as setting "the gold standard in trade agreements to open free, transparent, fair trade, the kind of environment that has the rule of law and a level playing field."[92] This statement was made during her time as secretary of state in 2012, well before the final agreement was reached. At that time it was not predictable that four years later she would be competing closely for the nomination of her own party against perhaps the most left-wing member of the Senate, who had a history of skepticism toward international trade agreements; to be followed by a general election campaign against a Republican who was even more strongly motivated by protectionist sentiments. As it was, Obama did keep trying to push for a congressional vote on TPP throughout the campaign, but to no avail.[93] Hence, this agreement, which did include more worker and environmental protections than previous iterations of trade deals and which might have acted as a bulwark against China's expansive aggressive trade practices, proved to be only the flimsiest of legacies.[94]

It is unclear how a President Clinton would have treated TPP. It seems quite conceivable that she would have walked back from her walk back, perhaps after securing a tweak or two to the text, and then pressed for congressional ratification. President Trump, however, stuck to his campaign guns and quickly withdrew the US from the agreement. Along with his long-time antipathy to some forms of immigration, Trump had in fact also been a consistent critic of free trade deals, maintaining that the US was constantly outdone in those deals allowing other countries to benefit at the US's expense. From the 1980s onwards he had spoken out against trade agreements; this is exemplified by his hostility to NAFTA, which can be dated back to the time of the agreement's ratification in 1993. In October that year, at an event where former presidents Jimmy Carter, Gerald Ford, and George H. W. Bush all spoke in favor of ratifying the deal then being debated by Congress, Trump was one of the voices against the deal. Trump's speech was not kept as an exact transcript, but newspaper reporting at the time included him saying specifically of NAFTA, "It's a no-brainer. . . . The Mexicans want it, and that doesn't sound good to me," along with the more general refrain that "We never make a good deal."[95]

Trump's opposition to trade agreements was central to his political persona in 2016. In an op-ed piece in *USA Today* during the primary campaign in March 2016, candidate Trump explained his view that the "American worker is being crushed," and continued by arguing that "One of the factors driving this economic devastation is America's disastrous trade policies." Further, this "situation is about to get drastically worse if the Trans-Pacific Partnership is not stopped."[96] Citing data from a left-wing think tank with ties to organized labor, the Economic Policy Institute, the piece took specific aim at Ohio governor and rival for the nomination John Kasich as well as senators Marco Rubio of Florida and Ted Cruz of Texas. This populist break from conservative orthodoxy on the benefits of trade liberalization did not cause too much concern amongst Republican primary voters, and while congressional Republicans did not join this particular Trumpian chorus, protests against his anti-trade rhetoric were ineffective and it mattered little that some of his claims about the negative consequences of the TPP were directly refutable.[97]

The death knell for US participation in the TPP came in the first week of the Trump presidency, when he signed a presidential memorandum instructing the US Trade Representative to inform the other nations that the US "withdraws as a signatory of the TPP and withdraws from the TPP negotiating process."[98] Since the deal had not yet come into effect, Trump's actions did not immediately change any trading relationships; yet, as CNN reported at the time, the move "ends all hopes for a deal Obama wanted as a major part of his legacy."[99] If Obama had hoped to persuade people across the spectrum that trade agreements could be achieved in a way that benefited both business and workers, he failed in this task. Further to Trump's action, and reinforcing how Obama had ended being out of step with political time on trade, Senator Sanders, established as a leading voice of the liberal left, issued a statement saying that he was "glad the Trans-Pacific Partnership is dead and gone."[100]

Conclusion

Writing about Obama's efforts on climate just as Trump came into office, Meg Jacobs reflected on how "Obama maneuvered within the confines of the politically possible" and attempted to use executive powers forcefully; but in the end: "Executive action without political support will probably prove a thin reed on which to build a lasting legacy."[101] These words proved prescient not only with regard to climate policy but also immigration reform, as institutional fragmentation undermined Obama's capacity to act decisively. On climate and immigration, even at the time of maximum possible institutional opportunity, with Democrat majorities in both chambers of Congress, Obama's efforts were thwarted.

Importantly, on climate change issues and immigration reform the increased level of partisanship did not mean that all Democrats were on board with the administration's initiatives. On health care, if accompanied by many agonies throughout the process and grudging concessions to individual senators such as Ben Nelson of Nebraska, the administration and congressional leadership managed to maintain enough unity within the congressional caucus through 2009 to achieve legislative outputs. In contrast, a few hold-outs in the Senate in 2009 and 2010 helped undo the climate bill and the DREAMers Act.[102] The later effort at comprehensive immigration failed despite generating bipartisan support in the Senate. In this case, House Speaker Boehner placed the imperative on maintaining the appearance of unity in his caucus. The 2016 Republican presidential primary and the rise of Donald Trump demonstrated that the GOP's base rejected the direction taken by the Bush administration and the advice in the party's own post-mortem on the 2012 election.

Under President Trump the direction of policy on climate and immigration was decisively reversed, with the Republicans doubling down on their climate change denialism and immigration restrictionism. Here Obama's tepid legacy was overturned, though the courts delayed some of the measures and offered a limited protection to DACA beneficiaries, at least through 2019. The politics of trade remain more confused, with party lines still blurred. The GOP, previously the more reliable party of free trade, found its stance scrambled by the Trump administration. As it was, TPP was easy to reject since, like the Paris climate accord, it had not actually come into effect. More generally, despite actual and threatened tariff wars with China and the European Union, the Trump administration has been more circumspect in its actions than suggested by candidate Trump's promises of massive tariffs against imported goods. On other hand, it was also clear that President Trump was not going to stick to the path heading toward trade liberalization that had been followed by occupants of the White House dating back well before Obama.

Notes

1. Joe Klein, "The Full Obama Interview," *Time*, October 23, 2008, <http://swampland.time.com/2008/10/23/the_full_obama_interview/> (last accessed December 20, 2019).
2. Robyn Eckersley, "Ambushed: the Kyoto Protocol, the Bush Administration's Climate Policy and the Erosion of Legitimacy," *International Politics*, 44.2–3 (March 2007): 306–44, <https://link.springer.com/article/10.1057/palgrave.ip.8800190> (last accessed December 20, 2019).
3. Lawrence H. Goulder, "US Climate Change Policy: The Bush Administration's Plan and Beyond," *Stanford Institute for Economic Policy Research*, policy briefing, February 2002, <https://siepr.stanford.edu/sites/default/files/publications/policybrief_feb02_0.pdf> (last accessed December 20, 2019).
4. "In Depth: Environment," ongoing Gallup poll, n.d., <https://news.gallup.com/poll/1615/environment.aspx>; Monica Anderson, "For Earth Day, Here's How Americans View Environmental Issues," *Pew Research Center*, April 20, 2017, <http://www.pewresearch.org/fact-tank/2017/04/20/for-earth-day-heres-how-americans-view-environmental-issues/> (both last accessed December 20, 2019).
5. Barack Obama and Joe Biden, "New Energy for America," n.d., <https://www.energy.gov/sites/prod/files/edg/media/Obama_New_Energy_0804.pdf> (last accessed December 20, 2019).
6. "In Depth: Environment."
7. Barack Obama, "Proclamation 8364—Earth Day," April 20, 2009, <http://www.presidency.ucsb.edu/ws/index.php?pid=86048.com> (last accessed December 20, 2019).

8. John C. Berg, "Environmental Policy: the Success and Failure of Obama," in W. Crotty (ed.), *The Obama Administration: Promise and Performance* (Lanham, MD: Lexington, 2012).
9. United Nations Framework Convention on Climate Change Report 2009 (2010), March, <https://unfccc.int/resource/docs/2009/cop15/eng/11a01.pdf> (last accessed 20 December 30, 2019).
10. H.R. 2454—American Clean Energy and Security Act (2009), <https://www.congress.gov/bill/111th-congress/house-bill/2454.com> (last accessed December 20, 2019).
11. Judith Layzer, "Cold Front: How the Recession Stalled Obama's Clean-Energy Agenda," in Theda Skocpol and Lawrence Jacobs (eds.), *Reaching for a New Deal: Ambitious Governance, Economic Meltdown, and Polarized Politics in Obama's First Two Years* (New York: Russell Sage Foundation, 2011), 321–85, at 334.
12. Meg Jacobs, "Obama's Fight Against Global Warming," in Julian Zelizer (ed.), *The Presidency of Barack Obama: A First Historical Assessment* (Princeton, NJ: Princeton University Press, 2018), 62–77, at 66.
13. Ryan Lizza, "As the World Burns," *The New Yorker*, October 3, 2010, <https://www.newyorker.com/magazine/2010/10/11/as-the-world-burns> (last accessed December 20, 2019).
14. Anderson, "For Earth Day, here's how Americans view environmental issues."
15. Barack Obama, "Inaugural Address by President Barack Obama," The White House, Office of the Press Secretary, January 21, 2013, <https://obamawhitehouse.archives.gov/the-press-office/2013/01/21/inaugural-address-president-barack-obama> (last accessed December 20, 2019).
16. Barack Obama, "Remarks by the President in State of the Union Address," The White House, Office of the Press Secretary, January 20, 2015, <https://obamawhitehouse.archives.gov/the-press-office/2015/01/20/remarks-president-state-union-address-January-20-2015> (last accessed December 20, 2019).
17. Jacobs, "Obama's Fight Against Global Warming," 73; James Inhofe, *The Greatest Hoax: How the Global Warming Conspiracy Threatens Your Future* (Washington, DC: WND Books, 2012).
18. "Fact Sheet: President Obama's Climate Action Plan," June 25, 2013, <https://obamawhitehouse.archives.gov/the-press-office/2013/06/25/fact-sheet-president-obama-s-climate-action-plan> (last accessed December 20, 2019).

19. Tom Wels, "President Obama's Climate Action Plan: Not Even Close," *Huffington Post*, August 13, 2013, <https://www.huffingtonpost.com/tom-weis/obama-climate-plan_b_3744885.html> (last accessed December 20, 2019). For a summary of actions taken under the Climate Action Plan, see Ori Gutin and Brendan Ingargiola, August 5, 2015, "Fact Sheet: Timeline of Progress Made in President Obama's Climate Action Plan," Environmental and Energy Study Institute, <https://www.eesi.org/papers/view/fact-sheet-timeline-progress-of-president-obama-climate-action-plan> (last accessed December 20, 2019).
20. Lucy Perkins and Bill Chappell, "President Obama Unveils New Power Plant Rules in 'Clean Power Plan,'" *NPR*, August 3, 2015, <https://www.npr.org/sections/thetwo-way/2015/08/03/429044707/president-obama-set-to-unveil-new-power-plant-rules-in-clean-power-plan> (last accessed December 20, 2019).
21. Gregory Korte, "States Challenge Obama's Clean Power Plan as Rules Go Into Effect," *USA Today*, October 23, 2015, <https://eu.usatoday.com/story/news/politics/2015/10/23/24-states-file-legal-challenge-obamas-power-plan/74472236/> (last accessed 20 December 24, 2019).
22. Adam Liptak and Coral Davenport, "Justices Deal Blow to Obama's Efforts to Regulate Coal Emissions," *The New York Times*, February 10, 2016, A1.
23. Steven Groves, "Obama's Plan to Avoid Senate Review of the Paris Protocol," Heritage Foundation, September 21, 2015, <https://www.heritage.org/environment/report/obamas-plan-avoid-senate-review-the-paris-protocol> (last accessed December 20, 2019).
24. "Clinton Hails Global Warning Pact," *CNN*, December 11, 1997, <http://edition.cnn.com/ALLPOLITICS/1997/12/11/kyoto/> (last accessed December 20, 2019).
25. The Paris Agreement and NDCs (undated), United Nations Climate Change, <https://unfccc.int/process/the-paris-agreement/nationally-determined-contributions/ndc-registry>; Daniel Bodansky, *Legal Options for US Acceptance of a New Climate Change Agreement*, 2015, <https://www.c2es.org/document/legal-options-for-u-s-acceptance-of-a-new-climate-change-agreement/> (both last accessed December 20, 2019).
26. *The New York Times/CBS News* Poll on the Environment (November 30, 2015), <https://www.nytimes.com/interactive/2015/11/30/science/earth/01poll-document.html> (last accessed December 20, 2019).

27. Karlyn Bowman, "Public Opinion on the Environment and Global Warning: Is It Changing?" *Forbes*, April 20, 2017, <https://www.forbes.com/sites/bowmanmarsico/2017/04/20/public-opinion-on-the-environment-and-global-warming-is-it-changing/#7bd79d615445> (last accessed December 20, 2019).
28. Environmental Protection Agency, "EPA to Review the Clean Power Plan Under President Trump's Executive Order," EPA News Release, March 28, 2017, <https://www.epa.gov/newsreleases/epa-review-clean-power-plan-under-president-trumps-executive-order> (last accessed December 20, 2019).
29. Donald Trump (@realDonaldTrump) on Twitter, November 6, 2012, <https://twitter.com/keelingover/status/265903119974674432> (last accessed December 20, 2019).
30. "Promises about Climate Change on Trump-O-Meter," *Politifact*, n.d., <https://www.politifact.com/truth-o-meter/promises/trumpometer/subjects/climate-change/> (last accessed December 20, 2019).
31. "Donald Trump's Contract with the American Voter," n.d., <https://assets.donaldjtrump.com/_landings/contract/O-TRU-102316-Contractv02.pdf> (last accessed December 20, 2019).
32. Leigh Paterson and Reid Frazier, "Coal Country Picked Trump. Now, it Wants Him to Keep His Promises," *NPR*, January 1, 2017, <http://www.npr.org/2017/01/01/507693919/coal-country-picked-trump-now-they-want-him-to-keep-his-promises> (last accessed December 20, 2019).
33. Matt Egan, "Why Coal Jobs Aren't Coming Back, Despite Trump's Actions," *CNN Money*, January 24, 2017, <https://money.cnn.com/2017/01/24/investing/trump-coal-epa-regulation/?iid=EL> (last accessed December 20, 2019).
34. Lauren Debter, "Stock Market Slingshots Higher after Trump Victory Sparked Overnight Plunge," *Forbes*, November 9, 2016, <https://www.forbes.com/sites/laurengensler/2016/11/09/trump-wins-election-markets-live-blog/#2e662ce15e1d> (last accessed December 20, 2019).
35. Paris Agreement, Chapter XXVII, Environment, December 12, 2015, <https://treaties.un.org/Pages/ViewDetails.aspx?src=IND&mtdsg_no=XXVII-7-d&chapter=27&clang=_en> (last accessed December 20, 2019).
36. Donald Trump, "Statement by President Trump on the Paris Climate Accord," White House Press Office, June 1, 2017, <https://

www.whitehouse.gov/briefings-statements/statement-president-trump-paris-climate-accord/> (last accessed December 20, 2019).

37. Trevor Nace, "America is Officially the Only Nation on Earth to Reject the Paris Agreement," *Forbes*, November 7, 2017, <https://www.forbes.com/sites/trevornace/2017/11/07/america-is-officially-the-only-nation-on-earth-to-reject-the-paris-agreement/#2dd7ab1e4dc4> (last accessed December 20, 2019).

38. Anne Hidalgo and William Peduto, "The Mayors of Pittsburgh and Paris: We Have Our Own Climate Deal," *The New York Times*, June 7, 2017, <https://www.nytimes.com/2017/06/07/opinion/the-mayors-of-pittsburgh-and-paris-we-have-our-own-climate-deal.html> (last accessed December 20, 2019).

39. Lou Dubose, "Why Has Trump Appointed Perry to Energy?" *Newsweek*, February 20, 2017, <https://www.newsweek.com/why-has-trump-appointed-perry-energy-557971> (last accessed December 20, 2019).

40. World Health Organization, "WHO Calls for Urgent Action to Protect Health From Climate Change," n.d., <http://www.who.int/globalchange/global-campaign/cop21/en/>; Tom DiChristopher, "EPA Chief Scott Pruitt Says Carbon Dioxide is Not a Primary Contributor to Global Warming," CNBC, March 9, 2013, <https://www.cnbc.com/2017/03/09/epa-chief-scott-pruitt.html> (last accessed December 20, 2019).

41. Nadja Popovich, Livia Albeck-Ripka, and Kendra Pierre-Louis, "83 Environmental Rules Being Rolled Back Under Trump," *The New York Times*, June 7, 2019, <https://www.nytimes.com/interactive/2019/climate/trump-environment-rollbacks.html> (last accessed December 20, 2019).

42. Dena Adler, *US Climate Change Litigation in the Age of Trump: Year Two*, Sabin Venter for Climate Change Law, June 10, 2019, <https://blogs.ei.columbia.edu/2019/06/10/trump-climate-deregulation-tracker-2019/> (last accessed December 20, 2019).

43. Eric Lipton, "President's Rush to Deregulate Meets an Obstacle: The Courts," *The New York Times*, October 7, 2017, A1.

44. Robinson Meyer, "The Car Industry Squirms, as It Gets What It Asked For," *The Atlantic*, August 2018, <https://www.theatlantic.com/science/archive/2018/08/car-industry-trump-epa/566738/> (last accessed December 20, 2019).

45. Kif Leswing, "Bad for the Environment, Bad for the Economy," *Business Insider*, July 1, 2017, <https://www.businessinsider.in/

bad-for-the-environment-bad-for-the-economy-facebook-google-and-amazon-react-to-trumps-decision-to-withdraw-from-paris-climate-agreement/articleshow/58953538.cms> (last accessed December 20, 2019).
46. "The US Climate Alliance and Related Actions" (Fact Sheet 2017), Environmental and Energy Study Institute, August 2017, <https://www.eesi.org/files/FactSheet_US_Climate_Alliance_2017.08.pdf> (last accessed December 20, 2019).
47. The 11 million figure comes from the Census Bureau's estimates. One study by researchers at Yale released in fall of 2018 calculated that there might be more than 22 million undocumented individuals in the United States. See Mohammad Fazel-Zarandi, Jonathan Feinstein, and Edward Kaplan, "The Number of Undocumented Immigrants in the United States: Estimates Based on Demographic Modeling with Data from 1990 to 2016," September 21, 2018, <https://journals.plos.org/plosone/article?id=10.1371/journal.pone.0201193> (last accessed December 20, 2019).
48. "Top Voting Issues in 2016 Election," *Pew Research Center*, July 7, 2016, <http://www.people-press.org/2016/07/07/4-top-voting-issues-in-2016-election/> (last accessed December 20, 2019).
49. Barack Obama Acceptance Speech, Democrat National Convention, *C-Span*, August 28, 2008, <https://www.c-span.org/video/?c4599351/barack-obama-acceptance-speech> (last accessed December 20, 2019).
50. Shan Carter, Jonathan Ellis, Farhana Hossein, and Alan McLean, "Election 2008: On the Issues: Immigration," *The New York Times*, 2008, <https://www.nytimes.com/elections/2008/president/issues/immigration.html> (last accessed 20 December 08, 2019).
51. Mark Hugo Lopez, "The Latino Vote in the 2008 Election," *Pew Research Center*, November 7, 2008, <http://www.pewLatino.org/2008/11/05/the-Latino-vote-in-the-2008-election/> (last accessed December 20, 2019).
52. Jorge Ramos interview with Barack Obama, May 29, 2008, <https://www.jorgeramos.com/en/obamas-promise-may-2008/> (last accessed December 20, 2019).
53. Muzaffar Chishti, Sarah Pierce et al., "The Obama Record on Deportations: Deporter in Chief or Not?" Migration Policy Institute, January 26, 2017, <https://www.migrationpolicy.org/article/obama-record-deportations-deporter-chief-or-not>; Department of Homeland Security Yearbook of Immigration Statistics, <https://www.dhs.gov/immigration-statistics/yearbook> (both last accessed December 20, 2019).

54. For an estimate of the numbers forcibly removed and returned during the twentieth century and beyond, see Department of Homeland Security, *Aliens Removed or Returned: Fiscal Years 1892 to 2017*, <https://www.dhs.gov/immigration-statistics/yearbook/2017/table39> (last accessed December 20, 2019).
55. John Skrentny, "Obama's Immigration Reform: A Tough Sell for a Grand Bargain," in Theda Skocpol and Lawrence Jacobs (eds.), *Reaching for a New Deal: Ambitious Governance, Economic Meltdown, and Polarized Politics in Obama's First Two Years* (New York: Russell Sage Foundation, 2011), 273–320, at 281.
56. Julia Preston, "House Backs Legal Status for Many Young Immigrants," *The New York Times*, December 9, 2010, A38.
57. Scott Wong and Shira Toeplitz, "DREAM Act Dies in Senate," *Politico*, December 20, 2010, <https://www.politico.com/story/2010/12/dream-act-dies-in-senate-046573> (last accessed December 20, 2019).
58. Sandra Lilley, "Senate Immigration Bill Revealed: A Path to Citizenship, Shift to Employment-Based Visas," *NBC Latino*, April 16, 2013, <http://nbclatino.com/2013/04/16/senate-immigration-bill-revealed-a-path-to-citizenship-shift-to-employment-based-visas/> (last accessed December 20, 2019).
59. Seung Min Kim, "Senate Passes Immigration Bill," *Politico*, June 27, 2013, <https://www.politico.com/story/2013/06/immigration-bill-2013-senate-passes-093530> (last accessed December 20, 2019).
60. Ginger Gibson, "Boehner: No Vote on Senate Immigration Bill," *Politico*, July 8, 2013, <https://www.politico.com/story/2013/07/john-boehner-house-immigration-vote-093845> (last accessed December 20, 2019).
61. Seung Min Kim and Carrie Budoff Brown, "The Death of Immigration Reform," *Politico*, June 27, 2014, <https://www.politico.com/story/2014/06/how-immigration-reform-died-108374?o=2> (last accessed December 20, 2019).
62. Barack Obama, "Remarks by the President on Border Security and Immigration Reform," The White House, Office of the Press Secretary, June 30, 2014, <https://obamawhitehouse.archives.gov/the-press-office/2014/06/30/remarks-president-border-security-and-immigration-reform> (last accessed December 20, 2019).
63. Sarah Coleman, "Obama and Immigration Policy," in Julian Zelizer (ed.), *The Presidency of Barack Obama: A First Historical Assessment* (Princeton, NJ: Princeton University Press, 2018), 179–94, at 187.

64. Barack Obama, "Remarks by the President on Immigration," The White House, Office of the Press Secretary, June 15, 2012, <https://obamawhitehouse.archives.gov/the-press-office/2012/06/15/remarks-president-immigration> (last accessed December 20, 2019).
65. For a review of presidential authority on who to deport and the politics of DACA, see John D. Skrentny and Jane Lilly López, "Obama's Immigration Reform: The Triumph of Executive Action," *Indiana Journal of Law and Social Equality*, 2.1 (2013), Article 3, <http://www.repository.law.indiana.edu/ijlse/vol2/iss1/3> (last accessed December 20, 2019).
66. Department of Homeland Security, "Immigration Action," November 20, 2014, <https://www.dhs.gov/archive/immigration-action> (last accessed December 20, 2019).
67. Barack Obama, "Remarks by the President in Address to the Nation on Immigration," The White House, Office of the Press Secretary, November 20, 2014, <https://obamawhitehouse.archives.gov/the-press-office/2014/11/20/remarks-President-address-nation-immigration> (last accessed December 20, 2019).
68. Peter Schroeder, "Boehner: Obama will Cement 'Legacy of Lawlessness' with Immigration Order," *The Hill*, July 31, 2014, <https://thehill.com/homenews/house/213931-boehner-obama-will-cement-legacy-of-lawlessness> (last accessed December 20, 2019).
69. Warren Fiske, "Goodlatte: Obama Said 22 Times He Lacks the Power to Change Immigration Law," *Politifact*, April 25, 2016, <https://www.politifact.com/virginia/statements/2016/apr/25/bob-goodlatte/goodlatte-obama-said-22-times-he-lacks-power-chang/> (last accessed December 20, 2019).
70. Ibid.
71. Lawrence Hurley, "Split Supreme Court Blocks Obama Immigration Plan," *Reuters*, June 23, 2016, <https://uk.reuters.com/article/us-usa-court-immigration/split-supreme-court-blocks-obama-immigration-plan-idUKKCN0Z91P4> (last accessed December 23, 2019).
72. "Here's Donald Trump's, Presidential Announcement Speech," *Time*, June 16, 2015, <http://time.com/3923128/donald-trump-announcement-speech/> (last accessed December 23, 2019).
73. Linda Qui, "Donald Trump Repeats Pant on Fire Claims About Million Illegal Immigrants," *Politifact*, September 1, 2016, <https://www.politifact.com/truth-o-meter/statements/2016/sep/01/

donald-trump/donald-trump-repeats-pants-fire-claim-about-30-mil/> (last accessed December 23, 2019).
74. Donald Trump, "Remarks by President Trump on the Government Shutdown," White House, January 25, 2019, <https://www.whitehouse.gov/briefings-statements/remarks-president-trump-government-shutdown/> (last accessed December 23, 2019).
75. Anita Kumar and Caitlin Oprysko, "Trump Lashes Out after Border Defeat," *Politico*, February 15, 2019, <https://www.politico.com/story/2019/02/15/trump-national-emergency-border-wall-1170988> (last accessed December 23, 2019).
76. Eliana Johnson and Katie Galioto, "Trump Issues First Veto of his Presidency," *Politico*, March 15, 2019, <https://www.politico.com/story/2019/03/15/trump-veto-national-emergency-1223285> (last accessed December 23, 2019).
77. Sarah Cammarata, "Trump Accuses Democrats of Inaction on Border Security Hours after House Passes Funding Bill," *Politico*, June 26, 2019, <https://www.politico.com/story/2019/06/26/trump-border-security-bill-1382995> (last accessed December 23, 2019).
78. Donald Trump (@realDonaldTrump) on Twitter, September 14, 2017, <https://twitter.com/realdonaldtrump/status/908276308265795585> (last accessed December 23, 2019).
79. Michael Shear, Julie Hirschfeld Davies and Adam Liptak, "How the Trump Administration Eroded Its Own Legal Case on DACA," *The New York Times*, November 11, 2019, <https://www.nytimes.com/2019/11/11/us/politics/supreme-court-dreamers-case.html> (last accessed December 23, 2019).
80. NAFTA was supported by 132 Republicans and 102 Democrats in the House, with 34 Republican votes and 27 Democrat votes in the Senate.
81. Jake Tapper, "Obama Knocks Clinton, But Wouldn't Ax NAFTA," *ABC News*, February 24, 2008, <https://abcnews.go.com/Politics/Vote2008/story?id=4336481> (last accessed December 23, 2019).
82. Katharine Seelye and Jeff Zeleny, "Obama, Now on the Defensive, Calls 'Bitter' Words Ill-Chosen," *The New York Times*, April 13, 2008, A1.
83. Eddie Ashbee and Alex Waddan, "The Obama Administration and United States Trade Policy," *The Political Quarterly*, 81.2 (2010): 253–62, at 258.
84. Leo Gerard, "Finally, a President with the Guts to Enforce Trade Laws," *Huffington Post*, September 13, 2009, <http://www.

huffingtonpost.com/leo-w-gerard/finally-apresident-with_b_284985.html> (last accessed December 23, 2019).
85. Jim Abrams, "Obama Signs 3 Trade Deals, Biggest Since NAFTA," *NBC News*, 21 October, 2011, <http://www.nbcnews.com/id/44989775/ns/politics-white_house/t/obama-signs-trade-deals-biggest-nafta/#.XfeouTL7RTY> (last accessed December 23, 2019).
86. Congressional Research Service, "Trade Promotion Authority: Frequently Asked Questions," June 2019, <https://fas.org/sgp/crs/misc/R43491.pdf> (last accessed December 23, 2019).
87. Russell Berman, "A Big Win for Big Labor," *The Atlantic*, June 12, 2015, <https://www.theatlantic.com/politics/archive/2015/06/a-big-win-for-big-labor/395699/> (last accessed December 23, 2019).
88. Jonathan Weisman, "Trade Bill Wins Final Approval in the Senate," *The New York Times*, June 25, 2015, B1.
89. Danielle Kurtzleben, "AFL-CIO Head Richard Trumka Explains Why Labor Unions Hate Obama'sTrade Deal," *Vox*, April 20, 2015, <https://www.vox.com/2015/4/20/8445991/afl-cio-tpp-obama-trumka> (last accessed December 23, 2019).
90. Ibid.
91. Barack Obama, "Statement by the President on the Trans-Pacific Partnership," The White House, Office of the Press Secretary, October 5, 2015, <https://obamawhitehouse.archives.gov/the-press-office/2015/10/05/statement-president-trans-pacific-partnership> (last accessed December 23, 2019).
92. Glenn Kessler, "Fact Check: Clinton Did Call TPP the Gold Standard," September 27, 2016, *The Washington Post*, <https://www.washingtonpost.com/politics/2016/live-updates/general-election/real-time-fact-checking-and-analysis-of-the-first-presidential-debate/fact-check-clinton-dod-call-tpp-the-gold-standard/> (last accessed December 23, 2019).
93. Jeffrey Rothfeder, "Why Obama Is Still Trying to Pass the T.P.P.," *The New Yorker*, September 18, 2016, <https://www.newyorker.com/business/currency/why-obama-is-still-trying-to-pass-the-t-p-p> (last accessed December 23, 2019).
94. For a discussion of the TPP agreement and how it was a key part of the Obama administration's "pivot to Asia," see James McBride and Andrew Chatzky, "What is the Trans-Pacific Partnership (TPP)?" *Council on Foreign Relations*, January 4, 2019, <https://www.cfr.org/backgrounder/what-trans-pacific-partnership-tpp> (last accessed December 23, 2019).

95. Andrew Kaczynski, "Donald Trump Spoke Forcefully Against NAFTA at a 1993 Business Conference," *Buzzfeed News*, February 29, 2016, <https://www.buzzfeednews.com/article/andrewkaczynski/trump-spoke-against-nafta-at-1993-convention> (last accessed December 23, 2019).
96. Donald Trump, "Disappearing Middle Class Needs Better Deal on Trade," *USA Today*, March 14, 2016, <https://eu.usatoday.com/story/opinion/2016/03/14/donald-trump-tpp-trade-american-manufacturing-jobs-workers-column/81728584/> (last accessed December 23, 2019).
97. Robert Blackwill and Theodore Rappleye, "Trump's Five Mistaken Reasons for Withdrawing from the Trans-Pacific Partnership," *Foreign Policy*, June 22, 2017, <https://foreignpolicy.com/2017/06/22/trumps-five-mistaken-reasons-for-withdrawing-from-the-trans-pacific-partnership-china-trade-economics/> (last accessed December 23, 2019).
98. "Presidential Memorandum Regarding Withdrawal of the United States from the Trans-Pacific Partnership Negotiations and Agreement," The White House, January 23, 2017, <https://www.whitehouse.gov/presidential-actions/presidential-memorandum-regarding-withdrawal-united-states-trans-pacific-partnership-negotiations-agreement/> (last accessed December 23, 2019).
99. Eric Bradner, "Trump's TPP Withdrawal: 5 Things to Know," *CNN*, January 23, 2017, <https://edition.cnn.com/2017/01/23/politics/trump-tpp-things-to-know/index.html> (last accessed December 23, 2019).
100. Ibid.
101. Jacobs, "Obama's Fight Against Global Warming," 77.
102. It is instructive to view Joe Manchin's run for Senate in 2010 in West Virginia. One campaign advert highlighted a series of issues on which he would stand up to the administration if elected to the Senate, finishing with the line "I'll take dead aim at the cap and trade bill, because it's bad for West Virginia." See <https://www.youtube.com/watch?v=xIJORBRpOPM> (last accessed December 23, 2019).

4

America and the world

Understanding specific presidential legacy in foreign affairs can be problematic. Sometimes a major event can be identified with a particular president; for instance, the US-led invasion of Iraq in 2003 was very much the result of decisions made in the George W. Bush White House. But such self-contained cases are unusual, and even in that instance the tensions between Washington, DC and the Saddam Hussein regime pre-dated Bush. The escalation, if not the origins, of US involvement in the Vietnam War make the description of that conflict as "Johnson's war" understandable, yet even here the reality is less than clear-cut as the US intervention can be traced back to the Kennedy and even Eisenhower administrations.[1] Moreover, the ebb and flow of the international context makes the potential gap between pre-White House campaign promises and the outcomes that emerge once a candidate has shifted to be president particularly great. Presidents may be surprised by how difficult it is to put domestic campaign promises into action, but the problems of legislating in Washington are generally more predictable, if not necessarily more resoluble, than the curveballs that can be thrown by international developments. As he waited to take office in early January 2001 George W. Bush would have been frustrated to be told legislative inertia would mean that Social Security reform would not be part of his legacy—but he would surely have been astonished to have been told that his time in office would be defined by terrorist attacks to be committed nine months later, and that as a consequence he would authorize a military deployment that would be ongoing beyond his successor.

Moreover, even more than in domestic policy and politics presidential claims of achievement can be mocked by subsequent developments, as acutely seen with George W. Bush's very premature declaration on May 1, 2003 that "Major combat activities in Iraq have ended," with a "Mission Accomplished" banner in the background.[2] Bush's legacy with regard to Iraq proved to be very different than he had anticipated on that day and, as described below, it turned out that Obama too misjudged the nature of the conflicts and power dynamics in that country. Further, much of any president's legacy in foreign policy is likely to be a series of ongoing commitments rather than finished articles and however much a successor may wish to disentangle from those commitments it can sometimes be difficult to do so as a form of path dependency kicks in. Hence, while foreign policy legacies can be quite different than a president may have anticipated, so rolling back existing US commitments can be problematic, however much a new occupant of the White House might despair at the quagmire left to them.

From bending history to "We're America"

The historian Jeremi Suri has noted how Obama entered office offering "a liberal internationalist vision—emphasizing multilateralism, negotiation and disarmament," in contrast to the projection of hard military power that had characterized the presidency of George W. Bush.[3] In two major set-piece speeches in the first year of his presidency Obama elaborated on how important it was to put aside stereotypes and increase cooperation between nation-states, even those who were traditionally wary of one another, in order to solve global problems. First, in what became known simply as the "Cairo speech" in June 2009, President Obama stated his determination "to seek a new beginning between the United States and Muslims around the world, one based on mutual interest and mutual respect."[4] Then in December 2009, when accepting the Nobel Peace prize, Obama explained why he thought it necessary to engage diplomatically with even those governments that violated the norms of the liberal international order:

> I know that engagement with repressive regimes lacks the satisfying purity of indignation. But I also know that sanctions without outreach—condemnation without discussion—can carry forward only

a crippling status quo. No repressive regime can move down a new path unless it has the choice of an open door.[5]

It is also important to understand how Obama's emergence onto the national political stage was framed by the idea that he was a critic of the US's reliance on its military strength. Perhaps ironically, given that Hillary Clinton went on to become President Obama's first secretary of state, their differing views on the role of the US in world affairs was critical to Obama's victory over Clinton in the race for the 2008 Democratic presidential nomination.[6] Specifically, Obama's consistent opposition to the war in Iraq gave him traction against Clinton amongst activist Democrats when she appeared to be the odds-on favorite for the party's presidential nomination in late 2007.[7] Yet despite this anti-war stance being a key building block to Obama's political identity as he came onto the national political scene, this positioning should not be over-interpreted. The Nobel speech also included a bold assertion of the benefits of American power: "The United States of America has helped underwrite global security for more than six decades with the blood of our citizens and the strength of our arms."[8]

So, as described by Martin Indyk et al., Obama may have entered office aiming "to bend history's arc in the direction of justice and a more peaceful, stable world," but this ambition was tempered in practice by "innate realism and political caution."[9] Over time, that caution led to debate over whether the administration had a distinct "doctrine" or indeed any clear guiding philosophy. This debate was fueled by Hillary Clinton's (post-State Department) remark complaining about the lack of a quick decision to support the anti-Assad forces in Syria: "great nations need organizing principles, and 'Don't do stupid stuff' is not an organizing principle."[10] Within the administration there was frustrated pushback against Clinton's commentary, with senior advisors to the president noting that Clinton might heed how the Iraq invasion should have "taught Democratic interventionists like Clinton, who had voted for its authorization, the dangers of doing stupid shit."[11]

Hence, Obama's worldview was one that embedded pragmatism as much as idealism, as reflected in his professed admiration for Brent Scowcroft, George H. W. Bush's National Security Advisor.[12] Jeffrey Goldberg refers to Obama's foreign policy perspective as that of a "Hobbsean optimist"; that is, someone who understands that the world is a messy and violent place but calculates that most people are better than they are bad.[13] One aspect of this pragmatism was Obama's acknowledgment that US power was in relative decline, at least inasmuch as the draining wars in Iraq and Afghanistan, along with the economic woes that he had inherited, meant that a strategy of "multilateral retrenchment" was necessary, with US allies taking on an increased responsibility for maintaining the rules base of the liberal international order.[14] Yet, if this was a strategy, it is not clear what it meant in terms of the Obama presidency establishing and leaving a legacy; nor was it a framework likely to appeal to a successor proclaiming the virtues of "America First," who was committed to a build-up of the US military and a renewed assertion of American power.

In fact, during the campaign, candidate Trump suggested that not only would he reject the policies of his predecessor, but he wanted to disrupt the established liberal international order. Some saw this as a reason to celebrate, especially as Obama had "bequeathed to his successor an entire world in disarray."[15] Others saw Trump's casual talk of the value of alliances, his disinterest in the importance of a multilateral rules-based order, and his apparent dismissal of the value of US internationalism as a threat to "the core convictions of the postwar US global project."[16] In interviews with senior White House officials in the Trump administration, Jeffrey Goldberg cited one exchange in the following manner: "'Obama apologized to everyone for everything. He felt bad about everything.' President Trump, this official said, 'doesn't feel like he has to apologize for anything America does.'" This attitude was memorably encapsulated in the phrase, "The Trump Doctrine is 'We're America, Bitch.' That's the Trump Doctrine."[17]

Such apparently stark contrasts between an Obama worldview and a Trumpian perspective, however, can make analysis seem simpler than it is. In reality, seeking to provide some insight on Obama's legacy and its meaning with regard to the US's role in world affairs and the extent to which President Trump effectively reversed that is an intellectually fraught task. Should US actions in Afghanistan from 2009 through to the end of 2016 be seen as Obama initiatives, or are they better understood as efforts to manage an extended Bush legacy passed on again, in January 2017, to President Trump? On the other hand, there are sometimes foreign policy initiatives that can clearly be identified with a president and that their successor can choose to revoke; a prime example is Obama's commitment to a nuclear deal with Iran, and Trump's rejection of that deal. In this chapter, therefore, we think through what can reasonably be seen as Obama-era policies and assess how they fared under the eye of President Trump.

On taking office in 2009, the key priorities for the incoming Obama administration—at least as articulated during the campaign by the then candidate—were to draw down from Iraq and Afghanistan and work toward improving US relations with nations unsettled by the "War on Terror" and the tensions caused by the sometimes abrasive approach taken during the Bush years. This drawdown was not simply a goal for its own sake, but reflected a desire to refocus the priorities of US foreign policy, to be manifested by the "pivot to Asia." Further, if the Obama direction of travel was toward a more limited and pragmatic world role, there were also signs of willingness to reach out to America's traditional adversaries with overtures to Iran, Cuba and Burma to come. Yet it turned out that not everything could be resolved by diplomacy, and even if wary of new interventions the Obama administration found itself drawn into using the US military's capacity in Libya. Together with the expanded use of drones, the Libyan intervention showed an administration certainly prepared to flex its muscles and assert the primacy of the executive branch in foreign affairs.

The Asia pivot

Writing in the fall of 2011, Secretary of State Clinton noted that the Obama administration had invested its energies, in efforts "spanning the entire US government," in developing its relations across the Pacific region. She acknowledged that this had often been a "quiet effort" that did not grab the headlines, but was underpinned by an understanding that "the future of geopolitics will be decided in Asia, not in Afghanistan or Iraq, and the United States will be right at the center of the action."[18] She referenced the significance of the fact that her first overseas visit as secretary of state, in February 2009, was to Asia (she was the first secretary to do this since Dean Rusk in 1961). Clinton's destinations included Japan, South Korea, Indonesia, and China, in addition to demonstrating US support for and accession to the ASEAN Treaty of Amity and Cooperation. One key departure from the Bush years in terms of style, if not quite substance, was to "show up" at Asian events. There had been a notable absence during the Bush years of key officials in attendance at gatherings such as the ASEAN meetings.[19] The essential characteristics included emphasis on multilateralism, diplomacy and development. A crucial strand of this was the desire to tie emerging powers into the world order that the Western powers had shaped in the post-World War II years.[20]

It was this range of actions by administration officials that led to the presentation of Obama as America's first "Pacific President"— but this was in truth hardly the case, as others before him had made similar overtures, not least Richard Nixon. In a 2016 *Foreign Policy* essay, Michael Green at the Center for International and Strategic Studies argues that the Asia pivot had substance but was not as "new" as the administration claimed, since it relied on continuing and building on foundations laid by the Bush administration, including the Trans Pacific Partnership (TPP) agreement and embracing the G-20. There were some practical outreach aspects to the pivot. These included Obama joining the East Asia Summit, establishing the US-ASEAN summit, and a more sustained and coordinated focus on economic issues. In previous years, economic links had been more sporadic and US attention in the region was often taken up with security- and terrorism-related matters. Green argues that US relations with all countries in the region improved in the post-2009 Obama years, with the exception of the politically unstable Thailand. From a regional perspective, this warming may have occurred in part at least due to the unnerving rise of China, and so increasingly robust links with the US were one sensible means of response. Nonetheless, President Obama stated his commitment to supporting China's "core interests" in Asia, which was disconcerting for some. After the change in Chinese leadership, it was soon apparent that Xi Jinping was a tougher counterpart than his predecessor. Soon, Xi's China began to assert itself overtly in the region, and the Obama administration announced new military deployments to Australia.[21] In this context, former Obama staffer Ben Rhodes pointed out that the term "pivot" had been carefully chosen in order to signal an assertive strategy (rather than sounding like the US was in retreat or had to make either/or choices about where to be).[22] In 2012, Secretary of Defense Panetta announced that 60 percent of US naval forces would be deployed in the Pacific by 2020, rather than the 50/50 (Atlantic) split that was in place at the time.[23]

This illustrates how the pivot was complicated by relations with China and the ongoing question of whether to treat that nation as a potentially co-operative partner or as a hostile rival. As a candidate in 2008 Obama had refrained from the standard pattern of the "out party" China-bashing employed by candidates Clinton in 1992 and Bush in 2000, but part of the thinking behind the pivot was to look at the region with less of a focus on China.[24] And, initially, the emerging strategy was interpreted by Chinese leadership as "nothing but a containment policy aimed at China."[25] Obama's first visit to China, in November 2009, was not a success, at least in public relations terms. In his 2016 memoir, *Believer*, David Axelrod recounts how this visit to a "fierce, sophisticated and sometimes unscrupulous competitor" played out. The senior advisor to the president mapped out the administration's incentive for an outreach initiative to a country he referred to as "a very complicated piece of business." Even the individual interactions on the trip were stilted: American jokes were lost in translation, and freeform interactions such as Obama had requested caused concern among hosts who preferred scripted conversations with pre-prepared answers.[26] Matters did improve subsequently, although missteps and misinterpretations of each other's motives meant that as Obama's time in office drew to a close, "the US-Chinese security relationship and the Asia-Pacific region in general are far more tense today than they were at the start of 2009."[27]

Assessing how this stands as legacy, therefore, is complex. Clearly, such a foreign policy priority adjustment, away from the long-standing alignment with Europe, was a shift—geopolitically, strategically, and bureaucratically. Eyebrows were raised among America's traditional allies, but more regarding practical than intellectual concern as they worried whether sufficient resources existed to facilitate an East *and* West focus.[28] It was a strategy underpinned, in the words of Kurt Campbell, Assistant Secretary for East Asia and the Pacific, by the assumption that "the lion's share of the history of the 21st century is going to be written in Asia."[29] The term "congagement" was used to describe the Obama administration's policy mix of realist ideas of "containment" and liberal ideas of "engagement."[30] As time moved on, the pivot was recast as a "rebalance" to make it sound less assertive and the *New York Times* journalist Mark Landler, who covered the Obama administration extensively, offered qualified praise reflecting that regardless of the "name, the policy was a rare example of over-the-horizon thinking by an administration that, in other parts of the world, seemed to lurch from crisis to crisis."[31]

Yet, perhaps the most concrete manifestation of the strategy by the end of the Obama era was the Trans Pacific Partnership, viewed as the future "linchpin" of the US vision for trade in the region and as a counterweight to China's economic power; and the fate of that agreement remained uncertain, not ratified by Congress, when Obama left office. As described in Chapter 3, it was an agreement disavowed by both candidates Trump and Clinton in 2016 and was promptly abandoned by President Trump. As well as reflecting Trump's rejection of existing trade deals, the move also reflected his distrust of the types of multilateral international agreements pursued by the Obama administration.

Beyond this big picture, it is worth reflecting on the Obama administration's efforts to re-integrate Burma into the international community as an example of how an apparent success story and positive legacy can turn sour. As Burma showed some signs of moving away from military rule in the direction of democracy, the US moved toward loosening of existing trade sanctions. On an Asia-Pacific tour in November 2011, the President announced that Hillary Clinton would visit Burma.[32] Sending a secretary of state for the first time in fifty years to one of the world's most repressive countries was, in the words of

Freedom House director David J. Kramer, "a pretty big deal."[33] The president spoke of leading in Asia on human rights issues, encouraged by the "flickers of progress" evident in Burma's actions.[34] He built a personal rapport with Aung San Suu Kyi, in part when she visited Washington, DC in 2012 to receive her Congressional Gold Medal. The same year, the US eased previously crushing sanctions as a reward for Burma's efforts toward democratic progress. The two leaders met again a number of times, including when Obama visited the long-isolated nation in October 2016.

By the fall of 2017, however, claims of progress toward democracy and respect for human rights in the country looked considerably more problematic as the Rohingya crisis made international headlines, with the United Nations describing the military offensive in Rakhine province as a "textbook example of ethnic cleansing."[35] Ben Rhodes, who served as Deputy National Security Advisor for Strategic Communications, was known for his sometimes controversial approach to dealing with rogue nations—that is, to engage with them and then work toward persuading them to change their behavior. Rhodes had been instrumental in encouraging the President to take this approach with Burma, with the loosening of sanctions as rewards for diplomacy-related improvements.[36] According to Rhodes, if the Rohingya crisis had occurred on Obama's watch, the President would have been in regular touch with Ang San Suu Kyi in an effort to keep the fledgling democratic process on track.[37] And it was the case that the Trump administration stood relatively askance from events. As former US ambassador to Burma (2012–16) Derek Mitchell told the *Washington Post*, "there is not the kind of strong interest in the White House as there used to be."[38] Vice President Mike Pence called on the United Nations to take "strong and swift action" to end the violence against the Rohingya Muslims, but there was limited pressure applied directly.[39] Yet Rhodes's argument seems more of an effort to rationalize the investment, and subsequent disappointment, in the leadership of Ang San Suu Kyi rather than a serious effort to suggest that the Trump administration's disengagement explained why, two years after Obama left office, the "democratization" of Myanmar had to be deleted from Obama's CV.

As noted above, when she explained the reasoning behind the "pivot," Secretary Clinton directly referenced Iraq, indicating that this was not where the US's long-term strategic interests should be prioritized.[40] That did not mean, however, that the Obama administration was going to be able to deal quickly and effectively with its inheritance from the Bush years and move on from the conflict in Iraq and the wider Arab world. In the following section, we examine the Obama administration's legacy in Iraq, Libya, and Syria. These cases provide an examination of how the Obama White House dealt with the legacy of the defining decision of the Bush administration and how it responded to two international crises that burst into the open on its watch, with an intervention justified on humanitarian grounds in one case but a policy of "wait and see" adopted in the other, even as a brutal conflict left a huge toll of death and population displacement.

Iraq

Obama's policies toward Iraq, the drawdown of US forces, and the subsequent rise of ISIS make up a complex story, and one that illustrates the folly of making premature claims about the effects of decisions taken in very uncertain environments. Obama had campaigned on a withdrawal of US forces from Iraq, but in fact when he arrived in office that was already an existing commitment as a consequence of the Status of Forces Agreement with Iraq, which had been signed by US and Iraqi representatives in mid-November 2008. This agreement stated that US forces would leave Iraq by the end of 2011. The agreement was fulfilled, although throughout 2011 there was debate in both Washington and Baghdad about whether a force numbering between 10,000 and 24,000 should remain. The US ambassador to Iraq was amongst those urging that a presence numbering several thousand should be maintained in the country, but as the Iraqi government would not concede that US forces be exempt from Iraqi law, no agreement was reached.[41]

The withdrawal of US forces, however, far from marked the end of American actions in Iraq as turmoil, notably in the shape of ISIS, continued to roil that troubled country. By the summer of 2014 Obama had authorized US air strikes against ISIS in Iraq as the threat from that terrorist organization came into clearer view. Although he insisted, "As Commander in Chief, I will not allow the United States to be dragged into another war in Iraq," the actions he took made it clear that his legacy was to be a complex one, far from reflecting a straightforward implementation of his 2008 campaign promise.[42] In September 2014 Obama took the further step of authorizing air strikes against ISIS targets in Syria, with the White House issuing a statement that it would "welcome action by the Congress that would aid the overall effort" while noting that it did not believe it needed approval to extend the scope of the battleground.[43]

Famously, according to Donald Trump when speaking at a campaign rally in Florida in August 2016, one of Obama's legacies was ISIS itself, as Trump asserted of the then President: "He's the founder of ISIS," adding that the group "honors" him.[44] Trump's comments were clearly for performance rather than a serious contribution to the foreign policy debate; but the rise of ISIS, and the renewed US engagement in Iraq and expansion of action against the terrorist group into Syria, illustrate the difficulties of trying to judge a presidential legacy in international affairs at any fixed point in time. They also highlight the danger for a president of making grand claims that soon unravel. Speaking to David Remnick of the *New Yorker* in early 2014, Obama, in what Remnick described as an "uncharacteristically flip analogy," spoke of al Qaeda's spin off groups in the following terms: "The analogy we use around here sometimes, and I think is accurate, is if a jayvee team puts on Lakers uniforms that doesn't make them Kobe Bryant."[45] Obama later denied that he had been referring to ISIS with this comment, but it was a denial that carried little credibility.[46] As Obama's presidency drew to a close, the US-backed forces battling against ISIS in Iraq and Syria were making headway and recapturing territory that had been claimed as part of the "caliphate," but the fighting was ongoing as he left office.[47] Moreover, ISIS-inspired terrorism was witnessed in the US as well as in Europe, roiling domestic political stability.[48]

Libya

In her examination of Obama's foreign policy, Donette Murray notes how the intervention in Libya fitted with the administration's preference for mitigating human rights abuses when it could do so in a quite particular way: "In short, the administration judged that there were good reasons why the international community *should* act—both moral and practical—and these were reinforced by a belief that they *could* act."[49] The administration's actions in some ways came to be characterized by the phrase "leading from behind," a phrase used by an advisor to the president.[50] This was meant to convey that the administration recognized that an overly bullish attitude from the US in the international arena could be alienating, especially in the aftermath of the Iraq invasion. With specific regard to Libya it also seemed to reflect how Obama committed to action in the wake of the lead taken by the British and especially the French. Yet, this is a little misleading, for although the French and British took the lead in proposing to the UN that a no-fly zone be established—with the US initially reluctant to support this idea—when Obama did come on board, the administration then overtook its allies in proposing a wider mission involving a formal military intervention. Obama's personal involvement, and the degree to which this represented a bolder move than some in the administration were comfortable with, was illustrated by the decision to act against the advice of Secretary of Defense Robert Gates.[51] On the other hand, the President was clear about setting strict limits of what that intervention would comprise. Air strikes were not to be a stepping stone to further mission creep, with a sharp admonishment that there would be "no boots on the ground."[52]

In the very short term, this action was perceived a success. Writing in early 2012, Ivo Daalder, who was US Permanent Representative to NATO, and James Stavridis, Supreme Allied Commander Europe and Commander of the US European Command, commended the operation in Libya as a "model intervention." Led by the US, they added, the NATO "alliance responded rapidly to a deteriorating situation that threatened hundreds of thousands of civilians rebelling against an oppressive regime. It succeeded in protecting those civilians and, ultimately, in providing the time and space necessary for local forces to overthrow Muammar al-Qaddafi."[53] Speaking in October 2011, shortly after the death of Qaddafi, Obama reflected on what was seen as a successful intervention: "Without putting a single US service member on the ground, we achieved our objectives, and our NATO mission will soon come to an end." The president acknowledged "difficult days ahead" but added, "the United States, together with the international community, is committed to the Libyan people. . . . And now, we will be a partner as you forge a future that provides dignity, freedom and opportunity."[54] If not quite Obama's "mission accomplished" moment, this was a premature judgment on the future of Libya, at least in the medium term, and the commitment to help secure stability in that country proved to be less meaningful than it might have sounded. Similarly, Daalder and Stavridis, while urging NATO to learn the value of acting together and sharing responsibilities from the Libyan experience, made minimal reference in their article to either the US's or NATO's role in Libya once Operation Unified Protector was over.

As it turned out, the legacy of the Libya intervention was much more institutionally complex, politically damaging for the administration, and fraught for Libya itself than these happy preliminary assessments came close to understanding. Firstly, the conduct of the military action itself prompted questions about whether the administration had bypassed the Congress and a possible invocation of the War Powers Resolution. The administration dismissed this idea on the grounds that NATO forces and drones were the primary means of action, meaning that there was minimal risk of US casualties.[55] In justifying the refusal to consult Congress, Harold Koh, a legal advisor to the State Department who had been a sharp critic of what he had described as the Bush administration's undue expansion of executive authority, insisted: "We are not saying the War Powers Resolution is unconstitutional or should be scrapped or that we can refuse to consult Congress. We are saying the limited nature of this particular mission is not the kind of 'hostilities' envisioned by the War Powers Resolution."[56] The *New York Times* editorial page, while urging support for the intervention itself, described this line of reasoning as one that "borders on sophistry."[57] Whatever the merits of the rationale produced by the White House, it was a justification that created a precedent that would likely be welcomed by future presidents looking to continue controversial actions without asking for congressional approval.[58]

Secondly, the fate of Libya after Qaddafi's ouster very quickly turned sour, destabilizing that country with effects that in turn destabilized the administration and in fact continued to haunt Secretary Clinton during her ill-fated 2016 presidential bid. It turned out that the coalition of countries that had come together to prevent Qaddafi's forces from attacking those protesting the regime, and that had in the end helped overthrow that regime, had made few plans for the consequences of its actions. Alan Kuperman, making the case that it would have been better not to intervene at all, argued in 2015,

> In retrospect, Obama's intervention in Libya was an abject failure, judged even by its own standards. Libya has not only failed to evolve into a democracy; it has devolved into a failed state. Violent deaths and other human rights abuses have increased several fold. Rather than helping the United States combat terrorism, as Qaddafi did during his last decade in power, Libya now serves as a safe haven for militias affiliated with both al Qaeda and the Islamic State of Iraq and al-Sham (ISIS).[59]

Obama took a different lesson about the merits of the intervention, but acknowledged that post-intervention developments had been highly problematic. When asked in April 2016 what had been the "worst mistake" of his time in office, Obama replied: "Probably failing to plan for the day after, what I think was the right thing to do, in intervening in Libya."[60] As Dominic Tierney points out, this meant that the Obama administration's record in Libya and its strategy for a sustainable post-intervention framework were flawed in the same way that the Bush administration's planning had been in Iraq.[61] The cost in American blood and treasure was significantly less, and there was no legacy of an ongoing military commitment, but Libya was left with little effective internal authority and a collapsed political system. This does not mean that the bloody events in Libya were caused by the intervention, as there was clearly already an incipient civil war developing; nor even that the intervention made things worse.[62] But if the aim was to demonstrate that it was possible, in tightly constrained circumstances, to act in a humanitarian fashion without needing to worry about what happened next, then a legacy of the Libyan intervention was to suggest the folly of such an optimistic approach. Clear evidence of the failure in Libya came in the summer of 2016 when President Obama authorized air strikes in the city of Surt to combat the growing presence of ISIS in the city.[63] These strikes were conducted at the behest of the UN-backed Libyan government, but that was a government with little capacity to police its own borders.

Syria

Obama's actions, in keeping America distant from the conflict in Syria, were apparently in accord with public sentiment, with polls showing majorities disagreeing with the idea that the US had a responsibility to act. There was some evidence that the numbers shifted when the Assad regime's use of chemical weapons were factored into questions, but not in a decisive fashion.[64]

Defending his administration's actions, or inactions, with regard to Syria, Obama explained:

> It is very difficult to imagine a scenario in which our involvement in Syria would have led to a better outcome, short of us being willing to undertake an effort in size and scope similar to what we did in Iraq. And when I hear people suggesting that somehow if we had just financed and armed the opposition earlier, that somehow Assad would be gone by now and we'd have a peaceful transition, it's magical thinking.[65]

Whatever the merits of this argument, Obama's opponents, and even some normally supportive voices, felt that the White House had diminished America's credibility by not enforcing its proclaimed "red line" in August 2013. That line had apparently been drawn a year earlier when, toward the end of a wide-ranging twenty-minute briefing with the White House press corps, Obama had replied to a question about what action the administration proposed to take with regard to the deteriorating situation in Syria and the Assad regime's chemical weapons stockpile by saying the following:

> We have been very clear to the Assad regime, but also to other players on the ground, that a red line for us is we start seeing a whole bunch of chemical weapons moving around or being utilized. That would change my calculus. That would change my equation.[66]

When, therefore, in August 2013, compelling evidence emerged that the Assad regime had used chemical weapons that resulted in the deaths of nearly 1,500 people, the pressure on the administration to act increased.[67] Even some senior figures who had previously been skeptical of the merits of US action, such as Joint Chief of Staff Marty Dempsey, urged a military strike.[68] Yet, as the United Kingdom's parliament prohibited Prime Minister David Cameron from translating his support for strikes into actual military action and close Obama ally German Chancellor Angela Merkel advised caution, Obama decided that he would seek congressional authorization for strikes.[69] This authorization would remove any doubt about the constitutionality of the strikes and also mean that there was shared ownership of any long-term downside. Congress, however, never voted on the matter and those who felt that the US needed to back up its apparently unequivocal words with action were left frustrated. As it was, the move away from ordering the strikes was very much Obama's own decision, taken alongside fellow skeptic and Chief of Staff Denis McDonough, to the surprise and consternation of the senior foreign policy team.[70] In an essay that was largely favorable to Obama's conduct of foreign policy, Gideon Rose, editor of the journal *Foreign Affairs*, disparagingly commented on how this episode unfolded: "first casually announcing a major commitment, then dithering about living up to it, then frantically tossing the ball to Congress for a decision—was a case study in embarrassingly amateurish improvisation."[71]

By 2016, however, Obama saw this decision to step back from strikes against Syria in 2013 as one of his best:

> I'm very proud of this moment. . . . The perception was that my credibility was at stake, that America's credibility was at stake.
>
> And so for me to press the pause button at that moment, I knew, would cost me politically. And the fact that I was able to pull back from the immediate pressures and think through in my own mind what was in America's interest, not only with respect to Syria but also with respect to our democracy, was as tough a decision as I've made—and I believe ultimately it was the right decision to make.[72]

Others have defended the final decision, if not the decision-making process, by pointing to the manner in which the US's step back gave space for a Russian initiative that led to the organized removal of more chemical weapons from Syrian soil than would possibly have been achieved by limited air strikes.[73] In April 2014 Obama noted, "My job as Commander in Chief is to deploy military force as a last resort," before adding that many of his critics advocated military action without thinking through the consequences and that what had transpired with regard to Syria's chemical weapons illustrated the benefits of restraint, as "it turns out we're getting chemical weapons out of Syria without having initiated a strike."[74] Three months after this, Secretary of State John Kerry went as far as to claim: "Russia has been constructive in helping to remove 100 percent of the declared chemical weapons from Syria."[75] However, it was not long after Obama left office that the limits of these claims became evident as in April 2017 Assad's forces unleashed a sarin gas attack on the town of Khan Sheikhoun.[76] The eradication of the Assad regime's chemical weapons stockpile was manifestly not a legacy that Obama left to his successor.

As Obama's presidency drew to a close two former advisors to his National Security Council noted how events in Iraq and Libya had soured the ground for liberal interventionists and "undermined any American willingness to put values before interests." Yet, they added the administration had developed a "clear Syria policy," which involved air strikes against ISIS forces operating in the country and a continued effort to reach a negotiated settlement that would see the removal of Assad from power. They acknowledged that this was "frustrating" and that efforts toward the latter goal had proved "unsatisfying," but it remained the only "sensible course of action."[77] In this view, therefore, Obama's legacy was the least bad of a series of bad possibilities, although it neglected to reflect on the role the administration had played in creating an environment so unfavorable to intervention through its ill-thought-out actions in Libya.

When assessing Obama's legacy with regard to US policy in the Middle East, it is important to distinguish retrenchment from disengagement and also to understand retrenchment in a broader historical timeframe than a comparison with the mid-2000s. According to Derek Chollet, a former special assistant to Obama and a senior director at the National Security Council, when Obama decided against direct intervention he was not motivated by a desire to disengage, but acting out of a recognition that there was not an American solution to every problem. Moreover, despite the withdrawal of the US ground forces from Iraq, the "military footprint" in the region at the end of the Obama presidency remained "quite significant" as "even if you set aside the capabilities we have in theater to fight the ISIL campaign, more military men and women are deployed in the Middle East than before 9/11 in terms of our maritime and air presence."[78] Some commentators took a dimmer view. Krieg, for example, offers a damning verdict on the Obama legacy in the Middle East, noting how the efforts to use surrogate forces and technologies rather than acting more directly had led to a "loss of control and oversight, the inability to shape conflicts directly and the failure to develop sustainable and reliable long-term strategies for US national interests" that "undermined the position of the United States as the leading power in an increasingly apolar world."[79]

What does seem clear is that in the three cases of Iraq, Libya, and Syria, Obama's final legacy at the end of 2016 was one that no incoming president could explicitly embrace or repudiate in a comprehensive fashion. There were ongoing military operations against ISIS and related terrorist groups that would continue in one form or another along with political and diplomatic efforts to broker ceasefires and increased governmental stability. Barring a major intervention, there was little that Trump and his administration could do that would explicitly change the direction of these policies. One difference was that President Trump did prove prepared to use military force in response to clear evidence that the remaining chemical weapons had been employed as a weapon against civilians. In April 2018, acting with French and British forces, the US launched 105 missiles against targets in Syria. This was in fact the second strike, following the deployment of fifty-nine missiles in April 2017. Then Secretary of Defense James Mattis explained the increased volume of the second strike:

> Clearly, the Assad regime did not get the message last year. . . . This time, our allies and we have struck harder. Together, we have sent a clear message to Assad, and his murderous lieutenants, that they should not perpetrate another chemical weapons attack for which they will be held accountable.[80]

Yet, it is important to understand that these actions by the Trump administration, while enforcing Obama's "red lines" in a manner that Obama did not, represent only a limited rollback of the wider Syria policy. There was little follow-up to these strikes and no suggestion that the US commit a major force to help overthrow the Assad regime. Yet, as Alex Ward points out, the fact that the Trump administration could authorize these missile strikes without that leading to a wider US involvement does undermine Obama's rationalization of his actions.[81]

Iran

It is difficult to think of any aspect of the Obama legacy more categorically rejected by his successor than the Joint Comprehensive Plan of Action (JCPOA), known more informally as the Iran Deal. Implementation day was scheduled for January 16, 2016, the anniversary of the Shah's departure into exile. The JCPOA was a signal achievement of collective foreign policy by the US and key allies (Russia, France, China, the UK, Germany, and the EU).[82] Whilst the deal faced domestic political resistance in the

US, including from some Democrats who were sympathetic to Israeli concerns about the trustworthiness of the Iranian regime, it did not meet with meaningful bureaucratic opposition and made "tremendous sense technologically."[83] The decision by President Trump to withdraw the US from proceedings was immense, both symbolically and substantially.

In January 2009, Barack Obama came to power thirty years after the US-backed Shah was forced to flee Iran. Ever since the Islamic religious leader Ayatollah Khomeini returned from exile two weeks later in February 1979, US–Iranian relations had veered between non-existent and overtly hostile. On the 2008 campaign trail, Obama had visited Israel and the West Bank. During a press conference he talked about the "game-changing situation" that a nuclear Iran would be, stating that "the world must prevent Iran from obtaining nuclear weapons."[84] On the other hand, his suggestion that he would meet with the Iranian leader without first setting down preconditions, reflecting the idea that it was worth at least trying to engage with hostile regimes, drew criticism. On entering the Oval Office, President Obama stated that he wanted a new emphasis on respect in the conduct of US–Iranian relations.[85] In addition, he agreed that his first television interview as president would be with Arab television network Al Arabiya in February 2009.[86] This good-will gesture came during a period when Iran was considered to be noncompliant with its Nuclear Proliferation Treaty, as noted by the UN Security Council in 2006. As a result, Iran had been instructed to suspend its enrichment programs. The prospects for meaningful talks improved with a change in political leadership in Iran that saw President Ahmadinejad replaced by President Rouhani, the latter having a reputation as a more moderate figure. In September 2013 a historic phone call, hailed as a significant diplomatic breakthrough, took place between Presidents Rouhani and Obama; they discussed efforts to reach agreement over Iran's nuclear program. It was the first time leaders of the two countries had spoken for over thirty years.[87]

Evolving from the 2013 Joint Plan of Action after two years of tense, highly technical and dense negotiations, the Joint Comprehensive Plan of Action was created in Vienna on July 14, 2015, by six world powers (China, France, Russia, UK, US, and Germany, often referred to as the P5+1) and Iran. The American negotiators were always aware that any agreement could not be submitted to the Senate as a treaty for ratification, as there was zero chance of getting the supermajority needed for such confirmation. The team were surprised, however, by the actions of Republican Senator Tom Cotton of Arkansas, who penned an open letter to the Iranians baldly stating that any measure forced through as an executive action could be easily reversed by a future president. As it was, the US side used this as leverage to persuade the Iranians that they were taking political risks and they were at the limits of what they could offer.[88] The strength of domestic opposition was revealed in September 2015 when a Republican resolution in the Senate to reject the executive agreement was supported by a clear majority, but fell short of breaking a Democratic filibuster by two votes. Hence, while Obama celebrated "a victory for diplomacy, for American national security, and for the safety and security of the world," it was evident that the longevity of American participation in this deal was highly contingent on short-term political developments.[89]

The plan came into effect from January 16, 2016,[90] but was a target throughout the year for candidate Trump, who repeatedly referred to the JCPOA deal as "one of the worst deals ever," and labeled Iran as one of the biggest state sponsors of terrorism around the world.[91] This chimed with the view of many in his adopted party and he polled well on his promise to take the US out of the deal.[92] The nature of the deal called for regular recertification from the US, and in October 2017 President Trump announced that he would not again certify the agreement. In an address from the White House, Trump talked through the evolution of the "fanatical regime" with its "murderous past and present," outlining his reasons for distancing himself from "one of the worst and most one-sided transactions the United States has ever entered into." Then, in May 2018, the White House announced the US's formal withdrawal. Later in that month, Secretary of State Mike Pompeo gave a speech at the Heritage Foundation outlining the administration's frustration with Iranian behavior more widely in international affairs and denouncing the JCPOA as flawed and unworkable, as well as only offering a delay, rather than an end, to Iran's nuclear ambitions. In reference to the previous administration, Pompeo stated that "strategically, the Obama administration made a bet that the deal would spur Iran to stop its rogue state actions and conform to international norms." He continued, "that bet was a loser with massive repercussions for all of the people living in the Middle East."[93] In his 2019 State of the Union remarks, President Trump reminded the nation that his administration "had acted decisively to confront the world's leading state sponsor of terror: the radical regime in Iran" and put in place the "toughest sanctions ever imposed on a country."[94]

President Trump's decision to walk away from the JCPOA angered not only Iran, but also the other partners in the P5+1. The three western allies, France, Germany, and the UK, all lobbied to maintain this part of Obama's legacy and even sought ways to keep the agreement functioning without the US.[95] The Trump administration's repudiation of the pleas of its traditional allies was not perhaps intended as an explicit implementation of the "We're America, Bitch" doctrine, but the indifference shown to wider international opinion was indicative of a worldview quite different from that held by the preceding administration. It is difficult to establish a precise Obama legacy with regard to the somewhat intangible question of America's role as what might be termed a collaborative actor in the world, but it is worth briefly reflecting on the interaction between the US and international institutions during the Obama era to get some measure of how those relationships shifted in tone from January 2017 onwards.

The US and international organizations: NATO

Obama might be viewed as the least Atlanticist president in America's post-war history. On his watch US troop numbers in Europe were reduced to 30,000. That is, according to Major General Robert Scales, less than the amount of police in New York City.[96] Moreover, while never publicly hostile to NATO, the Obama administration did let its resentment about perceived shortfalls in European spending on defense be known. During the Obama years, the US continued to be the dominant global military power, one which continued to underwrite Europe's security long after the continent had regained its post-World War II composure. Only four of NATO's European partners met the agreed defense expenditure of 2 percent of GDP.[97] Nevertheless, whilst Obama did shine a light on the inequality in NATO contributions, he also, not least in his final speech to NATO in 2016, highlighted "what will never change." In other words, he reinforced America's "unwavering commitment" to Article 5, pledging each member state to consider an armed attack on one as an attack on all member states in Europe or North America.

In contrast, first as candidate and then as president, Trump openly and consistently questioned NATO's purpose and efficiency, calling it "obsolete" and calling out member states for not shouldering their share of the economic costs. This latter criticism echoed the Obama administration but was expressed in a much more aggressive tone. Embracing his moniker as the "Disrupter in Chief" at the 2018 summit, *Politico* reported that the President "disorientated NATO leaders" with a "whiplash performance" including overt criticism of members for not meeting their spending targets.[98] In early 2019, NATO Secretary General Jens Stoltenberg told Fox News that "the clear message from Donald Trump is having an impact."[99] The practical manifestation of this was that NATO allies promised to bring forward planned increases in defense spending. In Trumpian terms this was a win for the President and could be explained by the sharper elbows and implied threats that the Trump administration was prepared to employ in contrast to the ineffectual diplomatic pleading of the Obama era. The cost was frayed relationships and a loss of trust amongst key allies—notably Europe's economic powerhouse, Germany—with the tensions barely concealed at the February 2019 Munich Security Conference.[100]

The United Nations

The United States is the most powerful member and the largest contributor to the United Nations. In a pattern exacerbated during the George W. Bush administration, Republicans tended to perceive the UN with some suspicion (as they do many international organizations), viewing it as a potential threat or curb to American global power. That skepticism, however, is not universally shared, with most data that has been gathered illustrating how, overall, the majority of Americans polled were more supportive of the UN than not.[101]

In a broad expression of his foreign policy thoughts in a July 2008 speech at the Ronald Reagan Building in Washington, DC, candidate Obama outlined the grave challenges facing not only the United States but the world in the early twenty-first century. As he mapped out his vision it was abundantly clear that he was addressing a nation weary of war and international engagement. This acknowledged, he called for a new era of international cooperation. Speaking about the United Nations, he referred to its role in amplifying rather than constraining American values, and in addition he called for UN reform, "so that this imperfect institution can become a more perfect forum to share burdens, strengthen our leverage, and promote our values."[102] In a similar vein, in a September 2009 address to the UN, President Obama reiterated his administration's move away from the unilateral positions sometimes taken by the Bush administration and toward a more multilateral approach to common challenges including climate change, peace and nuclear non-proliferation,[103] even if only limited progress was ever made toward these goals. In contrast, speaking to the American Israel Public Affairs Committee, Trump claimed in 2016 that the UN "is not a friend of democracy." In addition, he dismissed the UN for "utter weakness and incompetence." Over time, he accused the organization of being a talking shop and of being no friend to America.[104]

Some insights into Obama's perception of the UN can be gleaned from his choices of US ambassador. Susan Rice and later Samantha Power were on a notably different diplomatic page to Bush appointee John Bolton.[105] Bolton's language with regard to the UN was overtly derisive. As it was, despite Trump's sometimes apparently dismissive approach to the UN and its world role, the choice of former South Carolina governor Nikki Hailey to be US ambassador to the UN was relatively uncontroversial. As with his NATO-related campaign rhetoric, President Trump walked back to some extent from the most inflammatory aspects of his earlier UN criticism.

Ending the Cold War? Relations with Cuba

If the Iran deal was the Obama administration initiative directly repudiated by the Trump administration that generated the most international attention, also of consequence was the loosening but then quasi-closing of US relations with Cuba. As Mark Landler recounts, the outreach to the Cuban regime was very centered around Obama himself rather than the wider foreign policy team.[106] With relatively little media focus on the ongoing negotiations, with the Vatican acting as a mediator Obama caused some surprise in December 2014 when he announced that the two countries would resume diplomatic relations. The following month the administration announced a series of measures designed to "facilitate travel" as well as allowing more remittances to be returned to Cuba and allowing US "financial institutions to open correspondent accounts at Cuban financial institutions."[107] Then, in March 2016, Obama became the first US president to visit Cuba in nearly ninety years. While there, he declared: "I have come here to bury the last remnant of the Cold War in the Americas."[108] Republicans in Congress made it clear that they opposed revoking trade sanctions, but initial polling suggested majority support for the administration's moves.[109] And at first it seemed as if candidate Trump was more in tune with the White House than Republicans on Capitol Hill, but in September 2016, campaigning in Miami, he said that he would try to undo Obama's actions. He explained that "all the concessions that Barack Obama has granted the Castro regime was done through executive order, which means they can be undone and that is what I intend to do unless the Castro regime meets our demands."[110]

When Trump took office the promise to reverse the easing of relations was vociferously supported by some leading Republican figures, notably Florida senator Marco Rubio, but there was counter-pressure from businesses hoping to develop new markets. For example, by "2017, ports in Virginia, Alabama, and Mississippi had signed agreements with Cuba to explore opportunities for increasing trade."[111] These negotiations saw limited progress, but for the first two years of the Trump presidency the actions taken to explicitly reverse the increase in commercial activity were limited. The most evident change was the surge of Americans visiting Cuba via cruise ships and eventually, in June 2019, the administration took a decisive step by effectively banning cruise ships from stopping at Cuban ports. In a statement explaining the decision, Secretary of Commerce Wilbur Ross maintained: "Cuba remains communist, and the United States, under the previous administration, made too many concessions to one of our historically most aggressive adversaries."[112] Prior to this, US diplomatic staff in Havana had been cut to a minimum following a bout of unexplained sickness amongst diplomats stationed there,[113] but diplomatic relations were at least formally maintained.

Conclusion

One theme that commentators mulled over at the end of the 2000s was whether the combination of the hit to the US economy inflicted by the 2008 recession and the seemingly endless loss of blood and treasure fighting wars in Iraq and Afghanistan had left the nation facing a long-term decline of its relative power, or at least its political capacity to exert its power.[114] In this context, while not explicitly using the language of decline, Obama did talk of rebalancing long-term priorities, with an emphasis on "mov[ing] beyond today's wars, and focus[ing] our attention and resources on a broader set of countries and challenges."[115] In real-world terms that shift in priorities was supposed to be manifested by the "pivot to Asia." The administration certainly showed a commitment to turn this rhetoric into some sort of tangible reality, but relations with China were a constantly complicating factor, with the administration caught between seeing China as primarily friend or foe. In this light, the TPP should not just be seen as a trade agreement but as a pact to bring together a dozen economies, including Japan as well as the US, in a manner that challenged China's growing economic and political ascendancy.[116] President Trump's subsequent withdrawal of the US from TPP was not designed to empower China, but in undoing several years of negotiation that decision diminished any immediate legacy of the "pivot."

In addition to a proposed strategic rebalancing of US priorities, Obama's 2008 campaign also proposed that, as president, he would meet with US adversaries, without pre-conditions if necessary. These suggestions had been denounced by opponents as naïve and were fulfilled with more caution than that campaign message suggested, but the dealings that did take place bore some fruit, at least on the terms and conditions that the administration set for itself. As Obama left office, Burma seemed back in the fold of "respectable" nations, some important channels had been opened to Cuba, and the JCPOA had brought to a successful climax an angst-ridden multi-party international negotiation. In a counter-factual world, a Hillary Clinton presidency would very likely have seen a further embedding of this legacy. The Iran deal would have been sustained so long as Iran stuck by its commitments and perhaps more progress would have followed in developing relations with Cuba. Events in Burma followed their own brutal dynamic, but given Clinton's personal investment as secretary of state in bringing the country back into the international fold, it seems likely at least that there would have been a serious effort to intervene as the situation deteriorated. As it was, in the real world of a Trump presidency, the resilience of those initiatives proved limited.

Further, Obama's hopes of freeing the US from the ongoing conflicts across Iraq and Afghanistan did not fully materialize. The nature of the conflicts, especially in Iraq, changed, but simply downsizing the US presence did not end the political and military entanglement. The problems were captured by the administration's sometimes floundering response to the Arab Spring. In an article that largely lauded the decisions made by Obama, the political scientist Marc Lynch reflected on the irreconcilable contradictions the administration faced in its dealings in the Middle East:

> Obama's approach to the Arab uprisings was both visionary and incoherent. The administration sympathized with the aspirations of the protesters and hoped to encourage democratic transitions. But it struggled to grasp the fact that the old order under attack was a US-backed regional order, defended by US allies concerned, above all, with keeping themselves in power. The right side of history, on which Obama hoped to place the United States, may have appealed to American values, but it viscerally challenged American

interests.[117] In this context any legacy was likely to be unsatisfactory. Helping dispose of a tyrant in Libya did not lead to political stability in that country, yet standing relatively aside as another hung on to power in Syria brought no end to the chaos.

In the end, the Obama administration may have tried to minimize doing "stupid stuff," but that has a limited capacity to leave a distinctive legacy. For President Trump the ends were at least straightforwardly defined, manifested by the language of "America First" and an embrace of Jacksonian principles. Obama's foreign policy decisions were far from inconsequential, but many of the consequences were not fully played out when he left office: And perhaps the two most Obama-like initiatives to negotiate complex multilateral settlements to complex problems, the JCPOA and the TPP, were also conceivably the two most prominent examples of legacy rollback.

Notes

1. David Kaiser, *American Tragedy: Kennedy, Johnson and the Origins of the Vietnam War* (Cambridge: Belknap, 2002).
2. Jarret Murray, "Text of Bush speech," *CBS News*, May 1, 2003, <https://www.cbsnews.com/news/text-of-bush-speech-01-05-2003/> (last accessed June 12, 2019).
3. Jeremi Suri, "Liberal Internationalism, Law and the First African American President," in Julian Zelizer (ed.), *The Presidency of Barack Obama: A First Historical Assessment* (Princeton, NJ: Princeton University Press, 2018), 195–211.
4. Barack Obama, "Presidential Remarks at Cairo University," The White House, Office of the Press Secretary, June 4, 2009, <https://obamawhitehouse.archives.gov/the-press-office/remarks-president-cairo-university-6-04-09> (last accessed January 2, 2020).
5. Barack Obama, "Nobel Lecture," December 10, 2009, <https://www.nobelprize.org/prizes/peace/2009/obama/26183-nobel-lecture-2009/> (last accessed January 2, 2020).
6. Dan Balz and Haynes Johnson, *The Battle for America: the Story of an Extraordinary Election* (New York: Penguin, 2008), 20–2, 78–81.
7. Gary Jacobson, *The Politics of Congressional Elections* (London: Pearson, 2012), 207–24; Gary Jacobson, "George W. Bush, the

Iraq War, and the Election of Barack Obama," *Presidential Studies Quarterly*, 40.2 (2012): 207–24.
8. Obama, "Nobel Lecture."
9. Martin Indyk, Kenneth Liebarthal, and Michael O'Hanlon, "Scoring Obama's Foreign Policy: A Progressive Pragmatist Tries to Bend History," *Foreign Affairs*, 91.3 (2012): 29–43, at 29–30; Martin Indyk, Kenneth Liebarthal, and Michael O'Hanlon, *Bending History: Barack Obama's Foreign Policy* (Washington, DC: Brookings, 2012).
10. Jeffrey Goldberg, "Hillary Clinton: 'Failure' to Help Syrian Rebels Led to the Rise of ISIS," The Atlantic, August 10, 2014. On whether there was, or was not, an identifiable "Obama doctrine" see Elliot Abrams, "The Obama Doctrine," The Weekly Standard, February 4, 2012, <https://www.weeklystandard.com/elliott-abrams/the-obama-doctrine-620953> (last accessed January 2, 2020); Simon Chesterman, "'Leading from Behind': The Responsibility to Protect, the Obama Doctrine, and Humanitarian Intervention after Libya," Ethics and International Affairs, 25.3 (2011): 279–85; Colin Dueck, The Obama Doctrine: American Grand Strategy Today (New York: Oxford University Press, 2015); Daniel Drezner, "Does Obama Have a Grand Strategy? Why We Need Doctrines in Uncertain Times," Foreign Affairs, 90.4 (July/August 2011): 57–68; Leslie Gelb, "The Elusive Obama Doctrine," The National Interest, 121 (2012): 18–28; Christian Henderson, "The 2010 United States National Security Strategy and the Obama Doctrine of 'Necessary Force,'" Journal of Conflict and Security Law, 15.3 (December 2010): 403–34; Robert Kaufman, "Prudence and the Obama Doctrine," Orbis, 58.3 (2014), 441–59.
11. Jeffrey Goldberg, "The Obama Doctrine," *The Atlantic*, April 2016, <https://www.theatlantic.com/magazine/archive/2016/04/the-obama-doctrine/471525/> (last accessed January 2, 2020).
12. Ibid.
13. Michael White, "Is Barack Obama Right to Criticise NATO's Free Riders? Of Course He Is," *The Guardian*, March 11, 2016, <https://www.theguardian.com/us-news/blog/2016/mar/11/barack-obama-right-criticise-natos-free-riders-course-he-is> (last accessed January 2, 2020).
14. Drezner, "Does Obama Have a Grand Strategy?" 58.
15. Matthew Kroenig, "The Case for Trump's Foreign Policy: The Right People, The Right Positions," *Foreign Affairs*, 96.30 (May/June 2017): 31.

16. G. John Ikenberry, "The Plot Against American Foreign Policy: Can the Liberal Order Survive?" *Foreign Affairs*, 96.30 (May/June 2017): 3.
17. Jeffrey Goldberg, "A Senior White House Official Defines the Trump Doctrine: 'We're America, Bitch,'" The Atlantic, June 11, 2018, <https://www.theatlantic.com/politics/archive/2018/06/a-senior-white-house-official-defines-the-trump-doctrine-were-america-bitch/562511/> (last accessed January 2, 2020).
18. Hillary Clinton, "America's Pacific Century," *Foreign Policy*, October 11, 2011, <https://foreignpolicy.com/2011/10/11/americas-pacific-century/> (last accessed January 2, 2020).
19. Niels Bjerre-Poulsen, "The Obama Administration's Pivot to Asia," in Eddie Ashbee and John Dumbrell, *The Obama Presidency and the Politics of Change* (London: Palgrave Macmillan, 2015), 307–27, at 308.
20. Ashlee Godwin, "US-UK Relations Under President Obama," in Clodagh Harrington, *Obama's Washington: Political Leadership in a Partisan Era* (London: UCL Press, 2015), 177.
21. Michael J. Green, "The Legacy of Obama's 'Pivot' to Asia," *Foreign Policy*, September 3, 2016, <http://foreignpolicy.com/2016/09/03/the-legacy-of-obamas-pivot-to-asia/> (last accessed January 2, 2020).
22. Bjerre-Poulsen, "The Obama Administration's Pivot to Asia," 309.
23. Godwin, "US-UK Relations Under President Obama," 187.
24. Mark Landler, *Alter Egos: Hillary Clinton, Barack Obama and the Twilight Struggle Over American Power* (London: W.H. Allen, 2016), 290–5.
25. Cheng Li, "Assessing US-China Relations Under the Obama Administration," *Brookings*, August 30, 2016, <https://www.brookings.edu/opinions/assessing-u-s-china-relations-under-the-obama-administration/> (last accessed January 2, 2020).
26. David Axelrod, *Believer; My Forty Years in Politics* (New York: Penguin, 2016), 413–14.
27. Thomas J. Christensen, "Obama and Asia: Confronting the China Challenge," *Foreign Affairs*, September/October 2015, <https://www.questia.com/magazine/1P3-3792991101/obama-and-asia-confronting-the-china-challenge> (last accessed January 2, 2020).
28. Jeremy Shapiro, personal interview (January 11, 2019).
29. Indyk, Lieberthal, and O'Hanlon, "Scoring Obama's Foreign Policy," 26; Aaron L. Friedberg, "China's Strategic Ambitions in Asia,"

Princeton paper, April 2007, <https://carnegieendowment.org/files/Friedberg_paper.pdf> (last accessed January 2, 2020).
30. Zalmay Khalilzad, "Congage China," Rand Corporation, January 1, 1999, <https://www.rand.org/pubs/issue_papers/IP187.html> (last accessed January 2, 2020).
31. Landler, *Alter Egos*, 289.
32. When Clinton visited in 2011 the US, along with the UK, did not recognize that the country's name had changed to Myanmar, despite the fact that the UN had done so. See "Who, What, Why: Should it be Burma or Myanmar?" *BBC News*, December 2, 2011, <https://www.bbc.co.uk/news/magazine-16000467> (last accessed January 2, 2020).
33. Steven Lee Myers, "Clinton's Visit to Myanmar Raises Hope and Concerns," *The New York Times*, November 30, 2011, <https://www.nytimes.com/2011/11/30/world/asia/clintons-visit-to-myanmar-raises-hopes-and-concerns.html> (last accessed January 2, 2020).
34. Chuck Todd, "Obama: 'Flickers of Progress' in Myanmar," *NBC News*, November 19, 2011, <https://www.nbcnews.com/video/obama-flickers-of-progress-in-myanmar-44461123685> (last accessed June 12, 2019); Indyk, Lieberthal, and O'Hanlon, *Bending History*, 60.
35. Stephanie Nebehay, "UN Sees 'Textbook Example of Ethnic Cleansing' in Myanmar," *Reuters*, September 11, 2017, <https://www.reuters.com/article/us-myanmar-rohingya-un/u-n-sees-textbook-example-of-ethnic-cleansing-in-myanmar-idUSKCN1BM0SL> (last accessed January 2, 2020).
36. Nahal Toosi, "The Genocide the US Didn't See Coming," *Politico*, March/April 2018, <https://www.politico.com/magazine/story/2018/03/04/obama-rohingya-genocide-myanmar-burma-muslim-syu-kii-217214> (last accessedJanuary 2, 2020).
37. Mark Gearan, "The Final Year," *Harvard Forum*, April 26, 2018, <https://iop.harvard.edu/forum/%E2%80%9C-final-year%E2%80%9D-inside-account-diplomacy-obama-administration> (last accessed January 2, 2020).
38. Ishaan Thahoor, "If Trump Wants to Unravel the Obama Legacy, He Could Start With Burma," *The Washington Post*, September 13, 2017, <https://www.washingtonpost.com/gdpr-consent/?destination=%2fnews%2fworldviews%2fwp%2f2017%2f09%2f13%2fif-trump-wants-to-unravel-obamas-legacy-he-could-start-with-burma%2f%3f&utm_term=.77774908da6d> (last accessed January 2, 2020).

39. David Brummstrom and Tommy Wilkes, "Trump Urges 'Strong and Swift Action' to End Rohingya Crisis," *Reuters*, September 20, 2017, <https://www.reuters.com/article/us-myanmar-rohingya/trump-urges-strong-and-swift-un-action-to-end-rohingya-crisis-idUSKCN1BV0CD> (last accessed January 2, 2020).
40. Clinton, "America's Pacific Century."
41. Michael Schmidt, "In Iraq, Diplomatic Perspectives on a Deal Not Made," *The New York Times* blog, October 24, 2011, <https://atwar.blogs.nytimes.com/2011/10/24/proponent-of-iraq-invasion-discusses-the-u-s-withdrawal/> (last accessed January 2, 2020).
42. Helene Cooper, Mark Landler, and Alissa Rubin, "Obama Allows Airstrikes Against Iraq Rebels," *The New York Times*, August 8, 2014, A1. For a *CBS News* report on renewed American actions in Iraq see Martin David, August 8, 2014, <https://www.cbsnews.com/video/obama-authorizes-limited-air-strikes-to-quell-isis-surge/> (last accessed January 2, 2020).
43. Mark Landler and Jonathan Weisman, "Obama is Ready to Order Strikes From Air in Syria," September 10, 2014, *The New York Times*, A1.
44. Nick Corasaniti, "Donald Trump Calls Obama 'Founder of ISIS' and Says it Honours Him," *The New York Times*, August 10, 2016, <https://www.nytimes.com/2016/08/11/us/politics/trump-rally.html> (last accessed January 2, 2020).
45. David Remnick, "Going the Distance: On and Off the Road with Barack Obama," *The New Yorker*, January 27, 2014, <https://www.newyorker.com/magazine/2014/01/27/going-the-distance-david-remnick> (last accessed January 2, 2020).
46. Peter Baker, "A President Whose Assurances Have Come Back to Haunt Him," *The New York Times*, September 9, 2014, A10.
47. Michael Schmidt and Eric Schmitt, "As ISIS Loses Its Grip, US and Iraq Prepare for Grinding Insurgency," The New York Times, July 25, 2016, <https://www.nytimes.com/2016/07/26/world/middleeast/isis-iraq-insurgency.html> (last accessedJanuary 2, 2020).
48. Lizette Alvarez and Richard Pérez-Peña, "Praising ISIS, Gunman Attacks Gay Nightclub, Leaving 50 Dead in Worst Shooting on US Soil," June 13, 2016, *The New York Times*, A1.
49. Donette Murray, "Military Action But Not As We Know It," *Contemporary Politics*, 19.2 (April 20, 2013), <https://www.tandfonline.com/doi/abs/10.1080/13569775.2013.785827> (last accessed January 2, 2020).

50. Ryan Lizza, "The Consequentialist," *The New Yorker*, May 2, 2011, <https://www.newyorker.com/magazine/2011/05/02/the-consequentialist> (last accessed January 2, 2020).
51. Ibid.
52. Landler, *Alter Egos*, 175–7.
53. Ivo Daalder and James G. Stavridis, "NATO's Victory in Libya," *Foreign Affairs*, 91.2 (March/April 2012), <https://www.foreignaffairs.com/articles/libya/2012-02-02/natos-victory-libya> (last accessed January 2, 2020)
54. Barack Obama, "Remarks by the President on the Death of Muammar Qaddafi," The White House, Office of the Press Secretary, October 20, 2011, <https://obamawhitehouse.archives.gov/the-press-office/2011/10/20/remarks-president-death-muammar-qaddafi> (last accessed January 2, 2020).
55. David Rohde, "The Obama Doctrine," *Foreign Policy*, 192 (March/April 2012): 64–9.
56. Charlie Savage and Mark Landler, "War Powers Act Doesn't Apply for Libya," *The New York Times*, June 16, 2011, A16.
57. "Libya and the War Powers Act: The Law Does Apply to the NATO Campaign, but That Is No Excuse to End It Prematurely," *The New York Times*, June 17, 2011, A34.
58. Conor Friedersdorf, "How Obama Ignored Congress, and Misled America, on War in Libya," The Atlantic, September 13, 2012, <https://www.theatlantic.com/politics/archive/2012/09/how-obama-ignored-congress-and-misled-america-on-war-in-libya/262299/> (last accessed January 2, 2020).
59. Alan Kuperman, "Obama's Libya Debacle," *Foreign Affairs*, March/April 2015, <https://www.foreignaffairs.com/articles/libya/2019-02-18/obamas-libya-debacle> (last accessed January 2, 2020).
60. Dominic Tierney, "The Legacy of Obama's 'Worst Mistake,'" *The Atlantic*, April 15, 2016, <https://www.theatlantic.com/international/archive/2016/04/obamas-worst-mistake-libya/478461/> (last accessed January 2, 2020).
61. Ibid.
62. Shadi Hamid, "Everyone Says the Libya Intervention Was a Failure. They're Wrong," *Brookings*, April 12, 2016, <https://www.brookings.edu/blog/markaz/2016/04/12/everyone-says-the-libya-intervention-was-a-failure-theyre-wrong/> (last accessed January 2, 2020).
63. Helene Cooper, "Stepping Up the Fight against ISIS, US Conducts Airstrikes in Libya," *The New York Times*, August 2, 2016, A4.

64. Bruce Drake, "US Aid to Syrian Rebels: Public Has Opposed American Involvement in the Past," *Pew Research Center*, June 14, 2013, <http://www.pewresearch.org/fact-tank/2013/06/14/u-s-aid-to-syrian-rebels-public-has-opposed-american-involvement-in-the-past/> (last accessed January 2, 2020).
65. Remnick, "Going the Distance."
66. Barack Obama, "Remarks by the President to the White House Press Corps," The White House, Office of the Press Secretary, August 20, 2012, <https://obamawhitehouse.archives.gov/the-press-office/2012/08/20/remarks-president-white-house-press-corps> (last accessed January 2, 2020).
67. Joby Warrick, "More than 1500 Killed in Syrian Chemical Attack," *The Washington Post*, August 30, 2013, <https://www.washingtonpost.com/world/national-security/nearly-1500-killed-in-syrian-chemical-weapons-attack-us-says/2013/08/30/b2864662-1196-11e3-85b6-d27422650fd5_story.html?utm_term=.3d9ba9077b8e> (last accessed January 2, 2020).
68. Ben Rhodes, "Inside the White House During the Syrian 'Red Line' Crisis," *The Atlantic*, June 3, 2018, <https://www.theatlantic.com/international/archive/2018/06/inside-the-white-house-during-the-syrian-red-line-crisis/561887/> (last accessed January 2, 2020).
69. Ibid.
70. Landler, *Alter Egos*, 204–8.
71. Gideon Rose, "What Obama Gets Right," *Foreign Affairs*, September/October 2015, <https://www.foreignaffairs.com/articles/2017-07-05/what-obama-gets-right> (last accessed January 2, 2020).
72. Goldberg, "The Obama Doctrine."
73. Derek Chollet, "Obama's Red Line, Revisited," *Politico*, July 19, 2016, <https://www.politico.com/magazine/story/2016/07/obama-syria-foreign-policy-red-line-revisited-214059> (last accessed January 2, 2020).
74. Barack Obama, "Remarks by President Obama and President Benigno Aquino III of the Philippines in Joint Press Conference," The White House, Office of the Press Secretary, April 28, 2014, <https://obamawhitehouse.archives.gov/the-press-office/2014/04/28/remarks-president-obama-and-president-benigno-aquino-iii-philippines-joi> (last accessed January 2, 2020).
75. *Meet the Press* transcript, *NBC News*, July 20, 2014, <https://www.nbcnews.com/meet-the-press/meet-press-transcript-july-20-2014-n160611> (last accessed January 2, 2020).

76. Rodrigo Campos, "Syrian Government to Blame for April Sarin Attack: UN Report," *Reuters*, October 26, 2017, <https://uk.reuters.com/article/uk-mideast-crisis-syria-un/syrian-government-to-blame-for-april-sarin-attack-u-n-report-idUKKBN1CV3GF> (last accessed January 2, 2020).
77. Steven Simon and Jonathan Stevenson, "How to Avoid a Syrian Quagmire," *The New York Times*, October 6, 2016, A27.
78. Derek Chollet, Jake Sullivan, Dimitri Simes, and Mary Beth Long, "US Commitments in the Middle East: Advice to the Trump Administration," *Middle East Policy*, 24:1 (Spring 2017), <https://onlinelibrary.wiley.com/doi/abs/10.1111/mepo.12248> (last accessed January 2, 2020).
79. Andreas Krieg, *Commercialising Cosmopolitan Security: Safeguarding the Responsibility to Protect* (London: Palgrave, 2016), 111.
80. Daniel Arkin, F. Brinley Bruton, and Phil McCausland, "Trump Announces Strike on Syria Following Suspected Chemical Weapons Attack by Assad Forces," *NBC News*, April 14, 2018, <https://www.nbcnews.com/news/world/trump-announces-strikes-syria-following-suspected-chemical-weapons-attack-assad-n865966> (last accessed January 2, 2020).
81. Alex Ward, "How Obama's 'Red Line' Fiasco Led to Trump Bombing Syria," *Vox*, April 15, 2018, <https://www.vox.com/2018/4/15/17238568/syria-bomb-trump-obama-russia> (last accessed January 2, 2020).
82. "US Department of State Joint Comprehensive Plan of Action," n.d., <https://2009-2017.state.gov/e/eb/tfs/spi/iran/jcpoa/> (last accessed January 3, 2020).
83. Jeremy Shapiro, personal interview (January 11, 2019).
84. Caren Brohan, "Obama Toughens Iran Stance, Backs Israel on Jeruselam," *Reuters*, June 4, 2008, <https://www.reuters.com/article/us-usa-politics-obama-mideast/obama-toughens-iran-stance-backs-israel-on-jerusalem-idUSN0444417220080604?pageNumber=3&virtualBrandChannel=0> (last accessed January 3, 2020).
85. Barack Obama, "Inaugural Address by President Barack Obama," The White House, Office of the Press Secretary, January 21, 2013, <https://obamawhitehouse.archives.gov/the-press-office/2013/01/21/inaugural-address-president-barack-obama> (last accessed December 20, 2019).
86. "Full Transcript of Obama's Al-Arabiya Interview," *NBC News*, January 27, 2009, <http://www.nbcnews.com/id/28870724/ns/

politics-white_house/t/full-transcript-obamas-al-arabiya-interview/#.WtnF8U0rJD8> (last accessed January 3, 2020).
87. Jeff Mason and Louis Charbonneau, "Obama, Iran's Rouani Hold Historic Phonecall," *Reuters*, September 28, 2013, <https://www.reuters.com/article/us-un-assembly-iran/obama-irans-rouhani-hold-historic-phone-call-idUSBRE98Q16S20130928> (last accessed January 3, 2020).
88. Wendy Sherman, "How We Got the Iran Deal," *Foreign Affairs*, 97.5 (September/October 2018): 186–97.
89. Jennifer Steinhauer, "Democrats Hand Victory to Obama on Pact with Iran," *The New York Times*, September 11, 2015, A1.
90. Iran sanctions archive, US Department of State, <https://www.state.gov/iran-sanctions/> (last accessed January 3, 2020).
91. "The Nuclear Deal Fuelling Tensions Between Iran and America," The Economist, July 22, 2019, <https://www.economist.com/the-economist-explains/2020/01/28/what-is-the-jcpoa> (last accessed January 3, 2020).
92. "Trump on the Issues," *Council on Foreign Relations*, n.d., <https://www.cfr.org/interactives/campaign2016/> (last accessed January 3, 2020).
93. Mike Pompeo, "After the Deal: A New Iran Strategy," US Department of State, May 21, 2018, <https://translations.state.gov/2018/05/21/secretary-of-state-mike-pompeo-after-the-deal-a-new-iran-strategy/> (last accessed January 3, 2020).
94. Donald Trump, "State of the Union Address," February 5, 2019, <https://www.whitehouse.gov/sotu/> (last accessed January 3, 2020).
95. Zachary Laub, "What is the Status of the Iran Nuclear Agreement?" *Council on Foreign Relations*, May 8, 2018, <https://www.cfr.org/backgrounder/impact-iran-nuclear-agreement> (last accessed January 3, 2020).
96. Rosemary Righter, "NATO's 'Obama Problem,'" *Politico*, February 17, 2017, <https://www.politico.eu/article/natos-obama-problem/> (last accessed January 3, 2020).
97. Andrew Moran, "Barack Obama and the Return of 'Declinism'?" in Eddie Ashbee and John Dumbrell, *The Obama Presidency and the Politics of Change* (London: Palgrave Macmillan, 2015), 265–87, at 271.
98. David M. Herszenhorn and Lili Bayer, "Trump Threatens to Pull Out of NATO Summit," *Politico*, July 13, 2018, <https://www.politico.eu/article/trump-threatens-to-pull-out-of-nato/> (last accessed January 3, 2020).

99. Jens Stoltenberg, "US Role in the World Alliance," January 27, 2019, <https://www.youtube.com/watch?v=6vktju0ksYE> (last accessed January 3, 2020).
100. Thomas Wright, "The Moment the Transatlantic Charade Ended," *The Atlantic*, February 19, 2019, <https://www.theatlantic.com/ideas/archive/2019/02/mutual-distrust-2019-munich-security-conference/583015/> (last accessed January 3, 2020).
101. "Seventy Years of U.S. Public Opinion on the United Nations," Roper Center, June 22, 2015, <https://ropercenter.cornell.edu/blog/seventy-years-us-public-opinion-united-nations> (last accessed January 3, 2020).
102. "Full Text: Obama's Foreign Policy Speech," *The Guardian*, July 16, 2008, <https://www.theguardian.com/world/2008/jul/16/uselections2008.barackobama> (last accessed January 3, 2020).
103. Ewen MacAskill, Luke Harding, and Matthew Weaver, "Barack Obama Signals New Direction in US–UN Relations," *The Guardian*, September 23, 2009, <https://www.theguardian.com/world/2009/sep/23/unitednations-obama-administration> (last accessed January 3, 2020).
104. Maya Rhodan, "Here Are All the Times Donald Trump Bashed the United Nations Before Speaking There," *Time*, September 18, 2017, <http://time.com/4946276/donald-trump-united-nations-general-assembly/> (last accessed January 3, 2020).
105. It should be acknowledged that Zalmay Khalilzad, who succeeded Bolton in spring 2007, did have a more multilateral approach than his predecessor.
106. Landler, *Alter Egos*, 311.
107. "Cuba Sanctions Factsheet," US Department of the Treasury, January 15, 2015, <https://www.treasury.gov/press-center/press-releases/Pages/jl9740.aspx> (last accessed January 3, 2020).
108. Barack Obama, "Remarks by the President to the People of Cuba," The White House, Office of the Press Secretary, March 22, 2016, <https://obamawhitehouse.archives.gov/the-press-office/2016/03/22/remarks-president-obama-people-cuba> (last accessed January 3, 2020).
109. Jeremy Diamond, "CNN/ORC Poll: Americans Side with Obama on Cuba," *CNN*, December 23, 2014, <https://edition.cnn.com/2014/12/23/politics/cuba-poll/index.html> (last accessed January 3, 2020).
110. Jeremy Diamond, "Trump Shifts on Cuba, Says He Would Reverse Obama's Deal," *CNN*, September 17, 2016, <https://edition.cnn.

com/2016/09/16/politics/donald-trump-cuba/index.html> (last accessed January 3, 2020).
111. William M. LeoGrande, "Reversing the Irreversible: President Donald J. Trump's Cuba Policy," *Idees d'Amériques* (Automne 2017/Hiver 2018), <http://journals.openedition.org/ideas/2258> (last accessed January 3, 2020).
112. Vanessa Romo, "Trump Administration Clamps Down on Travel to Cuba," *NPR*, June 4, 2019, <https://www.npr.org/2019/06/04/729825471/trump-administration-clamps-down-on-travel-to-cuba-bans-cruise-ships> (last accessed January 3, 2020).
113. John Hamilton, "Doubts Rise About Evidence That US Diplomats Were Attacked in Cuba," *NPR*, March 25, 2019 <https://www.npr.org/sections/health-shots/2019/03/25/704903613/doubts-rise-about-evidence-that-u-s-diplomats-in-cuba-were-attacked> (last accessed January 3, 2020).
114. Ty McCormick, "Declinism Is America and Mitt Can Too," *Foreign Policy*, October 8, 2012, <https://foreignpolicy.com/2012/10/08/declinism-is-america-and-mitt-can-too/> (last accessed January 3, 2020).
115. Moran, "Barack Obama and the Return of 'Declinism?'" 267.
116. Jane Perlez, "US Allies See Trade Deal as a Check on China," *The New York Times*, October 6, 2015, A12.
117. Marc Lynch, "Obama and the Middle East: Rightsizing the US Role," *Foreign Affairs*, September/October 2015, <https://www.foreignaffairs.com/articles/middle-east/obama-and-middle-east> (last accessed January 3, 2020).

5
Exercising presidential power

The issues that we have considered so far have revolved around different, if sometimes sprawling, policy domains, and the respective capacities of the Obama and Trump administrations to implement and undo a variety of policy initiatives. This chapter and the next will somewhat move away from that formula and will reflect on the manner in which presidents Obama and Trump exercised their presidential powers. As we have already explained, it is far from simple to make definitive judgments about the legacy imprint of presidential actions, even in relatively tangible policy areas. That difficulty is heightened with regard to assessing the inevitably singular manner in which individual presidents wield their authority. Even presidents that mostly snugly fit Skowronek's category of "articulation," who look to build on their predecessors' political and policy foundations, will look to establish their own brand of executive leadership and individual political identity. A hypothetical President Hillary Clinton would very likely have furthered Obama's agenda in many of the areas where we have instead looked at President Trump's efforts at reversal, but she would also have employed different skills and set a different tone than Obama in terms of applying the powers of the office. Hence, the fact that President Trump has been quite a different leader from Obama is not surprising. On the other hand, for even the most casual observer, the gulf between the rhetorical styles of the two men and their means of communication is quite extraordinary. We will catch up with that aspect of their presidencies in the next chapter. Here we focus on how they exercised their powers of office and dealt with the many obstacles hindering the effective application of those powers. In doing so we focus on the process of nominating and securing the confirmation of justices to the federal judicial bench, the manner in which the two administrations managed the inevitable scandals afflicting any modern presidency, and how they conducted the nation's foreign policy.

The judicial branch

One of the key opportunities a president sometimes gets to shape the country's future is with their nominations for places on the federal bench. The long-term importance of this power is at its most public and politicized when a Supreme Court vacancy arises. In his Senate confirmation hearings after being nominated to the Court by President George W. Bush, John Roberts demurred from the notion that justices should be likened to partisans. Instead, he insisted, "judges are like umpires. Umpires don't make the rules; they apply them."[1] And often the justices will be in agreement on how to apply the rules in cases where the political stakes are low, but the prevailing conventional wisdom as Obama entered office was that he would be dealing with a divided Court. This involved four justices inclined to find their way to a liberal answer and four more likely to alight on a conservative alternative in those cases that had a clearer ideological dividing line, leaving Justice Anthony Kennedy as the more idiosyncratic median figure.

The importance of Kennedy was manifested in an extremely high-profile manner in the *Obergefell v. Hodges* ruling of 2015, which granted a constitutional right to same-sex marriage. This right can legitimately be seen as a legacy of the Obama era, even though it resulted from the Court's actions rather than directly from the executive branch. Whilst the President himself had demonstrated some caution, initially at least, with regard to laying out his own position on gay marriage (something he was roundly criticized for by activist groups), the same-sex marriage ruling is considered a substantial part of his legacy.[2] Despite Obama's first election and early-days public position of being opposed to gay marriage, it was clear to anyone who had watched closely that this was more of a strategic than a personal stance. He was at pains to avoid alienating the large number of African American Christian voters who supported him but were overtly opposed to same-sex marriage. David Axelrod's 2015 memoir *Believer* confirmed this, and the President's chief political strategist outlines how Obama was encouraged to "evolve" his position over time, thereby avoiding a sudden shock for the socially conservative among his supporters.[3] By the time the Court took up the case Obama had fully "evolved" on the matter, but it was Kennedy's vote that was critical, with four liberals voting in favor of the civil rights issues and four conservatives against. As was so often the case, the decision of swing justice Anthony Kennedy was crucial, and in this instance he sided with the liberals effectively to declare that same-sex marriage was a constitutional right. The court ruling chimed with the progressive agenda of the Obama administration.

On the other hand, this perspective on the Court's dynamics was an oversimplification, as sometimes the Court's alignments could be constructed differently. It was Roberts, not Kennedy, who provided the critical fifth vote to uphold the Affordable Acre Act in 2012. Yet, a president's Supreme Court picks are a key part of their legacy and, whatever the disclaimers about seeking the best-qualified candidates, those picks are guided by ideological preference. A president who successfully nominates one or more justices to the Supreme Court gets the chance to help preserve not only key aspects of their own legacy that might come under legal challenge over time, but also to lean the court in one direction or another on critical issues, including such perennial political controversies as abortion rights, the scope of affirmative action policies and the meaning of the Second Amendment. On the other hand, the Court's capacity to rebuke the executive branch has been witnessed numerous times. One famous example of this came in 1952 when President Truman, trying to avert a strike in the steel industry during the Korean War while also attempting to maintain good relations with organized labor, issued Executive Order 10340. This gave the Secretary of Commerce the power to take control of the steel industry. In June 1952, however, in a 6–3 decision, the Supreme Court ruled this an unconstitutional act.

Perhaps the most famous (or even notorious) example of a president attempting to impose executive branch authority over the judicial branch came with Franklin Roosevelt's 1937 court packing plan.⁴ Some scholarship has questioned the extent to which that episode is correctly seen as an explicit power grab, but as public opinion and the Senate turned against FDR's plan, even that giant of presidential authority was defeated.⁵ This is a complex story, and FDR's frustrations with the Court's decisions with regard to key pieces of New Deal legislation were lessened by the "switch in time that saved nine," leading the President to reflect that he might have lost the battle in 1937, but he had won the war. Alternatively, it has been argued that the fractures in his political coalition that were exposed as a result of the plan did not properly heal, diminishing the capacity for further decisive progressive legislation.⁶

Whatever view is taken of the long-term consequences of Franklin Roosevelt's effort in 1937, the episode does clearly illustrate the institutional limits of a president's power to short-circuit the nomination and Senate confirmation process, with these limits very evident again in 2016. In fact, there is no institutional mechanism that guarantees a president will get the chance to fill a court vacancy, which left one-term president Jimmy Carter bereft of even that chance to leave a stamp on the future. Moreover, there have been cases when presidents have not got what they expected from their nominees. Notably, President Eisenhower's appointment of Earl Warren did not meet his expectations of a chief justice who would lead the court toward a conservative agenda. During his sixteen years on the bench Warren ruled in favor of outlawing school segregation and his Court was responsible for numerous other progressive decisions.⁷

In response, Eisenhower reportedly lamented that the nominations of Warren and William Brennan to the Court were his two biggest mistakes. At that time, however, nominations were not based simply on the ideological positions of potential justices; Eisenhower picked these two men with wider political deal-making in mind rather than because he had good reason to expect them to be faithful conservatives.⁸ More recently, and in the era in which Supreme Court nominations were recognized as not just political but highly ideological, George H. W. Bush nominated David Souter to the court. Bush's chief of staff, John Sununu, had advised the President that Souter would be a reliable conservative, but this was decidedly not the case.[9] Alongside wholly unanticipated developments such as these, there have been surprise choices. Arch-conservative President Reagan nominated the Court's first female justice, and Sandra Day O'Connor was notably moderate in her conservatism.[10] In order to understand the importance of each individual justice and hence the consequence of each presidential pick, it is worth reflecting on how one of Reagan's nominees, Robert Bork, was blocked by Senate, which finally led to Justice Anthony Kennedy filling that vacant place on the court. Bork's record suggested that he would have been a very conservative voice but, while Kennedy did often side with the conservative wing of the court, he was a more liberal vote on the hot-button culture war issues of abortion and same-sex rights.

As it was, Souter's example did mean that future Republican administrations were much more rigorous in their vetting of justices to ensure that there were no repeats, making it much more likely that a modern president will successfully gravitate toward a choice of justice that chimes at least broadly with his worldview. Bill Clinton was in fact somewhat disinclined to participate too actively in the selection of judges to the federal bench,[11] stating that he wanted "a judge with a soul."[12] In addition, Clinton declared that his only criteria for nomination was a candidate's stance on abortion, though in the context of post-Roe America this was hardly an incidental qualification; this red-hot political issue had become, and remains, the litmus test for any Supreme Court nominee. Nonetheless, the Clinton administration did not view the Supreme Court as a vehicle for social change. As Joe Klein stated, "it's enough to put people of demonstrated quality on the bench. We've gone across gender, race and national origin lines. And that is a legacy the president is proud of."[13] Such an approach was not continued during the George W. Bush years. The 43rd president moved quickly in announcing that he would no longer consult with the American Bar Association on prospective nominees, as his predecessors had done. Instead, the White House would look to the explicitly conservative Federalist Society for advice and guidance.[14] The Bush choices of John Roberts and Samuel Alito were well received by social conservatives, along with virtually all the other 325 federal bench justices that took their seat on Bush's watch.[15] Yet even Bush found his presidential authority rebuked when he initially nominated White House counsel Harriet Miers to replace the retiring Sandra Day O'Connor to the Supreme Court. In this instance, the skepticism of senior congressional Republicans to endorse Miers was reinforced by the Federalist Society's objections and her nomination did not move forward.[16]

As a Senator, Obama made his opposition to the Roberts and Alito nominations clear at the time. In both cases he acknowledged the intellectual accomplishments and capacity of the candidates but highlighted his concerns with regard to their respective voting records. Coming down on the side of those with power would be a problematic aspect of their respective tenures, as he argued from a liberal perspective.[17] During the campaign Obama had spoken of his preference for justices with "empathy to understand what it's like to be poor, or African American, or gay, or disabled, or old," provoking Republicans into responding that judges should apply the law as it was written rather than through the lens of their own experience.[18] But Obama did not view the Courts generally as a means of bringing change, and his administration was slow off the mark with regard to filling positions on the federal bench.[19] Nevertheless, it was not long after entering the Oval Office that he got his own opportunity to appoint a justice to the highest court. With a gender imbalance of eight men to one woman, a female nomination was likely and, for many, a welcome development. The appointment of Sonia Sotomayor, then serving on the US Court of Appeals for the 2nd Circuit, in August 2009 offered an undeniable shot in the arm for the administration, and the Latina's liberal credentials were evident from the outset. Her nomination had led to a further round of debate about the importance of "empathy," as she had previously noted how her decision-making was likely to some degree to be "based on my gender and my Latina heritage."[20] In the end, however, she was confirmed by 68 votes to 31.

One year later, President Obama's second Supreme Court choice, Elena Kagan, the administration's Solicitor General, was approved. Some of Obama's more liberal supporters were initially disappointed, as they had hoped for a bolder pick even though the nominee was a known Democrat. As it was, Kagan was explicit about her partisan preferences during her confirmation hearings, but insisted that this would not affect her capacity to judge impartially.[21] Her nomination was confirmed by 63 votes to 37.

Such rapid changes of personnel offer a reminder of the substantial and sustained reinforcement that a president can acquire via other branches of government. The arrival of two justices within a brief period also undid any assumptions that the Roberts Court was a static entity. Yet, with these two choices Obama did not really have the chance to alter the overall ideological balance of the Court. While the two retiring justices, David Souter and John Paul Stevens, had both been nominated by Republican presidents, both were firmly in the liberal wing of the Court on those issues that divided the justices along mostly predictable ideological lines. The unexpected death of Justice Antonin Scalia in February 2016, however, seemed to offer Obama a chance to change the make-up of the Court in a more profound manner as Scalia, if not the most deeply conservative member of the Court, had over the years provided perhaps the Court's most assertive, and often intellectually robust, line of conservative reasoning. Replacing Scalia with a more liberal line of jurisprudence would have involved a rebalancing of a central institution of American governance. This would have been a legacy of substance and would have provided liberals with some comfort given their losses across so many of the country's elected institutions during the Obama years.

What happened after Scalia's death, however, laid bare the extent to which the Court was perceived to be, and was, a political institution. It also showed that the electoral setbacks suffered by the Democratic Party, notably the Republican takeover of the Senate in the 2014 midterm elections, had consequences beyond legislative stalemate. The deeply partisan environment resulted in President Obama's March 2016 nomination of the moderate Merrick Garland being stonewalled for the remainder of the Obama term. In the immediate aftermath of Scalia's death, Congressional Republicans made clear their determination to avoid facilitating the scale of legacy reinforcement that would come with an extra liberal on the Court. This saw an explicit power play by Senate Majority Leader Mitch McConnell of Kentucky, who made plain that the

Senate would not begin hearings on Garland's nomination, never mind bring things to a vote. When announcing Garland's nomination Obama made it clear that his choice had been influenced by a desire to pick a nominee who had previously garnered bipartisan praise for his work: "It is tempting to make this confirmation process simply an extension of our divided politics.... But to go down that path would be wrong."[22] That appeal carried little weight. In the summer of 2016, McConnell bragged: "One of my proudest moments was when I looked Barack Obama in the eye and I said to him, 'You will not fill this Supreme Court vacancy.'"[23]

It is also important to understand that Republican obstructionism with regard to judicial nominees extended beyond Garland's fate. The Supreme Court is, by definition, at the top of the federal judicial system, but the circuit and district courts also make many critical decisions, with the judges on those courts also nominated by the executive branch and confirmed by the Senate. The Pew Research Center's analysis revealed that 324 of the Obama administration's nominees were confirmed to those courts, bringing a considerably greater degree of diversity to the make-up of the federal bench. Of the successful nominees, 208 were white, 58 black, 31 Hispanic, and 18 Asian, with a further 9 non-white judges appointed. Thus 36 percent of these appointments were non-white, compared with 24 percent under President Clinton and 18 percent under President George W. Bush. Moreover, this increased diversity extended to gender, with 42 percent of Obama-era appointees being female compared to 28 percent under Clinton and 22 percent for Bush.[24]

The process of confirming nominees in the Senate, even for these positions below the Supreme Court, had, however, become increasingly fractious. Through to the end of 2014 Democrats enjoyed a Senate majority but the GOP had used its power to filibuster executive nominations, including some for positions on the federal bench. Democrat frustration came to a head in late 2013 as Republicans delayed the confirmation of three Obama nominees to the US Court of Appeals for the District of Columbia Circuit. In November 2013, then Senate Majority Leader Democrat Harry Reid from Nevada broke with decades of precedent to end the capacity of a minority to filibuster judicial nominees for positions below the Supreme Court. In the short term, this manoeuvre boosted the rate at which Obama nominees got confirmed. In 2014 eighty-nine judicial nominations were confirmed, making it the most productive year of the Obama presidency in this regard.[25] Yet, while those lifetime appointments should be viewed as part of the Obama legacy, the Democrats' tactics came with a long-term price tag. During the Senate debate in November 2013, then Minority Leader McConnell warned his opponents that they had broken an institutional norm in a manner that could leave them vulnerable to a future change in the partisan balance of power, and he accurately predicted: "We look forward to having a great election in 2014."[26]

Reid's actions centered on Senate procedure, but the *New York Times* reported that Obama "applauded" Reid's initiative. At the time Obama's words were slightly more nuanced than suggested by that description, as he focused on the behavior of the Senate GOP, noting, "today's pattern of obstruction, it just isn't normal," rather than explicitly celebrating how the diminishing of the filibuster would have the effect of facilitating the passage of his executive branch choices.[27] Yet, he did reflect on how Senate obstructionism was preventing him from fulfilling his constitutional duties and filling not just judicial seats but a variety of posts throughout the administration. As presaged by McConnell's comments, however, the 2014 midterm elections did empower the Republicans in Senate as well as the House and the final two years saw obstructionism with regard to Senate confirmation of judicial nominees reach new heights. In his final two years in office, Obama managed to get only two circuit court and eighteen district court judges confirmed. This compared to totals of sixty-eight and seventy-three for George W. Bush and Bill Clinton respectively, remembering that they also faced a Senate controlled by the opposite party.[28]

Moreover, as McConnell organized resistance to Obama's judicial nominees the make-up of the courts, and most obviously the Supreme Court, came to be an important theme on the 2016 campaign trail. As candidate Trump became the surprise Republican nominee, he soon realized the currency of a possible conservative court appointment. The Federalist Society listed twenty-one names as potential contenders and at some rallies, Trump went so far as to say that even if voters had reservations about him, they should still vote him in because they would get the conservative justice they so desperately wanted.[29] The media was full of coverage of those on the religious right who struggled with Trump's own character and actions, not least around the time of the "Pussygate" tapes. Social conservatives drew comfort from two sources, one of which was Mike Pence as the devout Christian vice presidential candidate. The other was the list of Federalist Society suggestions to replace that "Schwarzenegger of jurisprudence," Antonin Scalia.[30] Naming potential Supreme Court justices in this manner during a campaign was unprecedented, but proved to be an effective strategic move in what was often a disorganized campaign.

It is difficult to quantify precisely how much impact this had on voting behavior, but there is evidence that the prospect of filling Scalia's seat was a more powerful motivating factor for conservatives than liberals.[31] Certainly, Scalia's death, which seemed like an unexpected opportunity in early 2016 for Obama to shift the balance of the Supreme Court and hence extend his legacy, ended up becoming an important organizational tool for candidate Trump to keep hold of part of the conservative coalition that might have looked askance at the Republican nominee's personal lifestyle. In short, some religious Trump supporters were willing to make what some described as a Faustian deal in order to maintain a post-Scalia conservative balance on the court.[32] Some liberals also used the benefit of hindsight to argue that President Obama should have predicted how McConnell would behave and hence used his nominating power to put forward a candidate who would appeal to the party's base support, rather than "a middle-aged, white male centrist," and championed this nomination on the basis of "ideological grounds" rather than "procedural norms." Such a strategy would not have persuaded McConnell, but just might have made it "easier to mobilize the Democratic base in outrage" throughout the election cycle.[33]

Whatever the merits of second-guessing Garland's nomination, once Trump took office, the list of twenty-one he had announced during the campaign was shortened to eight, and forty-nine-year-old Neil Gorsuch was chosen. At this point, under existing Senate rules, it was still possible to filibuster a Supreme Court nominee, as Reid's manouver in 2013 had left that norm in place. In what was perhaps an unsurprising move in the circumstances, McConnell, with his party holding a majority of 52 to 48, moved to revoke that norm, preventing the Democrats from holding Gorsuch hostage. As a regular churchgoer, married to his college sweetheart, this constitutional originalist and social conservative could hardly have contrasted more to the president that nominated him. Illustrating the exaggerated reaction that Supreme Court news can cause, those less enamoured with the Trump win and Gorsuch appointment demonstrated their concerns for future bodily autonomy by stocking up on contraceptives. Such a knee-jerk reaction was not unusual, as was demonstrated when gun enthusiasts stocked up after both Obama victories.[34] Liberal dismay, however, was raised a further notch when Trump was fortunate enough to be provided with a second Supreme Court nomination opportunity within sixteen months of taking office. In June 2018, eighty-two-year-old Anthony Kennedy announced his retirement from the court after thirty years of service. The departure of this Reagan appointee, considered by so many to be the key swing justice between the two polarized groups within the court, was viewed as potentially game-changing. Not only did it mean that gay marriage and other relatively "new" developments might be under threat, but also more embedded political thorns such as *Roe v. Wade*. Even before his absence it was clear that state-level political actors were attempting to tighten abortion rights and on the campaign trail Trump promised his base that he would appoint pro-life justices. The potential threat to *Roe v. Wade* is a perennial concern for progressives; hence there are laws on the books in eight states that preserve a woman's right to an abortion should the 1973 ruling be overturned.[35]

With Kennedy's retirement, President Trump browsed his Federalist Society list of names for a second time. In July 2018 he settled on Brett Kavanaugh as his nominee. In its reporting, the *New York Times* described Kavanaugh as "a politically connected member of Washington's conservative legal establishment," with his nomination likely to stir an "epic confirmation battle" given the high stakes of "potentially cementing the court's rightward tilt for a generation."[36] Using the 2007 Epstein model, Nate Silver's 538.com website predicted that if placed on the Supreme Court, Kavanaugh would sit ideologically to the right of Samuel Alito and Neil Gorsuch, but would likely be less conservative than Clarence Thomas. This conclusion was based not only on the voting record of the individual but also the ideological position of the president who appointed him, along with those of the relevant senators and related actors.[37] One consequence was that Chief Justice Roberts would become the new median voice on the Court. On many issues where Kennedy had ruled with the conservatives, such as campaign finance, business regulation, voting cases, gun rights, religious liberty and the like, this would not shift the likely opinions from the Court. Elsewhere, however, shifting the median point from Kennedy to Roberts was potentially hugely significant—and not just with regard to abortion rights. Other areas in the spotlight included capital punishment and solitary confinement, religious anti-discrimination law, and possibly gay rights and race-based affirmative action.[38]

As it was, Kavanaugh's confirmation battle was "epic," though not for the reasons initially expected. As the confirmation hearings proceeded, it was evident that Republican senators were likely to stay on board. There was considerable focus on the isolated pro-choice Republican senators, notably Susan Collins and Lisa Murkowski, who had bucked their leadership before over repealing Obamacare; but it looked as if McConnell had held his caucus together. Then, however, allegations that Kavanaugh was guilty of sexual assault when in high school emerged. Further allegations of sexual misconduct by Kavanaugh as a university student also became public. For his part, Kavanaugh strongly denied all the allegations. President Trump stood by his man, defending Kavanaugh's integrity and then, at a rally in Mississippi, mocking one of the accusers. In the end, with the allegations remaining unproven, the Senate confirmed Kavanaugh by a 50 to 48 vote.[39]

Beyond the Supreme Court, the Trump administration proved very effective at getting nominees to the rest of the federal bench confirmed. When Obama left office there were 112 vacancies on the federal bench. This number compared with fifty-three vacancies when Obama entered office, with that disparity reflecting the effectiveness of Republican obstructionism over the last quarter of Obama's time in office.[40] Trump taunted his predecessor: "When I got in, we had over 100 federal judges that weren't appointed. I don't know why Obama left that. It was like a big beautiful present to all of us. Why the hell did he leave that. . . . Maybe he got complacent."[41] By mid-September 2019, 150 Trump nominees had been confirmed to lifetime positions on the federal bench, compared to ninety-six for Obama at a similar point in time. President Trump tweeted a *New York Times* report to note the landmark: "This week, the Senate passed a milestone in confirming the 150th Federal Judge of Mr. Trump's Administration to a lifetime appointment, far outstripping Barack Obama's pace and fulfilling pledges by Mr. Trump and Mr. O'Connell to remake the Federal Judiciary . . ."[42] The extent to which this had changed the overall political complexion of the federal bench should not be exaggerated, since 60 percent of the judgeships that had been filled by Trump nominees by that stage replaced previous Republican nominees. Nevertheless, between January 2017 and July 2019 the percentage of judges appointed by a Republican president had risen from 41 to 52 percent. Moreover, all but one of Trump's nominees had been members of the Federalist Society at some point.[43] One further clear difference between Obama and Trump was in the demographic make-up of their nominees. While less than 40 percent of federal judges appointed by Obama were white men, that number jumped back up to 70 percent under Trump.[44]

As discussed in the next chapter, President Trump confounded expectations of how a president should behave on an almost daily basis. One of the ways in which he defied convention was to explicitly attack judges when they made decisions he did not like. Barely two weeks into his presidency, Trump responded furiously when a federal judge put a temporary halt to the hastily imposed ban on people arriving into the US from seven Muslim majority countries. Trump tweeted, "The opinion of this so-called judge, which essentially takes law-enforcement away from our country, is ridiculous and will be overturned!"[45] At the end of 2018, Trump's continued critiques brought rebuke from the Chief Justice of the Supreme Court, John Roberts. Trump had attacked a decision from the Ninth Circuit as a "disgrace" and labeled the presiding judge as "an Obama judge." This prompted Roberts to retort that it was wrong to refer to "Obama judges or Trump judges, Bush judges or Clinton judges. What we have is an extraordinary group of dedicated judges doing their level best to do equal right to those appearing before them. . . . The independent judiciary is something we should all be thankful for."[46] There was, however, little subsequent evidence that Trump had taken this reprimand to heart.

This overt presidential hostility to decisions taken by the judicial branch was not, however, unprecedented. George W. Bush, for example, had made clear his frustration when the Supreme Court ruled that detainees in Guantanamo Bay did have some legal protections. Yet, it was President Obama who elevated criticism of the court to a new level when, in January 2010, in his State of the Union address, he rebuked the Supreme Court's decision in the case of *Citizens United v. Federal Elections Commission*. Obama prefaced his critique of that decision, which undid the McCain-Feingold campaign finance reform act, by acknowledging "all due deference to the separation of powers," but his words were perceived as especially provocative given that several of the justices were in the audience. Justice Samuel Alito, who was part of the majority in that case, was widely reported to have mouthed "not true" in response to Obama's comments.[47] Nevertheless, even if Obama had already made clear that criticisms of the judiciary were quite within bounds for a president, Trump's consistent attacks had a potentially more corrosive effect. As explained by Russell Berman,

> The tangible impact of Trump's attacks on the judiciary has been more limited than some initially feared. . . . It has . . . responded to . . . legal defeats as the system intended—through appeals within the federal courts themselves. But little by little, tweet by tweet, Trump is contributing to a shift in how the judiciary is perceived as an institution, from one prized for its independence from the partisan brawl to one that's no less political than its sister branches of government.[48]

It might be said that Trump's refrains simply echoed a suppressed reality about how the courts often seemed to work, with justices regularly managing to find a way to their initially preferred conclusion. Even so, his disregard for the norms of presidential rhetoric was striking and perhaps helps to explain why his administration so quickly and often found itself accused of substantive, as well as symbolic, wrongdoing.

Scandal management

One key test of a president's leadership style is how they respond when their administration is hit by scandal. This almost inevitable occurrence obliges the Oval Office resident to utilize their political and communication skills, not least in managing the issue-associated fallout. Barack Obama's bold claim that "We're probably the first administration in modern history that hasn't had a major scandal in the White House," has been repeatedly challenged.[49] It is clear that events perceived to be scandalous occurred on his watch.[50] However, one indisputable fact remains: During his eight years in the Oval Office, no special prosecutor was appointed to investigate high-level executive wrong-doing. Even some of President Obama's detractors acknowledged his character traits. In his memoirs, Secretary of Defense Robert Gates was highly critical of his Commander in Chief. Nonetheless, he clarified his position in relation to the President as an individual, stating that he was "a man of personal integrity."[51] In an interview at the University of Chicago, former senior advisor to President Obama David Axelrod pointed out that the administration had had "no major scandals" since coming to power in 2009. He credited the ban on revolving door politics for this, stating that the situation under the Obama regime was "light years" away from that of his predecessors.[52] This was not a legacy continued by his successor.

On January 21, 2009, President Obama signed Executive Order 13490. This stated that full-time non-career presidential and vice-presidential appointees were barred after leaving the administration from "lobbying" an executive branch official "covered" by the Lobbying Disclosure Act or any non-career SES appointment for the remainder of the administration.[53] Additionally, all senior officials subject to the statutory one-year cooling-off period on lobbying and advocacy communications to their former agencies were required to abide by such cooling-off periods for two years.[54] When President Trump took office in 2017, he signed Executive Order 13770.[55] Announced with fanfare as part of his "drain the swamp" initiative, Trump's order on managing undue special interest influence was notably similar to the one it superseded. In due course, the Trump administration received a range of criticism for not adhering to its own ethics rules, including a series of formal complaints from government watchdog group Public Citizen.[56] As it turned out, this was the least of President Trump's ethics violation worries. Following in the footsteps of every leader (save Obama) since Richard Nixon, he was obliged to contend with that most unsettling of challenges to presidential power, a special prosecutor investigation. The nation had experienced a welcome hiatus from this lengthy and expensive process during the Obama years, but that is not to overlook the ongoing scandal allegations made against the 44th president at a time when fake news and the distortion of truth was on the rise.

Undermining the presidency: Benghazi

Throughout President Obama's eight years in office, there were regular calls from opposition politicians and hostile media for his impeachment. Motivations ranged from pressuring him to release his birth certificate to rage at his decision to stop defending the Defense of Marriage Act.[57] In the vast majority of these instances, hyperbole outweighed meaningful rationale and the efforts came to nothing. Yet there were episodes when some mud at least did stick, and the term "Benghazi" is probably one that is most synonymous in the public mind with scandal in relation to the Obama administration. However, of the usual associated ingredients, be they influence peddling, corruption, greed, sex, or a novel interpretation of the law, none were present in this scenario. In fact, the events behind the scandal clamor were more serious and grave than the routine misbehaviors that leading political actors pursue.

On September 11th 2012, four Americans, among others, were killed in two separate attacks on the US consulate and the nearby CIA compound in the Libyan city of Benghazi. The story was one of chaos and drama with a tragic outcome. Information surfaced immediately that those on the ground in Benghazi had been requesting additional security but to no avail. Republicans cried foul and claimed that the administration was involved in a cover-up of its incompetence.[58] Amongst those killed was US Ambassador Chris Stevens, who was the first ambassador to be murdered in service since 1979. This directly involved then Secretary of State Hillary Clinton, and critics understandably wanted to understand why American personnel had been left so perilously in harm's way.

Furthermore, the timing of the attacks inevitably made them a major political flashpoint, coming as they did less than two months before the 2012 elections. Initially the administration stated that the situation had occurred as a result of an inflammatory video posted online, and US Ambassador to the UN Susan Rice declared as much in a television interview five days later.[59] Republicans were clearly, and justifiably, unhappy with this explanation, immediately claiming that a more likely reason was the administration's failure to manage the security situation in Benghazi and even manage its policy in the region. As it was, the State Department's own Accountability and Review Board reported that "Systemic failures and leadership and management deficiencies at senior levels within two bureaus of the State Department . . . resulted in a Special Mission security posture that was inadequate for Benghazi and grossly inadequate to deal with the attack that took place."[60] Certainly the first response from the White House had been misleading, however unintentionally, and the issue became increasingly politicized as the President's opponents took the opportunity to castigate him for failing to protect American diplomats in a volatile location and then lacking a transparent response when the difficult questions were asked. No less than ten investigations ensued, including those conducted by House and Senate Committees. Reports were duly produced, in a bitterly partisan environment. Not for the first time involving a Clinton, a crisis moment was presented as a liberal cover-up of the truth or a vast right-wing conspiracy, depending on the source. In the end, none of the ten investigations produced evidence to support claims of corruption or a concerted cover-up made against the administration.[61]

The incident did hurt Rice's chances of succeeding Clinton as secretary of state, and a potentially bitter confirmation fight in the aftermath of her television performance saw her withdraw from consideration for the post.[62]

While identifying causal factors to explain the 2016 presidential election result—which had huge implications for the resilience of Obama's legacy—is not a task for this book, it is important to reflect on how the murder of Ambassador Stevens and three other American personnel in Benghazi was politically damaging to Hillary Clinton for the next four years. Whatever the truth of what happened in the US Special Mission on that brutal day, the immediate response of the State Department to the first killing of a US ambassador since 1979 was, at the least, open to contention. Secretary Clinton's role and efforts to provide security to the Ambassador would provide fodder for Republican congressional investigations for a considerable period.[63] Of the numerous investigations, perhaps the noisiest was the House Select Committee on the Events Surrounding the 2012 Terrorist Attack in Benghazi. This held its opening hearings in September 2014, filing its final report in December 2016.[64]

In his memoir, Ben Rhodes describes how disorientating he and his colleagues found the conspiracy theories to be, and how odd the realization was that whatever the administration claimed, there were those who simply would not believe them. The term "Benghazi" became "an accusation that seemed to mean everything and nothing at the same time, shifting from one conspiracy theory to the next."[65] The story signified a growing trend in which, according to Rhodes, "the truth had become irrelevant."[66] The bogus scandal demonstrated how material found in the darker corners of the internet made its way into reports by higher-profile media sources such as Breitbart and Fox News. This, along with other "fake news" stories, as they would become known, would increasingly undermine the executive's ability to govern. White House staffer Derek Chollet decried what he saw as the "shameless and cynical way that Obama and Clinton's critics used the Benghazi attacks to score political points with their rank and file" in order to undermine the US in its world role.[67] Despite this challenge, and the catalogue of other accusations leveled against President Obama, one fact remained. The Obama White House did not have to contend with the enormous strain and potential depletion of power that comes with a special prosecutor investigation.

Nevertheless, since the Watergate era scandal management had become and remains a core component of presidential power. There is a pattern of sorts with the evolution of presidential scandal management, and this can often be more damaging than the original misdemeanour. From sexual indiscretion to electoral and executive impropriety, most modern presidents have had to run the gauntlet of an independent external investigation that operates with an elastic remit and bottomless funding. For a brief period at least, observers may have been forgiven for wondering if the prosecutor-free Obama administration had finally broken the post-Watergate mould. It had not.

The Mueller investigation

Donald Trump was a mere sixteen weeks into the job when Special Counsel Robert Mueller was appointed to investigate the possibility of meddling by a hostile foreign power in the 2016 election. As a result, the 45th president was deprived of any meaningful opportunity to experience a pre- and post-special prosecutor era of his administration. If the achievements of the first 100 days are the currency of the next, then the Trump administration was robbed of this potential benefit in part at least by the hyper-focus on the special counsel appointment and relentless speculation relating to what he would uncover. Hence, outcome aside, every day that the Mueller investigation continued increased the political damage done to the President. Such harm can occur in parallel with a president's popularity, as was the case in this instance. The Mueller investigation may have damaged the President's power, in that his reputation and international standing were impacted, but it did not negatively sway his supporters. His voter base remained unconditionally loyal, choosing to embrace the "witch hunt" narrative to explain the investigation. The president's detractors already had a low opinion of him, which was not altered by the Mueller probe.[68]

When considering damage control options, presidential advisor Steve Bannon reflected on how Bill Clinton had managed the extraordinarily intrusive investigation conducted by Kenneth Starr. When interviewed, Bannon stated his admiration for how the Clintons corralled the issue by building a legal and communications wall around it and distancing themselves from it. In Bannon's view, this was the optimum way forward in the face of such an existential threat to a president's power. Compartmentalizing the problem allowed the executive to remain functional and carry on with its agenda of running the country.[69]

In 2018, Donald Trump pardoned Lewis "Scooter" Libby of crimes he was convicted of by special counsel Patrick Fitzgerald, appointed during the George W. Bush years. The two had never met and the President justified his decision on the basis that he believed Libby had been unfairly treated by the special counsel.[70] The pardon was granted in April, the same month that former FBI director James Comey, who had appointed Fitzgerald in 2003, released a book highly critical of President Trump's behavior.[71] At that point, the Robert Mueller investigation was almost a year into its task and the President, in a norm-busting move, demanded that "the Department of Justice look into whether or not the FBI/DoJ infiltrated or surveiled" his campaign at the behest of the previous administration.[72] Such a direct intervention by a president was unprecedented, as was the use of the platform from which he made the request. For the 45th president, Twitter was the communication tool of choice. Perhaps unavoidably, Deputy Attorney General Rod Rosenstein asked the Department of Justice inspector general to follow up on the President's request.[73]

It is difficult to overstate the significance of Special Counsel Robert Mueller's appointment and investigation. On May 17th 2016, the former FBI director and Marine Corps platoon commander began his independent inquiry into possible US election meddling by a foreign government. The probe included Donald Trump's presidential campaign, with a remit to search for potential collusion with (Russian) election interference. At the time, President Trump tweeted that Mueller's appointment would "hurt our country."[74] There is little doubt that Team Trump, if not the man himself, was mindful of where such an investigation could lead. Pundits were swift to roll out the Watergate comparisons, not least because within Mueller's first month on the job, Trump associates were publicly discussing the President's desire to fire him.[75] It is possible that President Trump, new to the job and to politics, with his light grasp of history, may not have realized the abuse of power connotations that such a threat embodied. When Richard Nixon decided to have Watergate special prosecutor Archibald Cox fired in 1973 he led the nation toward a constitutional crisis, taking a dramatic further step toward his own political downfall. As was the case in both instances, the President could not fire the special counsel directly. He could order his Attorney General to do so, and if faced with a resignation, he could ask the Deputy Attorney General, and then the Solicitor General. In the context of Watergate, Nixon finally had his bidding done by the third in line, Robert Bork; the decision was declared illegal by the US Supreme Court a fortnight later.

Twitter rants aside, President Trump refrained from enacting his own Saturday Night Massacre, and the Mueller probe rumbled on. By the time the investigation was completed in spring 2019, Mueller's team had charged thirty-four individuals and three companies.[76] Over time, the level of public support for the investigation remained steady. Approximately halfway through the process, 61 percent of those polled in March 2018 by Pew stated that they were "very" or "somewhat" confident that Mueller's probe would be fair. The number saying that they were not very confident (19 percent) and not at all confident (18 percent) tallied with Trump's average poll ratings of 40 percent from the same time period.[77] A Washington Post/ABC poll taken a month later resulted in a higher support of 69 percent for the Russia probe. This increase may be explained by the especially dramatic developments relating to the investigation in April 2018, when the home and office of President Trump's personal lawyer Michael Cohen were raided by the FBI. The poll took place as the alleged payback of $130,000 to adult entertainer Stormy Daniels was under scrutiny, and the public clearly drew a distinction between investigation of election fraud and hush money for a 2006 affair. Of those polled, 70 percent supported Mueller investigating the former and 58 percent the latter.[78]

The scope of the special counsel's suite of investigations inevitably meant that a swift conclusion was unlikely. The White House clearly thought so too, despite presidential attorney Rudy Giuliani's assertion that the probe would be done "in a week or two."[79] Trump lawyer Ty Cobb, known for promoting a cooperative approach with the seventy-three-year-old Republican and his team, was replaced in mid-2018 by Emmet Flood, who had represented Bill Clinton during his 1990s impeachment proceedings and was known for his adversarial approach. As the midterm elections loomed, the administration worked to move the investigation along as swiftly as possible. This was not necessarily because it would loom large as a priority issue for voters as they headed to the polls; however, Republicans were tipped to lose their Congressional majority on November 6th, putting the President in a far more vulnerable position. A lengthy Mueller investigation was deemed unlikely, not least due to the $1 million a month price tag. Nonetheless, in such polarized times it was crucial that Lady Justice did not peep from under her blindfold. If this made for slow progress, then so be it. From the administration's perspective, the ongoing challenge to its power and prestige were deeply damaging.

Leadership in foreign policy

Presidential leadership in foreign affairs does not always play out as forecasted, especially when judged against the expectations created during the inadequate time normally given to debating international affairs during a presidential election campaign. Moreover, events can quickly and sharply change the perceptions and actions of the incumbent of the White House. President George W. Bush, for example, in a campaign debate with Vice President Al Gore, famously spoke of the US needing to act as a "humble nation" rather than an "arrogant" one in order to win the "respect" of the world.[80] This was perhaps misinterpreted to mean that Bush favored a more isolationist foreign policy, likely to prefer keeping the US out of the international arena. That is certainly not what his foreign policy legacy turned out to be. Clearly the terrorist attacks of 9/11 explain the nature of the interventions in

Afghanistan and also, to some extent, provided a rationale for those in his administration looking to justify the invasion of Iraq in 2003.[81] Yet, even prior to 9/11, it was evident that "humble" did not mean modest; nor did it signify that the US would not aggressively pursue its own interests.[82]

Similarly, much of candidate Obama's rhetoric on the campaign on foreign affairs was over-interpreted by some of his more liberal supporters who ended up being disappointed by aspects of his leadership in foreign policy, which they saw as more muscular than they anticipated. Candidate Obama's message was one that appealed to those looking for a change from the sometimes brash foreign policy leadership exercised by Bush's team. On the campaign trail he promised an end to executive branch justifications for practices at the least very close to torture, along with ending the practice of detaining "enemy combatants" at Guantanamo Bay. The former was fulfilled with an executive order on January 22, 2009, stipulating that interrogation could only be conducted in accord with Army Field Manual guidelines and that any legal advice permitting interrogation techniques beyond those guidelines issued between September 2001 and January 2009 was to be ignored. In summer 2014, in advance of a Senate Intelligence Committee report on the CIA's activities, Obama again spoke out against what had happened: "When we engaged in some of these enhanced interrogation techniques, techniques that I believe and I think any fair-minded person would believe were torture, we crossed a line."[83] In his inaugural address, Obama had laid out how American power needed to be both tempered by an understanding of the needs of other nations and reinforced through taking the high ground: "[O]ur power alone cannot protect us, nor does it entitle us to do as we please. . . . our power grows through its prudent use; our security emanates from the justness of our cause, the force of our example, the tempering qualities of humility and restraint."[84]

Yet, if these messages along with his dove-like stance on the Iraq war led to the perception that Obama was to be a timid leader in foreign affairs, such an impression was misleading. Critics were certainly frustrated by the inaction as Syria burned, and some accused him of weakness when challenged by Russian aggression. For example, as the crisis in Crimea grew and Russian annexation of Ukraine territory became a reality, Republican Senator Bob Corker of Tennessee—who was to become Chair of the Senate Foreign Relations Committee—complained: "Our administration is creating an air of permissiveness," and stated that there was a "need to show long-term resolve."[85] It would, however, be mistaken to view Obama's unwillingness to commit US forces as a sign of a president afraid to exert executive branch authority. Hence, at times, critics fumed as they accused the administration of acting imperially. As noted in Chapter 4, the Obama White House was dismissive of congressional protests that the intervention in Libya needed congressional authorization. In September 2014, reflecting on the Libyan intervention and the emerging military actions against Islamic State, Jack Goldsmith, who had served as assistant attorney general in the Office of Legal Counsel in the Bush administration, noted:

> Future historians will ask why George W. Bush sought and received express congressional authorization for his wars (against al Qaeda and Iraq) and his successor did not. They will puzzle over how Barack Obama the prudent war-powers constitutionalist transformed into a matchless war-powers unilateralist.[86]

This comment contains its share of partisan-inspired hyperbole, but it is based on the actuality of the Obama administration's ambiguous attitude toward a congressional role in foreign policy-making. In turn, this reflects how Obama's legacy with regard to the conduct of foreign policy did not match the expectations of those who championed him as the unalloyed antidote to George W. Bush's willingness to push the boundaries of legality.

The contradictions between the Obama administration's desire to take what might be termed the moral high ground and its willingness to assert American power in controversial ways was highlighted by the use of drones to conduct military strikes, notably in Pakistan, Yemen, and Somalia. Obama's use of drones significantly expanded a program that had begun under the Bush administration. For Obama's liberal supporters, the decision to "embrace an official program of targeted killing of suspected terrorists was one of the most surprising developments" of his time in office.[87] This was despite the fact that candidate Obama had stated in summer of 2007 that he would be willing to act in a foreign country even if the government of that country did not endorse the action. Referring explicitly to Pakistan, he said: "If we have actionable intelligence about high-value terrorist targets and President Musharraf won't act, we will."[88] Nevertheless, the scale of drone strikes in Pakistan in the face of strong internal popular opposition was striking. In the early years of the administration, as Pakistan became a focus of US drone strikes, the number of strikes in that country peaked at 122 strikes in 2010, with one estimate of 830 casualties.[89] Moreover, the anxieties about the value of these strikes was particularly acute given how the use of drone warfare in Pakistan was increasingly influenced by CIA assessments, with attacks carried out against the advice of successive US ambassadors to Pakistan.[90] Pakistani resentment was on public display when Secretary of State Hillary Clinton visited Pakistan in late 2009. Reporting suggested that she handled difficult situations in as dignified a manner as possible but that she was left unable to appease angry audiences who challenged her about the missile strikes.[91]

For his part, Obama was clearly aware of the potential abuses that came with the use of drones and explicitly addressed that matter in a speech at the National Defense University in May 2013. First, he acknowledged the issues raised by the use of drones as a means of conducting warfare:

> this new technology raises profound questions—about who is targeted, and why; about civilian casualties, and the risk of creating new enemies; about the legality of such strikes under US and international law; about accountability and morality.

Next, if not accepting the estimates of some non-governmental organizations about numbers of civilian casualties, Obama did concede that "it is a hard fact that US strikes have resulted in civilian casualties" and he referred to how, as Commander in Chief, he had to live with "these heartbreaking tragedies." Still, he argued that drones were preferable to alternative means of warfare and insisted: "Our efforts must be measured against the history of putting American troops in distant lands among hostile populations."[92]

An in-depth *New York Times* report detailed how personally involved Obama was in the decision-making with regard to the use of drones, but also noted how some advisors worried that the emphasis on this type of technological solution to the problem of al Qaeda, even though successful in killing many senior figures in that terrorist organization, had substituted for the development of long-term strategies to combat the appeal of anti-American preaching.[93] More generally, Andreas Krieg maintains that the use of drones was consistent with the administration's efforts to maintain an active presence in a fraught international environment while "externalizing the burdens of warfare."[94]

To further understand the somewhat conflicting nature of Obama's leadership in foreign policy and the manner in which he left a legacy that simultaneously illustrated a willingness to exert executive authority while also demonstrating an underlying institutional weakness, it is also worth briefly revisiting the circumstances in which the Obama administration signed the US up to the JCPOA, or the Iran nuclear deal, which was discussed in Chapter 4. In the context of Obama's substantive foreign policy legacy, we noted in that discussion how relatively simple it was for President Trump to undo that deal. One reason for this was that the deal was implemented as an "executive agreement" rather than as a formal treaty. From Obama's perspective there was minimal value in trying to formalize the deal as a treaty, since there was zero chance of it receiving sixty-seven votes in order to be ratified in the Senate. Hence the political rationale for declaring the deal an agreement, even though it contained "economic and national security implications" that precedent would have suggested meant "the deal is at least the *kind* of agreement that has been negotiated as a treaty in the past."[95] The process was further complicated by the manner in which the administration appeared to make a concession to opponents in Congress, but did so in a way always likely to leave the administration able to implement its will. That is, in April 2015 the White House agreed that there would be an opportunity for a congressional vote on the looming final deal, but that this would be a vote on whether to strike down the deal. Critically, even if there was a majority for that position, Obama retained the authority to veto the measure.[96] This effectively meant that there needed to be a two-thirds majority *against* the deal to deny it coming into force, rather than the two-thirds majority that would be needed in favor if it had been presented to the Senate as a treaty. In this immediate context, therefore, the administration's actions look like an attempt to do an end run around congressional capacity to check the executive branch's actions. From a broader perspective, however, it also illustrates the manner in which the extension of partisan conflict to foreign as well as domestic affairs has diminished the capacity of any White House to negotiate international deals that stand a serious chance of being ratified as treaties by the Senate. Hence, as was often the case with the administration's actions in domestic affairs, the turn to an expansive use of executive authority to implement the JCPOA reflected an inherent weakness of the contemporary presidency as well as a willingness to push executive authority to its limits.

So Obama's leadership legacy in foreign affairs was ambiguous. His was not an explicitly muscular style of leadership in the fashion of his predecessor, but nor was it one that shrank from asserting the priorities of the executive branch when it was determined to do so. The decision to ignore the requirements of the War Powers Resolution with regard to the intervention in Libya, yet to ask for congressional approval for missile strikes against the Assad regime in summer 2013, demonstrate intellectual and institutional inconsistency but also a consistent prioritization of political calculations. Overall, categorizing the fundamentals underpinning Obama's foreign policy leadership is perplexing. He was by no means the "dove" that many, perhaps including the Nobel Prize committee, had initially anticipated, but his time in office saw the constrained use of American power in both real and rhetorical terms. That was a legacy that was not embraced by his successor, though the evidence of the opening thirty months of Trump's presidency suggested its own contradictions.

During the campaign, candidate Trump made some extraordinary statements that seemed to embrace the use of torture and question the value of the US's traditional alliances.[97] Moreover, he made little effort to claim that the US role in the world was not simply based on its power but also on its moral leadership. Famously, just after assuming the presidency, he said in an interview that he would not criticize Russian president Vladimir Putin's style of leadership, as the US also had a "lot of killers"—going on to ask the interviewer, rhetorically, "What, do you think our country is so innocent?" This led conservative columnist Jonah Goldberg to reflect that "if Obama had ever suggested the same, conservatives would have pounced," and the writer continued to lament that while the US had often fallen short of its ideals, the problem with Trump's language was that "he often sounds like he has contempt for those ideals in the first place."[98]

This was a stark rejection not just of Obama's approach, but of the public position traditionally taken by US presidents throughout the country's history. Critics of US foreign policy actions might argue that Trump was in fact simply being more honest about US motives than his predecessors, but appealing to American virtue was an established feature of presidential rhetoric. Obama had in fact sometimes been ambivalent in his expression of the inherent goodness of American exceptionalism, particularly when addressing non-American audiences, but he was explicit about the value of the US maintaining a leading role in international affairs.[99] In this framing, while "America First" was not an embrace of isolationism, it was a turn away from the idea that the US was either a role model or a nation with a particular responsibility to provide leadership in a turbulent world. Moreover, on an individual level, Trump sometimes appeared admiring of political leaders in authoritarian regimes. Hence, regardless of the merits of a policy of negotiating directly with the North Korean regime, Trump's language lauding personal praise on Kim Jong-un contrasted with his verbal jabs at leaders of the US's traditional allies such as Angela Merkel of Germany.[100]

In other ways, President Trump took Obama's legacy and ran with it. In the summer of 2016, British columnist and commentator Simon Jenkins reflected on the US's use of air power, which had just left scores of civilians dead in Syria, observing that "Obama's wars remain unresolved and immoral." He mused that at least the election of Trump would likely lead to a decline in the use of drones, given what he saw as the more isolationist noises being made by the candidate.[101] This, however, did not come to pass. Under Trump, the use of drones continued and in some cases accelerated.[102] Strikes in Pakistan had dwindled to three in Obama's final year in office; focus had switched to Yemen, with forty-three strikes in 2016, and Somalia, with thirteen strikes that year. Under Trump the rate of strikes in Yemen continued at a similar pace during 2017 and 2018, while in Somalia there were eighty strikes by the end of 2018 and a further fifty-five in the opening nine months of 2019.[103]

On the other hand, the Trump administration did change some of the practices of the Obama era. Firstly, it reduced the already limited transparency about the use of drones and the numbers of civilian casualties from US strikes.[104] In the summer of 2016, Obama did issue an executive order laying out stricter ground rules for when and how US strikes would be carried out in places where the US was not a formal combatant. The order also required that the US government offer an estimate of the number of civilian casualties from any such strikes. President Trump rolled back that order in March 2019.[105] Secondly, Trump reduced White House oversight of the drone program and loosened restrictions on the CIA's ability to use drones under rules that were less restrictive than those observed by the Pentagon.[106] Depending on perspective and intellectual starting point, these moves could be seen as an extension of the logic of the Obama administration's position or a reversal of safeguards put in place to constrain the potentially excessive use of American power. These clashing interpretations are more a reflection of the ambiguous nature of Obama's legacy than of the direction of travel under the Trump administration.

Conclusion

As we have seen, the Obama administration ran into many institutional roadblocks, particularly in its last years after the GOP had taken control of the Senate in addition to the House. This meant that the frustration caused by the relentless probing of Hillary Clinton's record as secretary of state by House

Republicans was now multiplied by the manner in which Senate Republicans slowed the confirmation of judges to the federal bench to a trickle. This was not a new story for the modern American presidency. The scandals may have been very different but the Iran-Contra and Lewinsky affairs disrupted and stymied the second terms of presidents Reagan and Clinton respectively. George W. Bush too found his second mandate haunted by the failure of the effort at Social Security reform and then the botched practical response and the profoundly misjudged public reaction to the devastation wrought by Hurricane Katrina. Clearly, maintaining a composed and effective leadership equilibrium over an eight-year presidency is an almost impossible task. On the other hand, the chaos that engulfed the Trump administration from its opening week was unprecedented. President Clinton had quickly become mired in controversy over the issue of gays serving in the US military and the withdrawal of his original nominees to be Attorney General and Assistant Attorney General for Civil Rights, and his approval rating had dropped from 58 percent when he entered office to 37 percent by June 1993.[107] Yet, Donald Trump's approval rating was only 45 percent when he took office and his first week was marked by chaos at the nation's airports as the first iteration of the "travel ban" was put in place.[108]

Another indicator of disorganization came with the high turnover of senior figures in the administration in its opening years. This was exemplified by the comings and goings of the supposed gatekeeper to the Oval Office, the chief of staff. The Clinton administration, known for its disorganization, saw two people in that role during the first term. The much tighter ship of the Bush administration saw Andrew Card serve over five years from January 2001, while there were two permanent chiefs of staff in Obama's opening mandate. Reince Priebus, Trump's first chief of staff, lasted only 192 days before being replaced by General John Kelly, who was seen as a figure more likely to be assertive in guarding against unfiltered and un-evidenced information being passed on to the President. He had limited success in that task and lasted less than eighteen months in the job. At the start of 2019 Mick Mulvaney took over as acting chief of staff and he remained in that role, with the same title, as the year drew to a close. Unsurprisingly, Trump denied that this high turnover rate signaled problems in the White House. In late summer 2018, after announcing the impending departure of White House Counsel Don McGahn by tweet to the reported surprise of McGahn himself, Trump further tweeted: "The Fake News Media has it, purposely, so wrong! They love to portray chaos in the White House when they know that chaos doesn't exist—just a "smooth running machine" with changing parts!"[109] Extensive reporting, however, reinforced the picture of what was clearly visible chaos.[110] In September 2018 the *New York Times* published an anonymous op-ed piece by someone described as a senior official in the administration. The article praised some of the policy initiatives taken over the previous two years, such as tax cuts and efforts at deregulation, but described "the president's leadership style" as "impetuous, adversarial, petty and ineffective." Further, the author asserted,

> Meetings with him veer off topic and off the rails, he engages in repetitive rants, and his impulsiveness results in half-baked, ill-informed and occasionally reckless decisions that have to be walked back.[111]

Yet, in at least one critical, legacy-establishing arena, the Trump administration proved more effective than its predecessor. As reported by the *New York Times* in the fall of 2019, President Trump celebrated "his success confirming his judicial appointments, an achievement crucial to maintaining his hold on conservatives and on evangelical voters," even as his presidency again grew mired in scandal and controversy.[112] To an important group of conservatives, the Trump administration's effectiveness in remaking the federal judiciary provided a rationale for continuing to endorse a president whose personal behavior they privately considered reprehensible. Trump might sour the national conversation for eight years, but the judges that he and Senate Republicans placed on the federal bench could serve for decades.

The fact that these judicial nominations and confirmations took place against a backdrop of repeated scandals illustrated the importance of continuing Republican control of the Senate. This majority also seemed a bulwark for President Trump as impeachment proceedings gathered pace in the House over the emerging story in fall 2019 of efforts by the President to encourage the Ukrainian government to investigate the activities of former Vice President Biden's son, Hunter Biden, when he held a position with a Ukrainian gas company.[113] That scandal blew up almost as soon as the storm over the Mueller investigation appeared to have blown over. In the end, Trump's presidency survived the Mueller investigation. The final Mueller report sent somewhat mixed messages. It detailed numerous instances that might have constituted obstruction of justice and warned that the Russian threat to American democratic practices was a real one.[114] But Mueller did not conclude that there had been direct collaboration between the Trump campaign and Russian state operatives in his report and in testimony to Congress he explained: "Based on Justice Department policy and principles of fairness, we decided we would not make a determination as to whether the President committed a crime."[115] As it turned out, both President Trump's supporters and opponents took the report as vindication of their pre-existing position. To Trump's champions, the President was cleared of any wrongdoing and it was time to investigate the investigators for malicious intent. As read by the President's opponents, Mueller's report provided ample evidence that team Trump had happily let the Russian state intervene on its behalf in 2016 and had then engaged in multiple episodes of obstruction of justice. The report did not, however, provoke an immediate existential threat to the Trump presidency in the form of impeachment. That was yet to come.

Notes

1. John Roberts, "Judges, Umpires and Politicians," *C-Span*, September 12, 2005, <https://www.c-span.org/video/?c4681275/john-roberts-judges-umpires-politicians> (last accessed December 13, 2019).
2. See for example Kerry Eleveld, *Don't Tell Me to Wait: How the Fight for Gay Rights Changed America and Transformed Obama's Presidency* (New York, Basic Books, 2015).
3. David Axelrod, *Believer: My Forty Years in Politics* (New York, Penguin, 2015).

4. Marian McKenna, *Franklin Roosevelt and the Great Constitutional War: The Court Packing Crisis of 1937* (New York: Fordham University Press, 2002).
5. Judge Glock, "Unpacking the Supreme Court: Judicial Retirement, Judicial Independence, and the Road to the 1937 Court Battle," *Journal of American History*, 106.1 (2019): 47–71.
6. For a discussion of these perspectives see Michael Nelson, "The President and the Court: Reinterpreting the Court-Packing Episode of 1937," *Political Science Quarterly*, 103.2 (Summer 1988): 267–93.
7. Information available at <https://www.supremecourt.gov/about/members_text.aspx> (last accessed December 13, 2019).
8. Ed Lazarus, "Four Enduring Myths About Supreme Court Nominees," *Time*, May 26, 2009, <http://content.time.com/time/specials/packages/article/0,28804,1900851_1900850_1900845,00.html> (last accessed December 13, 2019). See also James Simon, *Eisenhower versus Warren: The Battle for Civil Rights and Civil Liberties* (New York: Liveright Publishing, 2018).
9. Jeff Greenfield, "The Justice Who Built the Trump Court," *Politico*, July 9, 2018, <https://www.politico.com/magazine/story/2018/07/09/david-souter-the-supreme-court-justice-who-built-the-trump-court-218953> (last accessed December 13, 2019).
10. "Sandra Day O'Connor, First Female Justice and Moderate Swing Vote, Retires," *PBS Newshour*, July 1, 2005, <https://www.pbs.org/newshour/politics/law-july-dec05-oconnor_07-01> (last accessed December 13, 2019).
11. David O'Brien, "Clinton's Legal Policy and the Courts: Rising From Disarray or Turning Around and Around?" in Bert Rockman and Colin Campbell (eds), *The Clinton Presidency: First Appraisals* (New York: Chatham House, 1996), 139.
12. Jeffrey Toobin, *The Nine: Inside the Secret World of the Supreme Court* (New York: Anchor, 2008), 42.
13. O'Brien, "Clinton's Legal Policy and the Courts," 139.
14. On its website the Federalist Society describes itself as a "group of conservatives and libertarians" that is "emphatically" committed to the idea that it is the "duty of the judiciary to say what the law is, not what it should be." See <https://fedsoc.org/about-us> (last accessed December 13, 2019).
15. Jeffrey Toobin, *The Oath: The Obama White House and the Supreme Court* (New York, Anchor, 2012), 121.

16. Jeffrey Toobin, "The Conservative Pipeline to the Supreme Court," The New Yorker, April 17, 2017, <https://www.newyorker.com/magazine/2017/04/17/the-conservative-pipeline-to-the-supreme-court> (last accessed December 13, 2019).
17. Barack Obama (Senator) on Samuel Alito, C-Span, January 26, 2006, <https://www.c-span.org/video/?c4580879/sen-barack-obama-samuel-alito; Barack Obama (Senator) on John Roberts Jr., C-Span, December 15, 2005, <https://www.c-span.org/video/?c4455704/senator-barack-obama-senate-session-dec-15-2005> (both last accessed December 13, 2019).
18. Robert Alt, "Sotomayor's and Obama's Identity Politics Leave Blind Justice at Risk," US News and World Report, May 27, 2009, <https://www.usnews.com/opinion/articles/2009/05/27/sotomayors-and-obamas-identity-politics-leave-blind-justice-at-risk> (last accessed December 13, 2019).
19. Risa Goluboff and Richard Schragger, "Obama's Court?" in Julian Zelizer (ed.), The Presidency of Barack Obama: A First Historical Assessment (Princeton, NJ: Princeton University Press, 2018), 78–94.
20. Sheryl Gay Stolberg, "Sotomayor, A Trailblazer and a Dreamer," The New York Times, May 26, 2009, <https://www.nytimes.com/2009/05/27/us/politics/27websotomayor.html> (last accessed December 13, 2019).
21. Ariane De Vogue and Devin Dwyer, "Hearing Gives Glimpse of Kagan's Views on Hot Issues," ABC News, June 30, 2010, <https://abcnews.go.com/Politics/Supreme_Court/elena-kagan-issues-supreme-court-hearings-give-glimpse/story?id=11052847> (last accessed December 13, 2019).
22. Jeff Stein, "President Obama: Supreme Court Process 'Beyond Repair' if GOP Refuses Hearing," Vox, March 16, 2016, <https://www.vox.com/2016/3/16/11245572/obama-scotus-garland-senate> (last accessed December 13, 2019).
23. Ron Elving, "What Happened with Merrick Garland in 2016 and Why It Matters Now," NPR, June 29, 2018, <https://www.npr.org/2018/06/29/624467256/what-happened-with-merrick-garland-in-2016-and-why-it-matters-now> (last accessed December 13, 2019).
24. John Gramlich, "Trump Has Appointed a Larger Share of Female Judges Than Other GOP Presidents, but Lags Obama," Pew Research Center, October 2, 2018, <http://www.pewresearch.

org/fact-tank/2018/10/02/trump-has-appointed-a-larger-share-of-female-judges-than-other-gop-presidents-but-lags-obama/> (last accessed December 13, 2019).

25. Al Kamen and Colby Itkowitz, "The Nuclear Option and Its Fallouts," *The Washington Post*, December 17, 2014, <https://www.washingtonpost.com/politics/the-nuclear-option-and-its-fallout/2014/12/17/abea2be6-8631-11e4-a702-fa31ff4ae98e_story.html?utm_term=.3dd82ccd5f62> (last accessed December 13, 2019).

26. Paul Kane, "Reid, Democrats Trigger 'Nuclear' Option: Eliminate Most Filibusters on Nominees," *The Washington Post*, November 21, 2013, <https://www.washingtonpost.com/politics/senate-poised-to-limit-filibusters-in-party-line-vote-that-would-alter-centuries-of-precedent/2013/11/21/d065cfe8-52b6-11e3-9fe0-fd2ca728e67c_story.html?utm_term=.251ce090b03b> (last accessed December 13, 2019).

27. Jeremy Peters, "Senate Vote to Curb Filibuster Power to Stall Nominees," *The New York Times*, November 22, 2013, A1.

28. Russell Wheeler, "Confirming Federal Judges During the Final Two Years of the Obama Administration: Vacancies Up, Nominees Down," *Brookings*, August 18, 2015, <https://www.brookings.edu/blog/fixgov/2015/08/18/confirming-federal-judges-during-the-final-two-years-of-the-obama-administration-vacancies-up-nominees-down/> (last accessed December 13, 2019).

29. Steve Benen, "Trump's Promise: 'I Will Appoint Judges That Will Be Pro-Life,'" *The Rachel Maddow Show: The MaddowBlog*, May 11, 2016, <http://www.msnbc.com/rachel-maddow-show/trumps-promise-i-will-appoint-judges-will-be-pro-life> (last accessed December 13, 2019).

30. Rolando Del Carmen and Craig Hemmens, *Criminal Procedure and the Supreme Court* (Maryland, Rowman & Littlefield, 2010), 334.

31. Elving, "What Happened with Merrick Garland."

32. John K. White, "Donald Trump and the Republican Party: The Making of a Faustian Bargain," Conference paper presented at the Political Studies Association, Glasgow, April 2017, <https://www.psa.ac.uk/sites/default/files/conference/papers/2017/Donald%20Trump%20and%20the%20Republican%20Party_0.pdf> (last accessed December 13, 2019).

33. Eric Levitz, "In Hindsight, Democrats Really Mishandled That Merrick Garland Thing," *New York Magazine*, June 26, 2018, <http://nymag.com/intelligencer/2018/06/in-hindsight-obama-shouldnt-have-appointed-merrick-garland.html?gtm=top> (last accessed December 13, 2019).

34. Aaron Smith, "Obama's Re-Election Drives Gun Sales," *CNN*, November 9, 2012, <https://money.cnn.com/2012/11/09/news/economy/gun-control-obama/index.html> (last accessed December 13, 2019).
35. Josh Gerstein and Jennifer Haberkorn, "It's Not Just Abortion: Five Issues Likely to be Affected by Kennedy's Exit," *Politico*, June 27, 2018, <https://www.politico.com/story/2018/06/27/anthony-kennedy-retirement-supreme-court-cases-680104> (last accessed December 13, 2019).
36. Mark Landler and Maggie Haberman, "Former Bush Aide is Trump Pick for Court," *The New York Times*, July 10, 2018, A1.
37. Oliver Roeder and Amelia Thomson-DeVeaux, "How Four Potential Nominees Would Change the Supreme Court," *FiveThirtyEight*, July 6, 2018, <https://fivethirtyeight.com/features/how-4-potential-nominees-would-change-the-supreme-court/> (last accessed December 13, 2019).
38. Alvin Chang, "Brett Kavanaugh and the Supreme Court's Drastic Shift to the Right," *Vox*, September 14, 2018, <https://www.vox.com/policy-and-politics/2018/7/9/17537808/supreme-court-brett-kavanaugh-right-cartoon> (last accessed December 13, 2019).
39. For a timeline on the Kavanaugh confirmation process, see Sophie Tatum, "Brett Kavanaugh's Confirmation: A Timeline," *CNN Politics*, 2018, <https://edition.cnn.com/interactive/2018/10/politics/timeline-kavanaugh/> (last accessed December 13, 2019).
40. John Gramlich, "With Another Supreme Court Pick, Trump is Leaving His Mark on Higher Federal Courts," *Pew Research Center*, July 16, 2018, <http://www.pewresearch.org/fact-tank/2018/07/16/with-another-supreme-court-pick-trump-is-leaving-his-mark-on-higher-federal-courts/> (last accessed December 13, 2019).
41. "Remarks by President Trump on the Infrastructure Initiative," March 29, 2018, <https://www.whitehouse.gov/briefings-statements/remarks-president-trump-infrastructure-initiative/> (last accessed December 13, 2019).
42. Jennifer Bendery, "Trump Has Confirmed 150 Lifetime Federal Judges. That's A Lot," *Huffington Post*, September 18, 2019, <https://www.huffingtonpost.co.uk/entry/trump-judges-courts-senate-rules-mcconnell-republicans_n_5d81397ee4b05f8fb6eee2e1?ri18n=true> (last accessed December 13, 2019).
43. Jennifer Bendery, "Unqualified and Ideological: A Guide to Trump's Worst Judges," *Huffington Post*, September 8, 2019, <https://www.

huffingtonpost.co.uk/entry/trump-courts-judges-abortion-lgbtq-voting-rights_us_5d669025e4b063c341f8fdc9> (last accessed December 13, 2019).

44. Russell Wheeler, "Trump's Judicial Appointments Record at the August Recess: A Little Less Than Meets the Eye," *Brookings*, August 8, 2019, <https://www.brookings.edu/blog/fixgov/2019/08/08/trumps-judicial-appointments-record-at-the-august-recess-a-little-less-than-meets-the-eye/> (last accessed December 13, 2019).

45. Amy Wang, "Trump Lashes Out at Federal Judge Who Temporarily Blocked Travel Ban," *The Washington Post*, February 4, 2017, <https://www.washingtonpost.com/news/the-fix/wp/2017/02/04/trump-lashes-out-at-federal-judge-who-temporarily-blocked-travel-ban/> (last accessed December 13, 2019).

46. "In His Own Words: The President's Attacks on the Courts," Brennan Center for Justice, June 5, 2017, <https://www.brennancenter.org/analysis/his-own-words-presidents-attacks-courts> (last accessed December 13, 2019).

47. Adam Liptak, "A Rare Rebuke, in Front of a Nation," *The New York Times*, January 28, 2010, A1.

48. Russell Berman, "The President Learns About Separation of Powers, And He Doesn't Like It," *The Atlantic*, January 13, 2019, <https://www.theatlantic.com/politics/archive/2019/01/donald-trump-brawls-james-robart-and-judiciary/580000/> (last accessed December 13, 2019).

49. Glenn Kessler, "Has the Obama White House Been Historically Free of Scandal?" *The Washington Post*, January 19, 2017, <https://www.washingtonpost.com/gdpr-consent/?destination=%2fnews%2ffact-checker%2fwp%2f2017%2f01%2f19%2fhas-the-obama-white-house-been-historically-free-of-scandal%2f%3f&utm_term=.a4fa6cff05ce> (last accessed December 13, 2019).

50. See for example "A Review of ATF's Operation Fast and Furious and Related Matters," US Department of Justice, September 2012, <https://oig.justice.gov/reports/2012/s1209.pdf>; "Review of Selected Criteria Used to Identify Tax-Exempt Applications for Review" (Internal Revenue Service targeting scandal), US Department of Treasury, September 28, 2017, <https://www.treasury.gov/tigta/auditreports/2017reports/201710054fr.pdf> (last accessed December 13, 2019).

51. Robert Gates, *Duty: Memoirs of a Secretary at War* (New York: Vintage, 2015).

52. David Axelrod, University of Chicago Institute of Politics video, posted on *Real Clear Politics*, February 17, 2015, <https://www.realclearpolitics.com/video/2015/02/17/axelrod_proud_of_the_fact_there_hasnt_been_a_major_scandal_in_obama_administration.html> (last accessed December 13, 2019).
53. The executive order included non-career individuals in the Senior Executive Service, and excepted service confidential policy-making appointees. See Executive Order 13490—Ethics Commitments by Executive Branch Personnel, The White House, Office of the Press Secretary, January 21, 2009, <https://obamawhitehouse.archives.gov/the-press-office/ethics-commitments-executive-branch-personnel> (last accessed December 13, 2019). TO HERE
54. Jack Maskell,, "Post-Employment 'Revolving Door' Laws for Federal Personnel," Congressional Research Service, January 7, 2014, <https://fas.org/sgp/crs/misc/R42728.pdf> (last accessed December 13, 2019).
55. White House Executive Order: Ethics Commitments by Executive Branch Appointeees, January 28, 2017, <https://www.whitehouse.gov/presidential-actions/executive-order-ethics-commitments-executive-branch-appointees/> (last accessed December 13, 2019).
56. Adam Eldeman, "Blizzard of Ethics Complaints Filed Against Trump Administration by Public Citizen," *NBC News*, March 26, 2018, <https://www.nbcnews.com/politics/white-house/blizzard-ethics-complaints-filed-against-trump-administration-public-citizen-n859246>; Citizens for Ethics (@CREWcrew) on Twitter, April 11, 2019, <https://twitter.com/i/web/status/1116317533122985992> (both last accessed December 13, 2019).
57. Alex Seitz-Wald, "Impeach Obama! Again!" *Salon*, May 10, 2013, <https://www.salon.com/abtest1/2013/05/10/impeach_obama_again/> (last accessed December 13, 2019).
58. Robin Wright, "Chris Stevens's Family Don't Blame Hillary Clinton for Benghazi," *The New Yorker*, June 28, 2016, <https://www.newyorker.com/news/news-desk/chris-stevenss-family-dont-blame-hillary-clinton-for-benghazi> (last accessed December 13, 2019).
59. Krishnadev Calamur, "Susan Rice Says Benghazi Claims Were Based on Information From Intelligence," *NPR*, November 21, 2012, <https://choice.npr.org/index.html?origin=https://www.npr.org/sections/thetwo-way/2012/11/21/165686269/susan-rice-says-benghazi-claims-were-based-on-information-from-intelligence> (last accessed December 13, 2019).

60. Accountability Review Board report (unclassified), US Department of State, <https://2009-2017.state.gov/documents/organization/202446.pdf> (last accessed December 13, 2019).
61. Lauren Gambino and David Smith, "House Benghazi Report Faults Military, Not Clinton, For Deaths," *The Guardian*, June 28, 2016, <https://www.theguardian.com/us-news/2016/jun/28/house-benghazi-report-clinton-attack-military> (last accessed December 13, 2019).
62. Reid Epstein, "Rice Withdraws for Secretary of State," *Politico*, December 14, 2012, <https://www.politico.com/story/2012/12/susan-rice-withdraws-for-secretary-of-state-085066> (last accessed December 13, 2019).
63. Natasha Ezrow, "13 Hours: What Actually Happened at the US Consulate in Benghazi," The Conversation, February 5, 2016, <http://theconversation.com/13-hours-what-actually-happened-at-the-us-consulate-in-benghazi-53832> (last accessed December 13, 2019). In January 2016 candidate Trump rented a cinema in order to put on free screenings of a film directed by Michael Bay, *13 Hours*, which dramatized the events in Benghazi. Tom LoBianco and Noah Gray, *CNN*, January 15, 2016, <https://edition.cnn.com/2016/01/15/politics/donald-trump-13-hours-iowa/> (last accessed December 13, 2019).
64. House of Representatives, Final Report of the House Select Committee on the Events Surrounding the 2012 Terrorist Attack in Benghazi (Washington, DC: US Government Publishing Office, 2016), <https://www.govinfo.gov/content/pkg/CRPT-114hrpt848/pdf/CRPT-114hrpt848.pdf> (last accessed December 13, 2019).
65. Ben Rhodes, *The World As It Is: Inside the Obama White House* (London, Random House, 2018), 243.
66. Ibid. 282.
67. Derek Chollet, *The Long Game: How Obama Defied Washington And Redefined America's Role in the World* (Public Affairs, New York, 2016), 113.
68. "How Popular is Donald Trump?" updating calculation of Trump's approval rating, *FiveThirtyEight*, <https://projects.fivethirtyeight.com/trump-approval-ratings/> (last accessed December 13, 2019).
69. Michael Wolff, *Fire and Fury: Inside the Trump White House* (London: Little Brown, 2018), 233.
70. Peter Baker, "Trump Pardons Scooter Libby in a Case That Mirrors His Own," *The New York Times*, April 13, 2018, <https://www.

nytimes.com/2018/04/13/us/politics/trump-pardon-scooter-libby.html> (last accessed December 13, 2019).
71. James Comey, *A Higher Loyalty: Truth, Lies, and Leadership* (London: Macmillan, 2018).
72. This was not the first time that accusations had been made against an incumbent administration. The George H. W. Bush campaign faced three years of independent counsel investigation costing $2.2 million to unearth evidence of its invasion of Bill Clinton's privacy.
73. "Trump Demands That Those Investigating Him be Investigated," The *Economist*, May 24, 2018, <https://www.economist.com/united-states/2018/05/24/trump-demands-that-those-investigating-him-be-investigated> (last accessed December 13, 2019).
74. Jake Tapper, Stephen Collinson, Dan Merica, "Trump Says Special Counsel Appointment Hurts Our Country," CNN, May 19, 2017, <https://edition.cnn.com/2017/05/18/politics/donald-trump-robert-mueller-appointment/index.html> (last accessed December 13, 2019).
75. "Trump Confidant Christopher Ruddy Says Mueller Has 'Real Conflicts' As Special Counsel," transcript, *PBS Newshour*, June 12, 2017, <https://www.pbs.org/newshour/show/trump-confidant-christopher-ruddy-says-mueller-real-conflicts-special-counsel> (last accessed December 13, 2019).
76. Susan Heavey, Sarah Lynch, and Jan Wolfe, "Factbox: Guilty Pleas, Indictments Abound in Trump-Russia Probe," *Reuters*, March 22, 2019, <https://www.reuters.com/article/us-usa-trump-russia-cases-factbox/factbox-guilty-pleas-indictments-abound-in-trump-russia-probe-idUSKCN1R32T5> (last accessed December 13, 2019).
77. "Public Confidence in Mueller's Investigation Remains Steady," survey report, *People Press*, March 15, 2017, <https://www.people-press.org/2018/03/15/public-confidence-in-muellers-investigation-remains-steady/> (last accessed December 13, 2019); "How Popular is Donald Trump?"
78. Scott Clement and Emily Guskin, "Post-ABC Poll: Majority of Americans Support Mueller's Probe of Russia-Trump Campaign," *The Washington Post*, April 13, 2018, <https://www.washingtonpost.com/gdpr-consent/?destination=%2fpolitics%2fpost-abc-poll-majority-of-americans-support-muellers-probe-of-russia-trump-campaign%2f2018%2f04%2f12%2ffd5326f6-3e87-11e8-8d53-eba0ed2371cc_story.html> (last accessed December 13, 2019).

79. David Graham, "Trump's New Strategy For Responding to Robert Mueller," *The Atlantic*, May 18, 2018, <https://www.theatlantic.com/politics/archive/2018/05/trumps-new-strategy-for-responding-to-robert-mueller/560723/> (last accessed December 13, 2019).
80. "THE 2000 CAMPAIGN; 2nd Presidential Debate between Gov. Bush and Vice President Gore," *The New York Times*, October 2, 2000, <https://www.nytimes.com/2000/10/12/us/2000-campaign-2nd-presidential-debate-between-gov-bush-vice-president-gore.html> (last accessed December 13, 2019).
81. Bob Woodward, *Plan of Attack* (New York: Simon and Schuster, 2004).
82. Ivo Daalder and James Lindsay, *America Unbound: The Bush Revolution in Foreign Policy* (Washington, DC: Brookings Institution Press, 2003).
83. Ray Sanchez, "Obama: US 'Crossed a Line' and Tortured after 9/11 Attacks," *CNN Politics*, August 3, 2013, <https://edition.cnn.com/2014/08/01/politics/obama-torture-comments/> (last accessed December 13, 2019).
84. Barack Obama, "President Barack Obama's Inaugural Address," The White House, January 21, 2009, <https://obamawhitehouse.archives.gov/blog/2009/01/21/president-barack-obamas-inaugural-address> (last accessed December 13, 2019).
85. Sam Frizzell, "Republicans Knock Obama on Russia, as Crimea Vote Gets Underway," *Time*, March 16, 2014, <https://time.com/26522/russia-crimea-ukraine-republicans-obama/> (last accessed December 13, 2019).
86. Jack Goldsmith, "Obama's Breathtaking Expansion of a President's Power to Make War," *Time*, September 11, 2014, <https://time.com/3326689/obama-isis-war-powers-bush/> (last accessed December 13, 2019).
87. Kathryn Olmstead, "Terror Tuesdays," in Zelizer, *The Presidency of Barack Obama*, 212–26.
88. Steve Holland, "Tough Talk on Pakistan From Obama," *Reuters*, August 1, 2017, <https://www.reuters.com/article/us-usa-politics-obama/tough-talk-on-pakistan-from-obama-idUSN0132206420070801> (last accessed December 13, 2019).
89. Peter Bergen, David Sterman, and Melissa Salyk-Virk, "The Drone War in Pakistan," *New America*, n.d., <https://www.newamerica.org/in-depth/americas-counterterrorism-wars/pakistan/> (last accessed December 13, 2019).

90. David Rohde, "The Obama Doctrine," *Foreign Policy*, 192 (March/April 2012): 64–9, at 67.
91. Declan Walsh, "Hillary Clinton Wraps Up Tough Mission in Pakistan," *The Guardian*, October 30, 2009, <https://www.theguardian.com/world/2009/oct/30/clinton-pakistan-drone-attacks> (last accessed December 13, 2019).
92. Barack Obama, "Remarks by the President at the National Defense University," The White House, Office of the Press Secretary, May 23, 2013, <https://obamawhitehouse.archives.gov/the-press-office/2013/05/23/remarks-president-national-defense-university> (last accessed December 13, 2019).
93. Jo Becker and Scott Shane, "Secret Kills List Proves a Test of Obama's Principles and Will," *The New York Times*, May 29, 2012, A1.
94. Andreas Krieg, "Externalizing the Burden of Warfare: the Obama Doctrine and US Foreign Policy in the Middle East," *International Affairs*, 92.1 (2016): 105.
95. Joshua Keating, "The Iran Deal Sets a Dangerous Precedent for Expanded Executive Power," *Slate*, September 11, 2015, <https://slate.com/news-and-politics/2015/09/iran-deal-and-executive-power-a-dangerous-precedent.html> (last accessed December 13, 2019).
96. Jonathan Weissman and Peter Baker, "President Yields, Allowing Congress Say on Iran Deal," *The New York Times*, April 15, 2015, A1.
97. Jenna Johnson, "Donald Trump on Water-Boarding: 'Torture Works,'" *The Washington Post*, February 17, 2016, <https://www.washingtonpost.com/news/post-politics/wp/2016/02/17/donald-trump-on-waterboarding-torture-works/>; Ashley Parker, "Donald Trump Says NATO is 'Obsolete,' UN is 'Political Game,'" *The New York Times*, April 2, 2016, <https://www.nytimes.com/politics/first-draft/2016/04/02/donald-trump-tells-crowd-hed-be-fine-if-nato-broke-up/> (both last accessed December 13, 2019).
98. Jonah Goldberg, "According to Trump, the US Is No Better Than Russia," *Los Angeles Times*, February 6, 2017, <https://www.latimes.com/opinion/op-ed/la-oe-goldberg-trump-moral-equivalency-putin-20170206-story.html> (last accessed December 13, 2019).
99. Jason Gilmore, "Translating American Exceptionalism: Comparing Presidential Discourse About the United States at Home and Abroad," *International Journal of Communication*, 8 (2014), 2416–37.

100. Uri Friedman, "The Disturbing Logic of Trump's Lovefest With Kim Jong Un," *The Atlantic*, June 1, 2019, <https://www.theatlantic.com/politics/archive/2019/06/why-doe-donald-trump-keep-praising-kim-jong-un/590830/> (last accessed December 13, 2019).
101. Simon Jenkins, "At Least President Trump Would Ground the Drones," *The Guardian*, July 22, 2016, <https://www.theguardian.com/commentisfree/2016/jul/22/president-trump-obama-republican> (last accessed December 13, 2019).
102. S. E. Cupp, "Under Donald Trump, Drone Strikes Far Exceed Obama's Numbers," *Chicago Sun Times*, May 8, 2019, <https://chicago.suntimes.com/news/2019/5/8/18619206/under-donald-trump-drone-strikes-far-exceed-obama-s-numbers> (last accessed December 13, 2019).
103. Drone Strikes: Yemen, *New America*, n.d., <https://www.newamerica.org/in-depth/americas-counterterrorism-wars/us-targeted-killing-program-yemen/>; Drone Strikes: Somalia, *New America*, n.d., <https://www.newamerica.org/in-depth/americas-counterterrorism-wars/somalia/> (both last accessed December 13, 2019).
104. Daniel Rosenthal and Loren Dejonge Schumlman, "Trump's Secret War on Terror," *The Atlantic*, August 10, 2018, <https://www.theatlantic.com/international/archive/2018/08/trump-war-terror-drones/567218/> (last accessed December 13, 2019).
105. "The Secret Death Toll of America's Drones," *The New York Times*, March 31, 2019, SR12.
106. Brett Max Kaufman, "Trump is Unshackling America's Drones Thanks to Obama's Weakness," *The Guardian*, September 17, 2017, <https://www.theguardian.com/commentisfree/2018/sep/17/the-cia-is-back-in-the-drone-business-trump-is-unshackling-americas-drones-thanks-to-obamas-weakness> (last accessed December 13, 2019).
107. Alex Waddan, *Clinton's Legacy: A New Democrat in Governance* (Basingstoke: Palgrave, 2002), 135–9; "Presidential Approval Ratings—Bill Clinton," Gallup poll, n.d., <https://news.gallup.com/poll/116584/presidential-approval-ratings-bill-clinton.aspx> (last accessed December 13, 2019).
108. "Presidential Approval Ratings—Donald Trump," Gallup poll, n.d. <https://news.gallup.com/poll/203198/presidential-approval-ratings-donald-trump.aspx> (last accessed December 13, 2019).

109. Emily Tillett, "Trump Insists White House is a 'Smooth Running Machine' in Wake of Don McGahn Ouster," *CBS News*, August 30, 2018, <https://www.cbsnews.com/news/trump-defends-white-house-as-a-smooth-running-machine-amid-don-mcgahn-ouster/> (last accessed December 13, 2019).
110. See for example Bob Woodward, *Fear: Trump in the White House* (New York: Simon and Schuster, 2018). For a more scurrilous but less reliable account see Wolff, *Fire and Fury*.
111. Anonymous, "I Am Part of the Resistance Inside the Trump Administration," *The New York Times*, September 5, 2018, <https://www.nytimes.com/2018/09/05/opinion/trump-white-house-anonymous-resistance.html> (last accessed December 13, 2019).
112. Carl Hulse, "President Celebrates Leaving His Mark on the Courts," *The New York Times*, November 7, 2019, A20.
113. John Haltiwanger, "A Ukraine Gas Company Tied to Joe Biden's Son is at the Center of the Trump-Whistleblower Scandal," *Business Insider*, November 19, 2019, <https://www.businessinsider.com/ukraine-gas-company-burisma-holdings-joe-bidens-son-hunter-explained-2019-9?r=US&IR=T> (last accessed December 13, 2019).
114. "Report on the Investigation Into Russian Interference in the 2016 Presidential Election," US Department of Justice, 2019, <https://www.justice.gov/storage/report.pdf> (last accessed December 13, 2019).
115. Dareh Gregorian, "Mueller Clarifies Comments on Whether He Could Indict Trump," *NBC News*, July 24, 2019, <https://www.nbcnews.com/politics/donald-trump/did-mueller-mean-trump-could-be-indicted-when-he-leaves-n1033901> (last accessed December 13, 2019).

6
Public communication and vision

The border of a rug in Obama's Oval Office included the quote: "The arc of the moral universe is long, and it bends toward justice."[1] The 44th president was clearly fond of these words, and often wove them into his speeches. When President Trump took office on a promise to "take our country back," he had the rug replaced. Standard refurbishment practice for a new administration, yet this seemed laden with symbolism, as the nation's first African American leader and his rug left the building. In contemporary politics, style is often superficially equated with substance, and this was among numerous gestures making it clear that Donald Trump wanted to overtly break with his predecessor in as many ways as possible.

In the canon of presidential leadership literature, the capacity to communicate ranks high. From Richard Neustadt's emphasis on the importance of persuasion to Fred Greenstein prioritizing it among his six traits for greatness, scholars tend to agree that the capacity to convey one's message fluently is vital both for winning and maintaining power even if there is disagreement on how much persuading can actually be done.[2] Greenstein speaks of the "atmospherics" of presidential communication when discussing the eloquence of a leader's oratory.[3] Hence, in this chapter we compare and contrast the communication styles of presidents Obama and Trump. Our purpose is not to examine the effectiveness of their respective approaches to the use of the bully pulpit, but to reflect on the differences between how they chose to speak to the public. Thus we do not attempt to assess whether either had a more "winning" method, but look at how "no-drama Obama" was succeeded by a president seemingly addicted to causing friction through a constant helter-skelter stream-of-consciousness commentary.

In order to provide a focus to this analysis, we will concentrate on how the two presidents addressed matters of race and key parts of the so-called culture wars. How did the first African American president deal with the issues raised by his own identity and the continuing evidence that his own election did not herald a post-racial settlement in American society? And what of the language of his successor, which often bordered on the racially incendiary? Indeed, in June 2016 Republican Speaker of the House Paul Ryan from Wisconsin called out Trump, then the prospective Republican nominee, for a "textbook definition of a racist comment" after Trump had said that a judge presiding in a case involving Trump University could not be impartial because of his Mexican ancestry.[4] Further, by looking at how the two men addressed the issues of abortion and LGBT+ rights rather than economic concerns, we have identified matters where political discourse is often emotionally heightened.[5]

On the campaign trail candidates for the White House often indulge their supporters with what they want to hear and try to persuade swing voters with grandiose promises and attractive, if sometimes ultimately insubstantial, soundbites. They certainly make claims about what they will do if they win office that pay little regard to their likely institutional capacity to deliver on their promises. In this context, Obama certainly fulfilled the dictum of Mario Cuomo, the former governor of New York, by campaigning in poetry but governing in prose.[6] On the other hand, few would describe Trump's campaigning style, let alone his time in office, as poetic. Throughout 2016 his diet of outlandish claims and unkeepable promises was reinforced by a consciously bullying persona. Yet, as commentators fulminated at what they perceived to be candidate Trump's lies and his consistently ad hominem style, his supporters mocked his political opponents and the media elites for taking his words literally but not giving serious pause to his ideas. This approach, Trump's advocates insisted, was to get things exactly the wrong way around, as his appeal was to those people who took the sentiments behind his words seriously but understood that the actual language was bombastic showmanship.[7]

One common aspect of the Obama and Trump presidential campaigns was the attention given to their respective rhetoric. They may have differed dramatically in terms of content and style but in both instances they won votes by delivering what was, to their respective bases, an underlying authentic message. In addition, as they traveled around the country and engaged in social media communication with audiences, they promised an alternative to the previous administration and all its perceived shortcomings. Hence Barack Obama was offering a distinct alternative to the George W. Bush agenda, which even Republicans were tiring of after years of expensive wars and an increasingly shaky economy. Clearly, campaign trail rhetoric inevitably offers observations on the legacy of previous incumbents. George W. Bush liked to use Harry Truman as his example of how much perceptions of legacy and success can alter over time. Nonetheless, the US public was ready for change by 2008, and this was clearly demonstrated in how John McCain avoided utilizing the President as he campaigned around the country.[8]

A key aspect of candidate Obama's campaign message was that he desired to draw a line under the Bush era. This included ending certain negative aspects of the legacy, including a withdrawal of US troops from Iraq, a drawdown from Afghanistan, and future use of "wisdom" in military deployment.[9] The positive campaign moving-on-from-the-legacy-of-his-predecessor messages included promoting a "green jobs" agenda (which was his way of transcending the earlier "it's the environment or the economy" dichotomy that voters felt they faced) and, of course, the promise to finally bring about reform of the country's health care system. America was not in good stead during those waning Bush 43 days, and there was a palpable desire for political change. The "skinny kid with the funny name" was unlikely to appeal to conservatives, but his message of "hope and change" was intensely seductive to many.[10] Nevertheless, despite the vitriol of some progressives toward the presidency of his predecessor, Obama avoided direct personal assaults on the outgoing president, instead focusing on the future and possible ways to unite a fractious nation operating in an unstable world.[11] Using the dual rhetorical functions of policy and visionary speeches, Obama successfully drew in a range of supporters. Policy wonks were impressed by his capacity to engage with the detail of health care reform, whilst the youth vote was enthralled with his ability to speak authentically to them and offer an optimistic future.

Donald Trump

In the context of political communication, if there is such a thing as rhetorical legacy rollback, then candidate Trump approached this with gusto. Conventional wisdom dictates that effective political messaging can be achieved via hope or fear.[12] Barack Obama chose the former route, whilst Donald Trump excelled at the latter. For every "Yes We Can" refrain from 2008, there was a resounding chorus of "American carnage" eight years later. From this, we can deduce that firstly, candidate Trump did not orchestrate the negative score but he and his team did pen the 2016 lyrics. The former had already been laid down by the Tea Party years earlier. A brief glance at the movement's placards dating back to 2009 reveals clear messages: "Taxed Enough Already," "Cut Government Spending: Fire a Politician," "No More Taxes, No More Spending," and many more.[13] Whilst Donald Trump had no direct affiliation with the Tea Party movement, undeniable synergies were present between their respective agendas. In addition, the contradictions of Trump's own political perspectives were reflected in the mish-mash of attitudes huddling under the Tea Party umbrella. Sarah Palin may have been the keynote speaker of choice, but the movement was not always united in a small-government conservative direction when it came to the status of some big-government programs such as Social Security and Medicare.[14] These internal contradictions and differences were put aside as it was clear that the Tea Party, and soon after, Donald Trump had a common goal: to overturn and undermine the Obama agenda as forcefully as possible.

If there was a link between the Palin-era Tea Party and the Trump campaign, it came in the shape of Steve Bannon. His ideology, influence and agenda were of paramount importance not only to Trump's victory but also to Hillary Clinton's loss. Bannon had been so impressed with the phenomenon that was Sarah Palin that when she asked him to shoot some videos for her coming up to the 2010 midterm elections, he went one step further. He made a movie-length documentary, *The Undefeated* (2011), on which he apparently spent $1 million of his own money.[15] Palin's decision not to run for the 2012 Republican nomination was a crushing disappointment to her supporters, who believed that she embodied a winning formula of the populist, socially conservative, telegenic soccer mom. With the speculation finally at an end, the Tea Party energy needed a direction. Breitbart News, hailed by its co-founder in 2007 as the "*Huffington Post* of the Right," provided a locus and platform for this charged but essentially leaderless movement.[16] With Breitbart users at his disposal, Bannon involved himself in a number of significant Clinton-bashing projects. The publication of the snappily titled *Clinton Cash: The Untold Story of How and Why Foreign Governments and Businesses Helped Make Bill and Hillary Clinton Rich* was facilitated by research at the conservative Government Accountability Institute. The GAI was co-founded by Bannon, whilst funded by the Koch Brothers and Robert Mercer. Bannon Film Industries then went on to fund a movie version of the book, which was shown at the Cannes Film Festival in 2016. As a *Time* reviewer observed, *Clinton Cash* was not aimed at conservatives, who already disliked and distrusted the Clintons. It was instead intended for "Environmentalists. Anti-nuke activists. Gay-rights advocates. Good-government folks," with a purpose to highlight claims that their party's nominee had, according to the film, received cash from "the darkest, worst corners of the world."[17]

Bannon's multifaceted attack on Hillary Clinton, for him the personification of the limousine liberals, was highly successful. From overt criticism of her and her policies to covert negative propaganda, the former secretary of state received multiple body blows. Anyone who had missed the book or movie version of *Clinton Cash* could digest it in graphic novel form, or simply head to Breitbart.com, where an entire section of the website was dedicated to Clinton and her alleged misdeeds. For every progressive horrified at stories of the Clinton Foundation and suspect donations, there was a conspiracy theorist rubbing their hands at the online traction that the Pizzagate fabrication gained.[18] High-profile controversial figures including Milo Yiannopoulos utilized their fame both on and offline via speaking tours and engagement with alt-right outlets such as Infowars.com and 4chan.org. What conspiracy theories Breitbart did not create, it promoted and shared with its audience, which included Donald Trump.[19] Importantly, in this context, Trump did little to distance himself from even the more fanciful and inflammatory social media memes promoting his candidacy on the political fringes.

Throughout the presidential campaign, even before he was hired as chief executive by Team Trump in August 2016, Bannon was firing on dual anti-Hillary and pro-Trump cylinders. The populist party disruptor was as scathing about the establishment GOP as he was about liberals and those he perceived as the Washington elite. It was difficult to see what, if any, common ground he may have had with Paul Ryan, whom Bannon described as being "born in a petri dish at the Heritage Foundation."[20] The House Speaker and his ilk were as anathema to the shoot-from-the-hip populist newcomers as were Hillary Clinton and Barack Obama. From their outsider perspectives, all of these "swamp dwellers" were to blame for the abysmal state of the nation. It was not clear initially what the Breitbart executive chairman, IGE founder, and vice president of Cambridge Analytica had in common with real-estate mogul Donald Trump. *The Apprentice* star did not at first glance appear to be the prime candidate for fighting the culture wars tooth and nail, as was clearly Bannon's purpose. Over time, however, the logic of the relationship became clearer. Bannon, the disheveled and profane ideas man, could never do front of house. Trump, on the other hand, possessed an enormous feel for television and, for some at least, huge charisma. These were key traits for a political candidate operating in a hyper-visual, post-print era of communication. Bannon explained the symbiosis of their relationship via his capacity to formulate Trump's feelings and emotions into a policy agenda. Bannon was always crystal clear about his own three-tier political vision: His agenda was to promote economic nationalism, a foreign policy to reinforce that nationalist message, and the dismantling of the administrative state. The "state," in his view, included the mainstream media, academia, and non-government organizations as well as establishment bureaucrats.[21]

Hence, as his campaign progressed, Trump's message sounded increasingly populist. One favorite refrain was crystalized in his election night tweet, which promised "the forgotten man and woman will never be forgotten again. We will come together as never before."[22] This is a fairly loose statement, but it struck a chord in the way that Richard Nixon's "silent majority" focus had decades earlier. In both instances, it was an effective means of reaching out to anxious white America. After years of liberal Democrat rule, with a progressive agenda highlighting health care reform and economic inequality but seemingly unresponsive to the apprehensions of those whose jobs were disappearing, the white working class felt as though a candidate was finally speaking to and for them. As Trump warmed to his campaign after leaving sixteen GOP opponents stunned and defeated, he channeled the Bannon message with increasing aplomb throughout the general election campaign. By November 2016, even on those topics where he came later to the party than most Republicans, such as abortion, overall Republican voters increasingly embraced his style and message.[23]

Even as late as 2016, Trump did not seem to be the social conservative's clear choice. Donor Robert Mercer had poured $11 million into a PAC which supported Ted Cruz. He had not, apparently, expected the Texas senator to win against Clinton, but along with so many others he came late to the realization that the experience-free candidate would actually win the GOP primary race.[24] In order to explain how even a billionaire might be willing to put $11 million on a losing bet, Mercer's perception of Clinton needs to be understood. Dating back to the 1990s, a group of low-profile conservatives had funded the "Arkansas Project," the aim of which was to destroy the reputation of Bill and Hillary Clinton. Back then, when the First Lady went on national television to talk of "a vast right-wing conspiracy," her claims were met with derision. However, the ongoing character assault was damaging both to the President and his wife. Accusations of everything from murder to drug-running were railed against them, and one of those promoting the conspiracy theories was Robert Mercer.[25] Twenty years on, there was a new opportunity to undermine the Clinton name and exploit the decades-old feeling among many Americans that the Clintons, as bad as each other, were not to be trusted.

Hence, there were two arcs of legacy rollback efforts taking place: one quite vast and ideological, the other more targeted and personal. Bannon and his associates were extremely focused on the dismantling of the "deep state" and no one personified this quite as precisely as the Clintons. The anti-Clinton agenda stretched back decades and went some way at least to explain why Hillary tended to present as suspicious and secretive. Experience had taught her to be both. From individual funders to Arkansas media and opposition politicians to special prosecutors, the Clinton-dismantling machine was multifaceted and highly effective. The Obama rollback efforts were, in a way, more straightforward. This agenda came more directly from Donald Trump. In interviews, Bannon did not tend to speak negatively about Obama, and post-election, his primary complaint was against the Republican establishment, which he said was trying to undermine the legitimacy of Trump's win. It is fair to surmise that Bannon's vision and political desires transcended simply unpicking what the 44th president had achieved. Unlike Donald Trump, he was clearly thinking on a far grander scale.[26]

Looking at the language of the campaign trail, much of Trump's to-dismantle list was simply focused on what Obama had done. From the signature achievements of Obamacare, the Paris Agreement, and the JCPOA Plan to the hot-button issues of abortion access and transgender rights, if Obama had implemented or promoted it, Trump seemed against it. This personalized approach thrilled voters who detested Obama, not only for his policy agenda but for his vision and his very presence in the Oval Office. The remainder of this chapter will examine some key issues where presidential tone and rhetoric played a key role in polarizing debates.

Talking about race

As the first African American president it was inevitable that Barack Obama's language and messaging around issues of race, be those messages explicitly or implicitly expressed, would be carefully scrutinized. When he left office his record on this front came under criticism from differing wings of the American political spectrum. Some felt that he had only timidly and hence inadequately addressed matters of racial inequity, as he had pandered too much to accommodate white prejudice. Others felt that Obama's attention to race at particular moments during his presidency was manipulative, as his very election had demonstrated that continued concentration on matters of race was unwarranted and that the country was best served by a "color-blind" attitude.[27] If, however, Obama's record lent itself to some ambiguity with regard to his legacy on the discussion of race and the continuing place for that discussion in American society, there was little mistaking the tone of his successor when he invoked race. As a candidate and then as president, Donald Trump regularly turned to racially inflammatory language. Democrats had previously challenged Republican presidential candidates for their alleged dog whistles to white prejudice. However, in comparison to Ronald Reagan's speech at Neshoba County Fair in Mississippi in 1980 or George H.W. Bush's use of the Willie Horton case in 1988, candidate Trump put aside the whistle and used a bull horn throughout 2016, maintaining his provocations into his time in the White House.[28]

In order to gauge President Obama's dialogue with regard to racial politics it is important to acknowledge that his election victories were not an indication that the US had reached a post-racial moment. His victory in November 2008 was unquestionably of huge historic importance, but Richard Johnson has illustrated how the assumption that voting in 2008 and 2012 could not have been divided along racial lines because Obama won is misguided, and the political science evidence emphasises how racial polarization—in particular, increased levels of racial resentment amongst some categories of white voters—impacted voting in 2016.[29] This helps explain Daniel Gillion's finding that Obama made fewer direct references to race in his public speeches than any other Democratic president since the end of World War II.[30] On the other hand, this fact should not obscure how he did sometimes engage with racial controversies. For example, when Professor Henry Louis Gates, an African American scholar at Harvard University, was arrested despite being at his own home in July 2009, Obama said that the police department "acted stupidly." He then acknowledged that he regretted this remark and organized what became known as the "beer summit" at the White House between Gates and the arresting officer, Sergeant James Crowley.[31] A further compelling public intervention came in the aftermath of the jury's acquittal of George Zimmerman following Zimmerman's trial over the death of the seventeen-year-old African American Trayvon Martin. Speaking in unusually personal terms, Obama did not dispute the jury's verdict or the conduct of the trial, but reflected on how the lived experience of African Americans inevitably impacted on how many in the black community interpreted events:

> You know, when Trayvon Martin was first shot I said that this could have been my son. Another way of saying that is Trayvon Martin could have been me thirty-five years ago. And when you think about why, in the African American community at least, there's a lot of pain around what happened here, I think it's important to recognize that the African American community is looking at this issue through a set of experiences and a history that doesn't go away.
>
> There are very few African American men in this country who haven't had the experience of being followed when they were shopping in a department store. That includes me. There are very few African American men who haven't had the experience of walking across the street and hearing the locks click on the doors of cars. That happens to me—at least before I was a senator. There are very few African Americans who haven't had the experience of getting on an elevator and a woman clutching her purse nervously and holding her breath until she had a chance to get off. That happens often.[32]

These comments drew praise, but also anger from those who felt that the President was stirring racial tension, and frustration from others who wished that Obama would more regularly and forcefully express these ideas.[33] As it turned out, as Obama's second term progressed the relationship between black Americans and law enforcement came into ever-sharper relief as the Black Lives Matter movement, which emerged in reaction to the Zimmerman verdict, gained national attention with protests marking the deaths of Michael Brown in Ferguson, Missouri, and Eric Garner in New York City. Obama's attempt to straddle the divided response to the Black Lives Matter protests was illustrated in a so-called Town Hall event organized by ABC News in the summer of 2016. This event took place very shortly after five white police officers had been killed in an ambush in Dallas when policing a Black Lives Matter demonstration which had been organized to protest against further incidents of black men being killed by police officers. At the Town Hall Obama appealed for unity and urged Black Lives Matter activists and the police to have some understanding of each other's perspective.[34] Overall, this episode is indicative of the "tightrope" that Obama regularly attempted to navigate as he talked in color blind or race neutral terms while fully aware of the continuing racial disparities in American society.[35] The difficulty of expressing his message successfully was illustrated by polls showing that during the second term a declining number of the population thought that race relations between white and black Americans were "very good" or "somewhat good."[36]

In contrast to Obama's efforts, however limited in their impact, to encourage dialogue and to use rhetoric to bridge racial divisions, candidate and then President Trump regularly stirred the pot of racial animosity. On occasion Trump proclaimed that the accusations of racism against him were false. Indeed, at the end of July 2019, Trump declared himself to be "the least racist person there is anywhere in the world": Yet this claim came amidst controversy as he tried to justify a series of comments over the summer of 2019 directed against Democratic members of Congress, which had drawn widespread condemnation for their racial overtones. These included deriding the city of Baltimore as "rat-infested" as part of an attack on Elijah Cummings, a veteran congressional Democrat representing the city.[37] And even if it was possible to see these comments through a non-racial lens, the same could not be said of his attacks on four House Democrats, collectively labeled "the squad" by the media for their sometimes abrasive challenges to their own party's leadership. Trump's tweet that these four women of color should all "go back" to the "crime-infested places from which they came" played into clear racist tropes and his comments were described in these terms by much of the media.[38]

It is worth noting that during his reality television star incarnation, Trump gave little or no indication of how forcefully the Obama legacy rollback on race would play out. When *The Apprentice* aired in the 2000s, Trump consistently rated highly among ethnic minority viewers and some of the show's winners included African Americans.[39] Trump's 1970s rental policies notwithstanding,[40] many observers were slow to categorize the Republican candidate as "racist" based on the dynamics of the show. PBS filmmaker Michael Kirk spent months interviewing Trump associates for his 2016 election documentary *The Choice*. Kirk deduced that Trump was not a racist but judged others on the basis of their economic success.[41] This seemed a plausible conclusion during *The Apprentice* years, but became less so once Trump associated himself with the anti-Obama "birther" conspiracy theory.

Harris polls conducted in 2010 showed that 25 percent of Americans believed that Barack Obama was not born in the US.[42] The internet had given birth to this conspiracy theory, and the rumor swirled around a small group of right-wingers mostly via email until it gained further traction via the Trump megaphone. In 2016, the *New York Times* stated that "facts hold a sacred place in western liberal democracies."[43] This claim has not aged well. So, when a high-profile popular culture icon promoted an item of fake news, the public were inclined to believe it—or, at least, those who were eager to embrace information that delegitimized a president that they saw as an interloper. For the next five years, Donald Trump utilized his platform to full effect, reiterating his alleged uncertainty in interviews with regard to the origins of the 44th president. "I'm starting to think he was not born here," he stated in 2011. Such sentiments were music to the ears of anti-Obama conservatives and in many ways were Trump's earliest efforts at de-Obamafication. What better way to undo the legacy of a president than to question his core legitimacy? This was an existential attack, one far more satisfying than simply criticizing a policy choice or administration priority.

If birtherism can be understood as the vulgarism of an outside provocateur, Trump's capacity to step outside the boundaries of normal, and by any conventional definition acceptable, behavior came in his reaction to the demonstrations and counter-protests that scarred Charlottesville, Virginia, in the summer of 2017. As neo-Nazis and white supremacists rallied in the city, ostensibly to protest at the impending removal of a statue of Robert E. Lee, explicitly racist and anti-Semitic chants were loudly proclaimed. Fighting broke out with counter-protesters and one woman in the counter-protests, but not involved in any skirmishes, was killed when a far right supporter deliberately drove his car into her. In the aftermath of this incident, Trump initially seemed to express some sympathy with the right-wing agitators, before then making the expected noise condemning Nazis. Yet he almost immediately gave an extraordinary press conference in Trump Tower in New York, where he referred to there being "very fine people on both sides."[44] This statement went beyond reversing the discourse of the Obama years. Presidents Reagan and George H. W. Bush had been accused of surreptitiously exploiting white prejudice for political gain, and George W. Bush was perceived by some to have been inadequately attuned to the disproportionate suffering of the African American community caused by Hurricane Katrina; yet all three of these presidents were very direct in their criticism of overt forms of racism and anti-Semitism. In this context, Trump rewound the presidential rhetorical clock to a time that most Americans thought had passed.

The travel ban

It is a matter of public record that George W. Bush left blank the tick box for "president" on the 2016 electoral ballot, a fact that may represent the distance traveled by his political party in the years since his 2009 departure. During his first year in office, Bush made history as the first president to deliver an entire weekly address from the Oval Office in Spanish. Although not fluent, he was lauded for his effort and for what was considered an authentic outreach to the American Latino community.[45] In this speech and many others, Bush spoke of strengthening relations with Mexico and applauded the Latino influence on American culture. As the 2000 census demonstrated, the Latino population had surpassed that of African Americans and therefore it was prudent for any Republican president to make an effort to capture some of this increasing voter demographic. Plenty of what the GOP mandate offered was in line with mainstream Latino values.[46] Eight years after President Bush stepped down, the immigration debate in the Tea Party-infused GOP had shifted, and the rhetoric of the 2016 election candidates reflected this. The contender with the most bullish slogans won the day, albeit with no support from his Republican predecessor. Trump's "Build the Wall" mantra struck a chord with many, along with his call for "a total and complete shutdown of Muslims entering the United States until our country's representatives can figure out what the hell is going on."[47]

In a February 2017 interview with *Today*'s Matt Lauer, when asked about President Trump's travel ban, George W. Bush stated: "I'm in favor of immigration policy that is welcoming and upholds the law."[48] It is a rule of thumb among former presidents not to publicly offer too many opinions on the policies of their successors, and Bush did not offer an overt criticism of the new administration. Nonetheless, the language Bush used had the effect of clearly distancing him from his Republican replacement. Bush also talked about the importance of people of all faiths being able to worship freely.[49] His Hawaiian-born successor pushed the rhetorical boundaries on immigration further than any president before him, coming as he did from Kenyan roots and a childhood spent abroad. Had she succeeded him, Hillary Clinton would likely have stayed in Obama's immigration policy lane, advocating comprehensive reform, with a focus on keeping families already in the US together. On the 2016 campaign trail, border security and terrorism featured high on the list of voter anxieties and the politics of fear won the day. The influence of Steve Bannon's clash of civilizations-based worldview was clear to see in Donald Trump's tone and rhetoric and, on entering the White House, in his actions.

On January 27th 2017 President Trump signed Executive Order 13769, which prevented Syrian refugees from entering indefinitely, and immigrants from seven majority Muslim countries for up to 120 days. The order was clearly a manifestation of the "extreme vetting" pledge from his "Contract with the American Voter."[50] Here, Elaine Kamarck's view of the President as the CEO of an industry he had never worked in rang true.[51] There was little or no evidence of advance consultation or planning, and the initial outcome and response was consternation. From a legal, bureaucratic, and logistical perspective this was an inevitable snafu, swiftly accompanied by political and diplomatic fallout. As one of the incumbent's earliest agenda items, the rollout of the plan suggested an administration that lacked a basic understanding of process. Viewed through the prism of Greenstein's organizational capacity criteria, this was a fail. The backlash transcended the liberal media and included international condemnation, even from those clearly eager to foster close ties with the new president. One such was British prime minister Theresa May, who was on a state visit to the US when the ban was implemented. Her response, stating "we do not agree with this kind of approach," was considered the bare minimum rebuke by many.[52]

Unsurprisingly, lawsuits began immediately, as those with visas and green cards were among the affected passengers. Within twenty-four hours, the Ninth Circuit Court of Appeals had partially and temporarily halted the travel ban. Already brimming with anti-Trump sentiment, the liberal media piled scorn on the President's action. Social media responses went into overdrive as protesters arrived at airports around the US to decry the ban and show support for those affected. The chaotic manner in which the travel ban was imposed and the anger with which Trump responded to the federal court rulings suggest that he was not fully aware of process and procedure. In these early days, which should have been the height of his presidential honeymoon, his administration was mired in difficulty and under widespread attack. His supporters did not waver in their positive opinion of him, despite the fact that he was unable to fulfill his "total and complete shutdown" pledge. Significantly, from the President's perspective, the nation was split in its response to the ban, and support for it was slightly higher than for the man himself, which remained fairly constant (around 44 percent) during this period.[53] National telephone polls saw averages of 51 percent in favor and 55 percent opposed to the policy. Polls tended to use slightly different language and not all referred to it as a ban. Overall, Trump's job approval rating tended to be pegged to the ban, therefore those who supported the ban supported the President, and vice versa.[54] Eventually, showing some capacity for learning, the administration managed to produce a third iteration of the ban that satisfied the Supreme Court, though the 5–4 decision was accompanied by a vigorous dissent written by one of Obama's nominees, Justice Sotomayor.[55]

The substance of Barack Obama's immigration legacy has been examined elsewhere in this book. Only a cursory glance is required to see the difference in content and intent between the leader who spent his childhood years in Indonesia and the insular, nationalistic rhetoric of his successor. Within a brief period, President Trump succeeded not only in undermining what the nation's first non-white president had achieved in immigration terms, but also what the predecessor from his own political party had established. Many Bush-era Republicans were pragmatic about the benefits of migrant labor. By the Trump years, it was those party members who believed, rightly or wrongly, that their economic status was being undermined by unfettered immigration whose voice was in the ascendant. Crines and Dolowitz discuss how Trump's *pathos*-driven rhetoric on the topic "expanded the range of what was allowable in public discourse, thereby pushing the boundary beyond what would have been previously considered civil."[56] Such presidential norm-busting, twinned with the no-holds-barred platform that social media provided, set the benchmark for the nation's political dialogue.

Reproductive rights

On the 2016 campaign trail, the Republican nominee took a highly personalized approach. In a similar way to Obama supporters in 2008, it was clear that many voters were enamored with Trump's character. In both cases, despite their radically different views on what America should be, Obama and Trump ran decidedly personal campaigns, and their direct communication with voters was a key element of their success. Alongside the medium of Twitter, it was at Trump campaign rallies where the Obama legacy rollback plans took center stage. From promises to Make America Great Again to anti-Clinton chants of "lock her up," the former reality television star had a masterful capacity to woo and direct his audiences. It was, however, on those hot-button "moral values" issues that many voters set their hopes on Trump to turn back, as they viewed it, the unbridled liberal progress of the previous eight years. It came as no great surprise to observers that candidate Trump warmed to a range of socially conservative themes as his 2016 election campaign progressed. Historically, no one could have mistaken citizen Trump for a feminist, but he had publicly stated his position on abortion as far back as his proposed presidential run in 1999 as "very pro-choice."[57] Earlier in his 2016 campaign, his rhetoric on the issue was muted, inconsistent, and at times completely removed from the Republican party line. When pressed in a MSNBC interview with Chris Matthews, he stated rather unconvincingly that he thought "there should be some sort of punishment" for women who sought abortions.[58] This flew in the face of the GOP platform position, which promoted abstinence, tax incentives for fostering and adoption, along with compassion for individuals seeking terminations, with punitive action reserved for abortion providers. The candidate swiftly distanced himself from those comments and took a more politically astute stance that was in line with the mainstream pro-life movement. Aligning himself with the nation's favorite Republican, he claimed "Like Reagan, I am pro-life, with exceptions."[59] This offered vital comfort to social conservatives who, despite their eagerness to redress the impact of the previous eight liberal years, were nervous about throwing their support behind someone with a personal history like Trump's. Hence, offering reassuring public communication on their key issues was crucial.

Holding out hope for various future conservative Supreme Court appointments required voters to display a steady nerve and strategic mindset. They also needed a more immediate demonstration of commitment from a candidate who was not their first choice. Clearly, this was a political marriage of convenience between the twice-divorced reality television star and his conservative base. During the honeymoon period, the President was quick to display his powers of political seduction. On January 23, 2017, a presidential memorandum reinstating the Reagan-era "Global Gag" rule was signed. This restored the conditions relating to US funding of international NGOs who offered abortion services or counseling. The 45th president was continuing a trend dating back decades, in which the Global Gag was revoked, or re-invoked, depending on who was in power. Whilst this international development issue did not impact American women directly, it sent a clear message with regard to the new administration's priorities. First and foremost, it rolled back a specific action of the previous president. Furthermore, the "America First" aspect of saving $500 million of tax dollars dovetailed nicely with the "moral values" message attached to withdrawing US support for NGOs who provided abortions and associated advice. Described by Amnesty International as "a devastating blow for women's rights," the executive action went further than those of Republican predecessors and referred to all global health aid.[60] This, along with his pledge to end federal funding for Planned Parenthood and choice of conservative stalwart Mike Pence for vice president, provided comfort and reassurance to religious voters unsure of the President's own commitment to their "moral values" concerns. A key, if distant, prize for this voting demographic was the overturning of the Supreme Court's ruling in *Roe v. Wade*.

This inability to allow an almost half-century-old ruling to settle demonstrates how, even by the early twenty-first century, America had "not made peace with the sexual revolution of the 1960s and 1970s."[61] No other "moral values" issue lit up both sides of the political spectrum in quite the same way as women's reproductive rights. After a period of issue stability, individual states increasingly took measures to restrict abortion rights. Research published by the Guttmacher Institute in 2019 demonstrated that eighteen states had laws that could be used to restrict abortion. In contrast, ten states had laws that protected such rights.[62] During the 2016 election campaign, 61 percent of voters who identified as "pro-life" told Gallup that they were unsure of candidate Trump's position on abortion. In 2019, twenty years on from his apparently unequivocal 1999 "I believe in choice" declaration, President Trump's public communication on this most emotive issue left voters in no doubt. Addressing a rally at Green Bay, Wisconsin in 2019, with an eye on his 2020 run, he talked of doctors and mothers who planned to "execute the baby."[63] Such language would inevitably play well with those who turned out in such impressive numbers for him in 2016, not least 81 percent of white evangelical Protestants, but overall the 65 percent of white Christians who supported him.[64] Presidential reference to "children being ripped from their mother's womb" in relation to late-term abortion legislation in New York and Virginia took place alongside moves in conservative states toward what were effectively near-total bans on abortion clinics operating.[65]

Presidential rhetoric on reproductive rights came a long way in the short time since the pro-choice position of the previous administration. Obama had faced challenges before and during his time in office with regard to his stance on abortion. In *The Audacity of Hope*, he outlined his fears that a ban on abortion would oblige women to seek illegal options.[66] On the 2008 campaign trail he highlighted the importance of contraception education for teenagers, as well as abstinence advice.[67] Here he sought to balance his position as a practicing Christian with being someone whose re-election victory Planned Parenthood would later refer to as "a resounding victory for women."[68] It was clear that Obama faced a greater challenge than his successor when dealing with the thorny issue of abortion. Firstly, Donald Trump was not held to the same standard as his political counterparts, as the "Pussygate" tape so clearly indicated. For any other presidential contender, such an undeniable embarrassment would have ended their campaign instantly. This was not the case for the businessman who had had outlined his adversarial strategy in *The Art of the Deal*. When attacked or exposed, his preferred response was to come out fighting. As he warmed to his anti-abortion base, if not to the cause itself, Trump increasingly owned the issue. Unlike his predecessor, he did not shy away from publicity on the day of his Global Gag executive action. In 2009, Barack Obama scheduled his executive order on January 23rd—one day after the *Roe v. Wade* anniversary. He took care to ensure that this occurred on a Friday evening, away from the media spotlight.[69] In contrast, Donald Trump reinstated the funding ban in front of a wall of cameras, surrounded by men. The image was shared hundreds of thousands of times online, frequently accompanied by the refrain: "Where are the women?"[70]

Rhetoric and LGBT + rights

On the campaign trail and later in the Oval Office, Donald Trump spoke more authentically about some issues than others. Regarding trade and immigration, for example, his positions were more consistently based on long-held views. On other issues, including those termed as "moral values" issues, in the early days at least, his tone was more muted, his rhetoric less certain. Over time, his position on key voter issues solidified as he warmed to conservative themes. He went from speaking for his evangelical base to sounding like one of their own. This occurred despite the dearth of evidence to suggest that he had strong (or any) views on hot-button issues such as transgender rights or reproductive health.

At the time Barack Obama came to office, national attention had been increasingly focused on gay and, more widely, LGBT+ rights. As discussed elsewhere in this book, Obama's legacy on LGBT+ issues has been described as monumental.[71] There were, without doubt, some hugely significant leaps forward for gay and transgender Americans on his watch. Clearly, this was not well received by everyone, although societal acceptance has evolved markedly in terms of tolerating, even embracing, such progress as gay Americans in the military and same-sex marriage. Efforts to track Donald Trump's position on gay rights show that, unlike those of his vice president, his views have not always been clear. It is fair to say that in comparison to some other recent aspirants to the GOP's presidential nomination such as Mike Huckabee, Ted Cruz, and Rick Santorum, Trump presented as at the very least undecided about his position on gay marriage and related issues. Consequently, he may have presented as a reasonable option for any gay conservatives pondering who to support.[72] Not everyone saw him this way, however: For example, in January 2017, *Salon* magazine published a piece which outlined why the Trump presidency would be "a paradise for the Christian Right."[73] It was unlikely that both of these conclusions could be accurate. Perhaps simple voting mathematics could explain the New Yorker's trajectory from being perceived as the gay-friendly candidate to a poster boy for the religious right. With 81 percent of the white evangelical vote behind him, it was clear that Trump was going to prioritize their agenda over the 14 percent of gay Americans who turned out for him on election day.[74] An early taste of red meat for the base was the choice of Mike Pence as vice-presidential nominee. The former governor of Indiana's track record on "culture wars" issues was enough to warm the heart of any religious conservative.

Gay marriage

In 2015, the Supreme Court ruled via *Obergefell v. Hodges* that the fundamental right to marry was guaranteed to all citizens under the 14th Amendment. The issue made its way up through the judiciary until a Supreme Court majority agreed to bring federal law into line with those states which had already progressed on the issue. Therefore, Barack Obama could not take personal credit for this development. Nonetheless, same-sex marriage activists on the whole considered Obama a champion of their cause and there is no doubt that through the tone and rhetoric emanating from the White House, he proactively created an environment sympathetic to progress on the matter. This view was reinforced when both of his Supreme Court appointments, Sonia Sotomayor and Elena Kagan, voted in favor of same-sex marriage in the *Obergefell* case. Here was a substantial and solid progressive aspect of the Obama legacy, which would be hard (although not impossible) for a successor to undo, should he wish to.

Any undoing would depend on the opportunities that would arise for Donald Trump to put a Supreme Court justice on the bench. On the subject of gay marriage, Trump had not been consistent in the past, which is just one reason why evangelicals were nervous about his nomination. Unlike Ted Cruz and other GOP candidates, Trump had used mild language on the topic and publicly stated that if elected, he would not plan on revisiting a decision that had been put to rest by the court. As a New Yorker who had previously identified with Democrats on various "moral values" issues, Trump did not always authentically talk the socially conservative talk on the campaign trail. Nonetheless, his position on the issue was, in his words, "evolving," and appeared to do so in a conservative direction as the 2016 election drew nearer.[75]

Military service

LGBT+ developments on Obama's watch included the repeal of "Don't Ask, Don't Tell" via bipartisan legislation in December 2010 as well as ensuring that federal contractors have guarantees against discrimination on the basis of their sexual orientation or gender identity.[76] This settled a long-standing and unsatisfactory arrangement dating back to the days of Bill Clinton and his trouble with social conservatives decades earlier. Back then, Clinton had dodged the policy bullet and created a compromise relating to gay Americans serving in the military that essentially pleased no one. The 2010 repeal was met with only muted objection, and a study commissioned by the Department of Defense and undertaken by the RAND Corporation found that gay Americans serving in the military "brought no meaningful harm" to the armed forces.[77]

Trump's own version of "Don't Ask, Don't Tell" is the issue of transgender Americans serving in the military. Like the contentious matter of transgender bathroom access, this may have only impacted a small proportion of the population, but the symbolism was enormous. Such matters acted as a lightning rod for those on both sides of the political fence to state their case and abuse their perceived opponents, not least via the global platform of Twitter. Back in 2010, despite being pressured by LGBT+ rights activists, Obama did not mention transgender Americans in relation to "Don't Ask, Don't Tell."[78] At that point, the decades-old language on this topic in the Department of Defense guidelines referred to transgender people as "sexual deviants." In 2015, then Secretary of Defense Chuck Hagel stated that the military should "continually review" its prohibition of transgender people in the armed forces. In 2016 Hagel's successor, Ashton Carter, announced that transgender Americans would be allowed to serve in the military and acknowledged that many already were, albeit not openly. The RAND Corporation estimated that there were approximately 2,450 trans Americans serving in an army consisting of 1.2 million active personnel and 800,000 reservists. Around sixty-five of those would seek to transition each year. The cost was estimated to be in the region of $3–4 million per year. The study concluded that the situation "would cost little and have no significant impact on unit readiness."[79]

Ashton Carter made a formal announcement on June 30th, 2016 stating that with immediate effect, transgender Americans may serve openly in the military. Now, this was only months before the presidential election and clearly an impending change of administration invariably brings the prospect of uncertainty. That uncertainty was enhanced when, in July 2017, again in a series of tweets, Trump announced that there would be a full reversal of the Obama-era progress on allowing transgender Americans to serve in the military in any capacity. The Pentagon was caught unawares, especially as this had not been something that Trump had publicly given attention to previously or discussed with his generals. In August 2017, the White House then sent a two-and-a-half-page executive memo to the Pentagon outlining three key requirements: Firstly, how to remove existing service-people where appropriate, secondly, instructions to reject any new transgender army applicants, and thirdly, to stop medical treatment spending on existing trans service members.

The RAND Corporation estimated that the financial cost to the military for transgender medical treatment would be 1/1000th of 1 percent of the nation's defense budget. Hence, this was less about saving money or reducing the readiness of the armed forces than about the culture wars and de-Obamafication, and here, Trump aimed to score a win with his base. Plus, he proved that it was actually possible to direct policy via social media. In response, Secretary of Defense Mattis requested a six-month study to consider the impact of trans Americans in the military. The same month, fifty-six retired generals and admirals wrote an open letter opposing the proposed ban. In autumn 2017, a series of lawsuits were issued (*Jane Doe v. Trump* and *Stone v. Trump* among others) and this resulted in ten federal judges blocking the attempted ban. Trump's policies went against the military's own recommendations regarding transgender service members. Moreover, he squandered political capital on an issue that had already been dealt with.

This unprecedented situation involved presidential efforts to overturn a predecessor's specific policy item initially via the emotive and non-binding medium of Twitter, which instigated a heated national conversation on the matter, and then moving to the more formal method of a presidential memorandum, followed by strong public responses, court cases, confusion, and stress for those impacted by the change in administration position. In January 2019, the Supreme Court ruled 5–4 in favor of allowing the Trump administration to limit transgender Americans from serving in the military.

Conclusion

It is unsurprising that presidential rhetoric and style differs from one president to the next. Even a new president who succeeds a like-minded president of the same party will likely have their own distinct approach to how they use the bully pulpit. Nobody, for example, tagged George H. W. Bush as the Great Communicator II. The advent of the age of social media has offered ever more ways for presidents to communicate to the public and hence to display their alternative means of charming voters. Yet even in this context the shift from Obama to Trump was a jarring one. It was not just that their messages on the matters discussed in this chapter of race and LGBT rights were so different, but across the whole scope of political and policy debates the tone in which they delivered those messages was far apart. The matter at hand is not that one was more effective than the other, or even more authentic. What is clear, however, is that, in the round if not on every occasion, Obama paid heed to the traditional boundaries of presidential behavior. On the other hand, while Trump could deliver speeches as might be expected in the wake of tragedy, he regularly flouted the norms of what it meant to be presidential.[80] The outlandish nature of much of his rhetoric is in fact well illustrated by the blowback he received when he did give what might be called the "expected" speech. For example, Trump was mostly praised for hitting the right note, at least in the immediate moment, in the aftermath of the Las Vegas mass shooting in October 2017. Yet his speech on this matter prompted a furious response from the "never Trumper" David Frum, a former speechwriter for George W. Bush. Frum attacked those commentators who simply took Trump's words at face value, adding:

> For once, Trump read the speech exactly as written. Perhaps his aides talked him into it. Because Trump is not a good reader, he read the speech wrong. And because it sounded wrong, he looked bad.[81]

Part of Frum's particular complaint was Trump's turn to piety in his speech, but a broader version of the argument is that this was an instance where President Trump was trying to act as the nation's healer, as is expected of a president at a time of natural disaster or an act of terror, yet this meant adopting a language and tone that was alien to him. And Trump was certainly more comfortable free-wheeling at rallies and unleashing provocations that inevitably stirred both his supporters and opponents.

One example of Trump's use of a rally to exploit cultural division came in September 2017. Trump was in Alabama, ostensibly in support of then sitting Senator Luther Strange as he sought to win the GOP's nomination for the forthcoming special Senate election in the state. The next day, however, the headlines were not about Strange but about Trump's attack on NFL players kneeling during the national anthem. That act of protest had been started by San Francisco quarterback Colin Kaepernick and his example had been followed by a handful of other players across the league. Their focus was on racial disparities and especially allegations of police brutality against African Americans. Hence President Trump's rhetoric, when he pronounced: "Wouldn't you love to see one of these NFL owners, when somebody disrespects our flag, to say, 'Get that son of a bitch off the field right now, out, he's fired,'" was widely interpreted through a racial lens.[82] Furthermore, rather than taking a step back from the political firestorm that followed, Trump embraced the melee and doubled down on his stance the following summer. That came even after the normal presidential invite to the White House for the team winning the Super Bowl was canceled for the 2018 winners, the Philadelphia Eagles, after several players said they would not attend in protest at Trump's language.[83]

Overall, both the style and substance of Trump's dialogue with the American public were extraordinary. His capacity and willingness to break the rules of acceptable discourse went well beyond reversing the norms and manner adopted and largely practiced by President Obama. As Trump neared the end of his third year in office, it remained unclear whether his embrace of provocation and open crudity to deride his opponents would be a political and presidential one-off or whether future presidents might see this as an attractive model, setting them free from the constraints of even pretending to represent and heal an entire nation.

Notes

1. Sam Dangremond, "The Oval Office Through the Years, in Photos," *Town and Country*, August 24, 2017, <https://www.townandcountrymag.com/society/politics/g12090469/oval-office-pictures-through-the-years/?slide=15>. Quote is from Martin Luther King, Jr., National Cathedral speech, March 31, 1968, <https://www.si.edu/spotlight/mlk?page=4&iframe=true> (last accessed December 13, 2019).
2. See for example Fred Greenstein, *The Presidential Difference: Leadership Style From FDR to Barack Obama* (Princeton, NJ: Princeton University Press, 2009); Richard E. Neustadt, *Presidential Power and the Modern Presidents: The Politics of Leadership From Roosevelt to Reagan* (New York: Free Press, 1991). On the limits of the power to persuade see George Edwards, *Overreach: Leadership in the Obama Presidency* (Princeton, NJ: Princeton University Press, 2012).
3. Greenstein, *The Presidential Difference*, 155.
4. Deirdre Walsh and Manu Raju, "Paul Ryan Rips Donald Trump Remarks as 'Textbook Definition of a Racist Comment,'" *CNN*, June 7, 2016, <https://edition.cnn.com/2016/06/07/politics/paul-ryan-donald-trump-racist-comment/index.html> (last accessed December 13, 2019).
5. For an examination of presidential rhetoric and economic matters, see B. Dan Wood, *The Politics of Economic Leadership: The Causes and Consequences of Presidential Rhetoric* (Princeton, NJ: Princeton University Press, 2007).
6. Paul Waldman, "Campaign in Poetry, Govern in Prose," *The American Prospect*, November 8, 2010, <https://prospect.org/article/campaign-poetry-govern-prose/> (last accessed December 13, 2019). For an examination of how some of Obama's early speeches after winning the presidency missed their intended mark, see Kathleen Hall Jamieson, "How Well Has President Barack Obama Chosen from Among the Available Means of Persuasion?" *Polity*, 45.1 (2013): 153–68.
7. Salena Zito, "Taking Trump Seriously, Not Literally," *The Atlantic*, September 23, 2016, <https://www.theatlantic.com/politics/archive/2016/09/trump-makes-his-case-in-pittsburgh/501335/> (last accessed December 13, 2019).

8. George W. Bush, *Decision Points* (New York: Virgin, 2010), 72–3.
9. Barack Obama, Address to Chicago Council on Global Affairs, April 23, 2007, <https://www.youtube.com/watch?v=a2r9rsewVRg> (last accessed December 13, 2019).
10. Barack Obama keynote address, DNC, 27 July 2004, <https://www.pbs.org/newshour/show/barack-obamas-keynote-address-at-the-2004-democratic-national-convention> (last accessed December 14, 2019).
11. See for example Barack Obama Victory Speech, *C-Span*, November 4, 2008, <https://www.c-span.org/video/?282164-2/barack-obama-victory-speech> (last accessed December 14, 2019).
12. Christopher Weber, "Emotions, Campaigns and Political Participation," *Political Research Quarterly*, 66.2 (2013), 414–28.
13. Shannon Travers, "What Would the Tea Party Cut?" *CNN*, April 13, 2011, <http://edition.cnn.com/2011/POLITICS/04/13/tea.party.cuts/index.html> (last accessed December 14, 2019).
14. Theda Skocpol and Vanessa Williamson, *The Tea Party and the Remaking of Republican Conservatism* (New York: Oxford University Press, 2012), 60–4.
15. *The Undefeated*, dir. Stephen K. Bannon (USA: Arc Entertainment, 2011); Joshua Green, *Devil's Bargain: Steve Bannon, Donald Trump and the Storming of the Presidency* (London: Scribe, 2018), 88.
16. James Rainey, "Breitbart.com Sets Sights on Ruling the Conservative Conversation," *Los Angeles Times*, August 1, 2015, <https://www.latimes.com/entertainment/la-xpm-2012-aug-01-la-et-breitbart-20120801-story.html> (last accessed December 14, 2019).
17. Philip Elliott, "Clinton Cash: A Scathing Broadside Aimed at Persuading Liberals," *Time*, May 12, 2016, <http://time.com/4328254/clinton-cash-movie-hillary-clinton-peter-schweizer-breitbart/> (last accessed December 14, 2019).
18. Joshua Gillin, "How Pizzagate Went From Fake News to a Real Problem for a DC Business," *Politifact*, December 5, 2016, <https://www.politifact.com/truth-o-meter/article/2016/dec/05/how-pizzagate-went-fake-news-real-problem-dc-busin/> (last accessed December 14, 2019).
19. Jon Swaine, "Offshore Cash Helped Fund Steve Bannon's Attacks on Hillary Clinton," *The Guardian*, November 7, 2017, <https://www.theguardian.com/news/2017/nov/07/steve-bannon-bermuda-robert-mercer>; see also <www.infowars.com>, <www.breitbart.com> (all last accessed December 14, 2019).

20. Green, *Devil's Bargain*, 188.
21. "Steve Bannon and Reince Priebus at 2017 Conservative Political Action Conference," *C-Span*, February 23, 2017, <https://www.c-span.org/video/?424394-102/reince-priebus-steve-bannon-make-joint-appearance-cpac> (last accessed December 14, 2019).
22. Donald Trump (@realDonaldTrump) on Twitter, November 6, 2012, <https://twitter.com/realdonaldtrump/status/796315640307060738?lang=en> (last accessed December 14, 2019).
23. Hannah Fingerhut, "How Republicans See the GOP on the Eve of the 2016 Election," *Pew Research Center*, November 2, 2016, <http://www.pewresearch.org/fact-tank/2016/11/02/how-republicans-see-the-gop-on-the-eve-of-the-2016-election/#> (last accessed December 14, 2019).
24. Green, *Devil's Bargain*, 132-133
25. Ibid. 132.
26. Charlie Rose interviews with Steve Bannon, 11, 12, September 13, 2017, <https://charlierose.com/episodes> (last accessed December 14, 2019).
27. For wide-ranging discussions of Obama's presidency and the place of race in his rhetoric, see Daniel Gillion, *Governing with Words: The Political Dialogue on Race, Public Policy, and Inequality in America* (New York: Cambridge University Press, 2016) and Melanye T. Price, *The Race Whisperer: Barack Obama and the Political Uses of Race* (New York: New York University Press, 2016).
28. On Reagan and race see Ian Haney-Lopez, "The Racism at the Heart of the Reagan Presidency," *Salon*, January 12, 2014, <https://www.salon.com/2014/01/11/the_racism_at_the_heart_of_the_reagan_presidency/> (last accessed December 15, 2019); on the Bush campaign and Willie Horton see Thomas Edsall with Mary Edsall, *Chain Reaction: The Impact of Race, Rights and Taxes on American Politics* (New York: W.W. Norton and Company, 1992), 222–4.
29. Richard Johnson, "Racially Polarised Partisanship and the Obama Presidency," in Eddie Ashbee and John Dumbrell, *The Obama Presidency and the Politics of Change* (London: Palgrave Macmillan, 2015), 161–80; John Sides, Lynn Vavreck, and Michael Tesler, *Identity: The 2016 Presidential Campaign and the Battle for the Meaning of America* (Princeton, NJ: Princeton University Press, 2019).
30. Gillion, *Governing with Words*.
31. Helene Cooper and Abby Goodnough, "In a Reunion over Beer, No Apologies, But a Cordial Plan to Have Lunch Sometime," *The New York Times*, July 30, 2009, A10.

32. Barack Obama, "Remarks by the President on Trayvon Martin," The White House, Office of the Press Secretary, July 19, 2013, <https://obamawhitehouse.archives.gov/the-press-office/2013/07/19/remarks-president-trayvon-martin> (last accessed December 14, 2019).
33. Scott Horsley, "Obama Breaks His Silence on Trayvon Martin Verdict," *NPR*, July 20, 2013, <https://choice.npr.org/index.html?origin=https://www.npr.org/2013/07/20/203816155/obama-breaks-his-silence-on-trayvon-martin-verdict> (last accessed December 14, 2019).
34. Maya Rhodan, "President Obama Defends Stance on Police, Black Lives Matter," *Time*, July 15, 2016, <https://time.com/4407362/president-obama-police-black-lives-matter-town-hall/last accessed December 14, 2019).
35. Roger Smith, Desmond King, and Philip Klinkner, "Challenging History: Barack Obama and American Racial Politics," *Daedalus*, 149.2 (2011): 121–35.
36. "In Depth: Race Relations," ongoing Gallup poll, n.d., <https://news.gallup.com/poll/1687/race-relations.aspx> (last accessed December 14, 2019).
37. Marianne Dodson, "Donald Trump Claims He is Least Racist Person in the World," *Daily Beast*, July 30, 2019, <https://www.thedailybeast.com/trump-claims-he-is-least-racist-person-in-the-world-after-repeated-racist-attacks> (last accessed December 14, 2019).
38. Abigail Tracy, "'They're as Different as People Come': The Complex Truth about the 'Squad,' Trump's Favorite Foil," *Vanity Fair*, August 16, 2019, <https://www.vanityfair.com/news/2019/08/the-squad-donald-trump> (last accessed December 15, 2019).
39. Joshua Green, "The Remaking of Donald Trump," *Vanity Fair*, July 6, 2017, <https://www.bloomberg.com/news/features/2017-07-06/the-remaking-of-donald-trump> (last accessed December 15, 2019).
40. Trump Management Company, Materials 1972–74, *FBI Records: The Vault*, <https://vault.fbi.gov/trump-management-company> (last accessed December 15, 2019).
41. Michael Kirk, "Behind the Headlines," event at the British Library, London, October 5, 2016.
42. CNN Opinion Research Poll on President Obama's Birthplace, *CNN*, August 4, 2010, <http://i2.cdn.turner.com/cnn/2010/images/08/04/rel10k1a.pdf> (last accessed December 15, 2019).

43. William Davies, "The Age of Post-Truth Politics," *The New York Times*, August 24, 2016, "https://www.nytimes.com/2016/08/24/opinion/campaign-stops/the-age-of-post-truth-politics.html> (last accessed December 15, 2019).
44. Glenn Thrush and Maggie Haberman, "Trump Gives White Supremacists an Unequivocal Boost," *The New York Times*, August 16, 2017, A1.
45. Paul Brinkley-Rogers, "Bush Gets Bravos for Speech in Spanish," *Latin American Studies*, May 6, 2001, <http://www.latinamericanstudies.org/immigration/bravos.htm> (last accessed December 15, 2019).
46. Robert Leiken, "Border Colleagues: on Migration, Bush and Fox Belong on the Same Side," *Brookings*, September 2, 2001, <https://www.brookings.edu/opinions/border-colleagues-on-migration-bush-and-fox-belong-on-the-same-side/> (last accessed December 15, 2019).
47. Jenna Johnson, "Trump calls for 'total and complete shutdown of Muslims entering the United States,'" *The Washington Post*, December 8, 2015, <https://www.washingtonpost.com/news/post-politics/wp/2015/12/07/donald-trump-calls-for-total-and-complete-shutdown-of-muslims-entering-the-united-states/> (last accessed January 8, 2020)
48. Cory Siemaszko, "George W. Bush: Free Press 'Indispensable' to Democracy," *NBC News*, February 27, 2017, <https://www.nbcnews.com/news/us-news/george-w-bush-free-press-indispensable-democracy-n726141> (last accessed December 15, 2019).
49. Ibid.
50. Donald Trump's Contract with the American Voter, n.d., <https://assets.donaldjtrump.com/_landings/contract/O-TRU-102316-Contractv02.pdf> (last accessed December 15, 2019).
51. Elaine C. Kamarck, *Why Presidents Fail: And How They Can Succeed Again* (Washington, DC: Brookings, 2016), 23.
52. Rowena Mason, "May Under Pressure to Condemn Trump's Immigration Ban," *The Guardian*, January 28, 2017, <https://www.theguardian.com/politics/2017/jan/28/may-under-pressure-to-condemn-trumps-immigration-ban> (last accessed December 15, 2019).
53. "How Popular is Donald Trump?" updating calculation of Trump's approval rating, *FiveThirtyEight*, <https://projects.fivethirtyeight.com/trump-approval-ratings/> (last accessed December 13, 2019).

54. Scott Clement, "Americans Are More Split on the Trump Travel Ban Than You Might Think," *The Washington Post*, February 13, 2017, <https://www.washingtonpost.com/news/the-fix/wp/2017/02/13/americans-arent-rejecting-trumps-immigration-ban-outright-but-it-has-a-tough-road-ahead/> (last accessed January 8, 2020).
55. Adam Liptak and Michael Shear, "Justices Back Travel Ban," *The New York Times*, June 27, 2018, A1.
56. Andrew Crines and David Dolowitz, "The Oratory of Donald Trump," in Andrew Crines and Sophia Hatzisavvidou (eds), *Republican Orators From Eisenhower to Trump* (London: Palgrave Macmillan, 2018), 293–4.
57. "*Meet the Press*: Trump in 1999: 'I am Very Pro-Choice,'" *NBC News*, October 24, 1999, <https://www.nbcnews.com/meet-the-press/video/trump-in-1999-i-am-very-pro-choice-480297539914> (last accessed December 15, 2019).
58. "*Hardball*: Donald Trump Advocates Punishment for Abortion," *NBC News*, March 31, 2016, <https://www.nbcnews.com/meet-the-press/video/trump-s-hazy-stance-on-abortion-punishment-655457859717> (last accessed December 15, 2019).
59. Nolan McCaskill and Jennifer Haberkorn, "Grand Old Primary: Trump Reverses Statement That Women Should Be Punished for Illegal Abortions," *Politico*, March 30, 2016, <https://www.politico.com/blogs/2016-gop-primary-live-updates-and-results/2016/03/donald-trump-illegal-abortions-punish-women-221391> (last accessed December 15, 2019).
60. White House Presidential Memorandum Regarding the Mexico City Policy, January 23, 2017, <https://www.whitehouse.gov/presidential-actions/presidential-memorandum-regarding-mexico-city-policy/>; Erika Guevera-Rosas, "Trump's Global Gag a Devastating Blow for Women's Rights," Amnesty International, January 25, 2017, <https://www.amnesty.org/en/latest/news/2017/01/trumps-global-gag-a-devastating-blow-for-womens-rights/> (both last accessed December 15, 2019).
61. Risa Goluboff and Richard Schragger, "Obama's Court?" in Julian Zelizer (ed.), *The Presidency of Barack Obama: A First Historical Assessment* (Princeton, NJ: Princeton University Press, 2018), 86.
62. "Abortion Policy in the Absence of Roe," Guttmacher Institute, 2019, <https://www.guttmacher.org/state-policy/explore/abortion-policy-absence-roe> (last accessed December 15, 2019).

63. Chris Cameron, "Trump Repeats a False Claim That Doctors 'Execute' Newborns," *The New York Times*, April 28, 2019, <https://www.nytimes.com/2019/04/28/us/politics/trump-abortion-fact-check.html> (last accessed January 8, 2020)
64. Lydia Saad, "Most 'Pro-Life' Americans Unsure About Trump's Abortion Views," Gallup, May 26, 2016, <https://news.gallup.com/poll/191573/pro-life-americans-unsure-trump-abortion-views.aspx?g_source=ABORTION&g_medium=topic&g_campaign=tiles> (last accessed December 15, 2019).
65. Cameron, "Trump Repeats a False Claim"; Andrew Hay, "Alabama Boycott Builds as States Retaliate Against Abortion Law," *Reuters*, May 17, 2019, <https://www.reuters.com/article/us-usa-abortion-alabama-boycott/alabama-boycott-builds-as-states-retaliate-against-abortion-law-idUSKCN1SM2V8> (last accessed December 15, 2019).
66. Barack Obama, *The Audacity of Hope* (Edinburgh: Canongate, 2008), 197–8.
67. Rebecca Sinderbrand, "Clinton, Obama Put Politics Aside to Discuss Faith," CNN *Politics Election Center*, April 14, 2008, <http://edition.cnn.com/2008/POLITICS/04/13/forum/index.html?iref=topnews> (last accessed December 15, 2019).
68. "Planned Parenthood: Obama Reelection Is 'Resounding Victory for Women,'" Planned Parenthood press release, January 28, 2013, <https://www.plannedparenthoodaction.org/pressroom/planned-parenthood-obama-reelection-resounding-victory-women> (last accessed December 15, 2019).
69. Edwards, *Overreach*, 45.
70. "Trump's order on abortion policy: What does it mean?" *BBC News*, January 24, 2017, <https://www.bbc.co.uk/news/world-us-canada-38729364> (last accessed December 15, 2019).
71. Simone Leiro, "President Obama Designates Stonewall National Monument," *White House Blog*, June 24, 2016, <https://obamawhitehouse.archives.gov/blog/2016/06/24/president-obama-designates-stonewall-national-monument> (last accessed December 15, 2019).
72. Maggie Haberman, "Trump Flouts GOP Dogma on Gay Issues," *The New York Times*, April 23, 2016, A1.
73. Alex Kotch, "When God Steps In: Why the Christian Right is Rejoicing Under Trump's Presidency," *Salon*, February 25, 2017, <https://www.salon.com/2017/02/25/why-the-christian-right-is-rejoicing-under-trumps-presidency_partner/> (last accessed December 15, 2019).

74. Gregory Smith and Jessica Martinez, "How the Faithful Voted: A Preliminary 2016 Analysis," *Pew Research Center*, November 9, 2016, <https://www.pewresearch.org/fact-tank/2016/11/09/how-the-faithful-voted-a-preliminary-2016-analysis/>; NBC News Exit Polls, *NBC News*, November 8, 2016, <https://www.nbcnews.com/card/nbc-news-exit-poll-trump-fails-peel-lgbt-voters-away-n680901> (both last accessed December 15, 2019).
75. Joshua Gillin, "Hillary Clinton Says Donald Trump 'Wants to Undo Marriage Equality,'" *Politifact*, November 3, 2016, <https://www.politifact.com/truth-o-meter/statements/2016/nov/03/hillary-clinton/hillary-clinton-says-donald-trump-wants-undo-marri/> (last accessed December 15, 2019).
76. "Repeal of 'Don't Ask, Don't Tell' (DADT): Quick Reference Guide," US Department of Defense, October 28, 2011, <https://archive.defense.gov/home/features/2010/0610_dadt/Quick_Reference_Guide_Repeal_of_DADT_APPROVED.pdf> (last accessed December 15, 2019).
77. Agnes Gereben Schaefer, Radha Iyengar Plumb, Srikanth Kadiyala, Jennifer Kavanagh, Charles Engel, Kayla Williams, and Amii Kress, "Assessing the Implications of Allowing Transgender Personnel to Serve Openly," RAND Corporation, 2016, <https://www.rand.org/pubs/research_reports/RR1530.html> (last accessed December 15, 2019).
78. Michelle Dietert and Dianne Dentice, "The Transgender Military Experience: Their Battle for Workplace Rights," *Journal of Workplace Rights* (April–June 2015): 1–12, <https://journals.sagepub.com/doi/pdf/10.1177/2158244015584231> (last accessed December 15, 2019).
79. Schaefer et al., "Assessing the Implications."
80. David Smith, Ben Jacobs, and Lauren Gambino, "Donald Trump Calls Las Vegas Shooting an 'Act of Pure Evil,'" *The Guardian*, October 2, 2017, <https://www.theguardian.com/us-news/2017/oct/02/donald-trump-condolences-las-vegas-shooting> (last accessed December 15, 2019).
81. David Frum, "A Presidential Speech Steeped in Hypocrisy," *The Atlantic*, October 2, 2017, <https://www.theatlantic.com/politics/archive/2017/10/a-speech-steeped-in-hypocrisy/541758/> (last accessed December 15, 2019).
82. Ken Belson and Julie Hirschfield Davies, "Trump Rebukes Athlete, A Star Posts 'U Bum,'" *The New York Times*, September 24, 2017, A1.

83. John Fritze, "NFL: Trump's Toughest Tweets Knocking Players for Kneeling During National Anthem," *USA Today*, September 9, 2018, <https://eu.usatoday.com/story/news/politics/2018/09/09/donald-trumps-toughest-tweets-kneeling-during-national-anthem/1248196002/> (last accessed December 15, 2019).

7
Conclusion: From "Renegade" to "Mogul"

Barack Obama's Secret Service codename was "Renegade." Whilst this may have chimed with supporters' interpretation of his refreshing outsider role, the more formal definition of the term would doubtless have satisfied his detractors. To those who opposed him he truly was a president who embodied the definition, as someone who "deserts and betrays an organization, country, or set of principles."[1] By the time he left office, as with all presidents aged by the experience, the freshness had gone after numerous institutional battles at home, and the reality that military deployments are difficult to disentangle had tested his opening set of principles to the limit. Yet, before reviewing Obama's achievements and failures and the resilience of the plans he was able to put into place, it is necessary to reflect on the importance of the very fact that he was elected and re-elected as president of a country with such a deeply troubled and violent racial history.

In his seminal 2004 speech at the Democrat National Convention, the Illinois senator reminded the audience that "in no other country on earth is my story even possible."[2] It is fair to assume that the first paragraph of any Obama political obituary will mention his heritage. Yet, racial reality continued to bite. While running on the idea of a post-racial ticket in the 2008 presidential election may have been politically necessary, there was little in America that could be categorized as post-racial before, during, or after the Obama years. Nonetheless, that apparent barrier to the highest office in the land was finally transcended, and this was a moment of profound significance not only for African Americans but for everyone who cared about social progress. It was also a watershed moment for those less pleased that the skinny kid with the funny name had attained the nation's highest office. The long shadows of the nation's racially fraught past remained distinctly present. In fact, even at the time of his election, there was evidence that many were not just unhappy but uncomfortable with the outcome. A Gallup poll, cited at the time of the election as showing grounds for positivity, found that 67 percent of respondents said that they were "proud" and "optimistic" as a result of the election outcome: Yet, while 32 percent of people who had voted for John McCain did express pride, 56 percent said that they felt "afraid" at the prospect of Obama's time in office.[3] That fear may have been motivated by partisanship rather than racial animus, but whatever the cause, it suggested a truth to Ta-Nehisi Coates's reflection that Obama was obliged to be "half as black" and "twice as good."[4] In turn, there was always a likelihood that politics could soon turn ugly once the presidential honeymoon period was over.

At the extreme, one remit of the Southern Poverty Law Center is to track serious and credible threats against the government, dating back to the Oklahoma City bombing of 1995. In its *Terror From the Right* report, conspiracies and right-wing plots were documented and until 2008 tended to average around two per year. At least correlated by the Obama victory was a spike in neo-Nazi threats and violence.[5] As the threats against President Obama became increasingly disturbing, a Presidential Threat Task Force was created inside the FBI to track and monitor assassination attempts that might be linked to domestic or international terrorism.[6] Amongst older African Americans the fear that something might happen to Obama was palpable. One scholar, Anthea Butler, explained: "somebody who's 70 or older, they're gonna be like, 'Honestly, we just want him to get out alive.'"[7] In the conservative media ecosystem fear and resentment was stoked continuously, even if the relevant pundits simultaneously denied that they had a racial axe to grind. Talk radio host Rush Limbaugh fretted about white decline, whilst on *Fox and Friends* Glenn Beck taunted Obama for "having a deep-seated hatred of white people."[8]

While Limbaugh and especially Beck might be seen as being on the fringes of conservative politics, the anger they expressed was brought into the mainstream by the emergence of the Tea Party, which infused the Republican Party throughout Obama's first term.[9] This in turn further morphed into Trumpian populism, with its racially antagonistic streak not too well hidden. In fall of 2015, when Trump's election to the White House still seemed a distant prospect, Anthea Butler pointed to one driver of his early surge in the polls for the Republican nomination: "I mean, here people are, acting so surprised about Donald Trump's popularity. Hello? He's the one who asked Obama for a birth certificate!"[10] Further to this, the best analysis in political science suggested that the 2016 vote did reflect a greater degree of racial rather than simply economic resentment.[11] This backlash against the fact of an African American president does not, of course, take away from the reality that Obama served two terms and left office with a 60 percent approval rating, but it suggests that building a lasting political coalition that would continue his policy project in the longer term was always going to be a highly fraught task.[12]

The "Renegade" era: opportunities and restraints

In truth, based on his voting record in Congress, Senator Obama sat on the center-left of the political spectrum, with a record similar to that of Hillary Clinton.[13] Health care reform and modest wealth redistribution were ambitious goals but did not amount to radical socialism, and by 2008 opposition to "dumb wars" was a widespread sentiment. Perhaps the fact that Obama did not pursue a Bernie Sanders-style agenda helps to explain the disappointment felt toward him by those on the left. In his *Requiem for the American Dream*, Noam Chomsky presented as equally underwhelmed by the "hope and change thing" as Sarah Palin.[14] Other leftist commentators also pointed to missed opportunities and the conservatism of some of Obama's choices to senior cabinet and advisory positions.[15] More centrist voices also expressed some concern that Obama might be too cautious. The *New York Times* acknowledged that Tim Geithner and Lawrence Summers, who were the central figures in Obama's economic team when he took office, had "demonstrated a capacity for good judgment and good ideas," but the editors added that both had "played central roles in policies that helped provoke today's financial crisis."[16]

One reason behind some liberal disappointment with the final scale of Obama's achievements might be that many commentators thought that the apparent mood of celebration at the emblematic importance of his victory was matched by an opportunity for his to be a transformative presidency in concrete policy terms, which in turn could lead to the building of a new majority political coalition. As it turned out, both the notion that there was a universal mood of welcome for Obama and the idea that there was an opening for radical political change and policy change were overstated. Nevertheless, there were grounds at the time for believing that the 2008 election represented a landmark event beyond the transfer of power between the parties. In the language of political science, the crisis that Obama inherited also seemed to offer an opportunity for him to be a president of "reconstruction."[17] Economic meltdown, arriving as it did on the back of war fatigue, increased public concern regarding key issues such as climate change, health care reform, income inequality and more, apparently presenting a window for presidential boundary-pushing, even cracking. The possibilities seemed to be recognized in what became a famous, or perhaps notorious, line by Obama's first chief of staff, Rahm Emmanuel, when, during the transition period, he stated: "You never want a serious crisis to go to waste. And what I mean by that, it's an opportunity to do things you think you could not do before."[18] In this spirit, also during the transition, *Time* magazine mocked up a picture of Obama as Franklin Roosevelt, the most transformative president of the twentieth century, with the banner headline: "The New New Deal."[19] The scholarly community was also anxious to chart the progress of this new venture, with titles such as *Reaching for a New Deal*.[20]

Yet, a thorough read of that last title, edited by leading political scientists Theda Skocpol and Lawrence Jacobs, illustrates not only the opportunity for change but also just how much opposition Obama was always likely to face when trying to pursue an ambitious policy agenda. At the start of 2009, Republicans were not in a strong institutional position in Washington, DC, with both executive and legislative branches controlled by Democrats; but GOP leaders quickly laid plans for how they could thwart the new president. At a dinner on the night of Obama's inaugural that January, leading Republican figures from both the Senate and the House met with strategists, lobbyists, and the pollster Frank Luntz. The most specific topic of their discussion was the issue of health care, but the wider theme was to plot how to undermine the credibility of the Democrats' forthcoming legislative agenda and to ensure that their party remained united in its opposition.[21]

Hence it was always likely naïve of those millions of Obama supporters to think that the new president, however talented, could straightforwardly bring meaningful change in the dysfunctional twenty-first-century mechanism that is the US government system, even at a time when the Democrats were in the ascendancy. But it is critical to stress that Obama *did* deliver on many of his campaign promises. In order to get some perspective on the achievements of Obama's opening two years in office, it is worth comparing his record with that of the previous Democratic incumbent of the White House, Bill Clinton, who also presided over a two-year period of unified partisan governance in Washington, DC.

The institutional similarities between the two presidencies should not be overstated. Obama's personal mandate was considerably clearer and, while the Democratic majorities in the House were similar in size through the 103rd and 111th Congresses, the latter session was marked by greater ideological coherence and higher levels of partisan loyalty amongst congressional Democrats as well as Republicans.[22] Critically in the Senate, Democrats, if briefly, had a potential sixty votes to get past the filibuster in 2009, which they had never enjoyed in 1993–4.[23] And before making claims that the Obama era was marked by greater achievement than that of Clinton, it is important to acknowledge that the legislative outcomes promoted by Clinton throughout 1993–4 were consequential. The 1993 budget, which increased taxes on the highest-earning Americans, was an important moment in controlling the deficit and contributed to the very short period of budgetary surplus at the end of the 1990s (and, reflecting the ensuing politics, it was the first substantive bill to pass without a vote from the minority party in the post-war period). NAFTA, which was ratified in 1993, was a landmark free trade agreement, and the Violent Crime Control and Law Enforcement Act of 1994 contained a temporary ban on nineteen types of assault weapon, funding for extra police officers, and money to give more teeth to the implementation of the Violence Against Women Act. For all this, that legislative session was at least equally renowned for the failure of Clinton's health care reform effort to make any serious progress through the congressional maze.[24]

The contrast between the failure of the Health Security Act and the successful passage of the Affordable Care Act provides the most obvious point of divergence between Clinton's opening two years as president and Obama's. Clinton's plan was more radical than the ACA, but Vice President Biden's colorful words did accurately capture a truth that the ACA was a big "deal."[25] Further, the American Recovery and Reinvestment Act was a near-$800 billion fiscal stimulus package enacted in early 2009.[26] The economic crisis that Obama inherited dwarfed the recession of 1990–1 that had framed Clinton's election campaign and so demanded a different scale of response. Hence, the contexts were quite different, but Clinton's successful efforts to reinvigorate the federal government as a driver of economic growth were limited by any standard. Despite considerable rhetoric about increasing investment in human capital through increased education spending, the actual expenditure commitments were limited by the emphasis on the deficit and the plan for a stimulus bill of just over $16 billion early in 1993 fell victim to the same refrain that fiscal constraint was the priority. In contrast, whatever the later laments that an even bigger package would have been appropriate, ARRA was a massively expansive project. Further, the Dodd-Frank Wall Street and Consumer Protection Act, which created the CFPB, was a significant challenge to existing banking and Wall Street practices.

This summary of the 1993–4 period offers its own cautionary tale of the dangers of imposing too much hindsight and not enough understanding of the contemporary circumstances when considering a president's legacy. Clinton's plans for economic stimulus and investment spending may look restricted, but the deficit was a primary concern in the early 1990s, as illustrated by President George H. W. Bush's politically disastrous breaking of his "no new taxes" pledge in the budget agreement of 1990 and then Ross Perot's emphasis on the issue in the 1992 election campaign.[27] Further, NAFTA had never been popular on the left, and free trade remained an issue that tended to divide Democrats in the White House from those outside it in a pattern that was repeated during Obama's time in office. And, two decades after its passage, the crime bill was remembered less for the assault weapons ban than for its punitive measures, which contributed to the expansion of the federal prison population and reinforced the era of mass incarceration.

One crushing similarity between the Clinton and Obama presidencies was the loss of Democratic Party control of Congress after only two years, and in both cases the scale of the rebuke was telling. In 1994 the Democrats lost control of the House for the first time in forty years, and in 2010 the party's losses in the House were the largest for any party in the post-war period. As Obama acknowledged, it was a "shellacking."[28] This left both of the presidents dealing with at least one at times overtly hostile chamber of Congress for 75 percent of their time in office. Furthermore, Obama had to operate in an environment where the Tea Party wave not only pushed the GOP agenda sharply to the right, but also succeeded in increasingly taking control of the political narrative. Their counterparts on the left, the Occupy Movement, never achieved anywhere near the same momentum.

In this less hospitable environment, the prospect of a new "New Deal" and an expansive legislative agenda evaporated. Obama did continue to talk of working with Congress, and in 2011 there were tentative negotiations between the White House and Republican House Speaker John Boehner's office about a "grand bargain" on taxes and entitlement reform. The reality, however, was that even if such discussions had led to an agreement there was little likelihood that either Obama or Boehner would have been able to persuade their own side of the merits of a deal with their opponents, such was the level of partisan hostility.[29] At the end of 2015, the administration did agree a budget deal with new House Speaker Paul Ryan that passed Congress on a bipartisan basis; this included the permanent extension of tax credits for low-income households that had originally been part of ARRA. Yet, important as such measures were to many Americans, it would be stretching thin evidence to make a claim that the last six years of Obama's presidency fulfilled the transformative promise that had been fleetingly in view in the early months of 2009.

As it was, at least in domestic affairs, the most far-reaching initiatives of Obama's presidency in its later years came through executive actions. As his second term progressed, Obama began referring to the notion that he had a pen and a phone that he could use to bring about change. At the start of 2014 he spoke, optimistically, of a "Year of Action." At an event in January of that year he explained,

> I am going to be working with Congress where I can to accomplish this, but I am also going to act on my own if Congress is deadlocked. . . . I've got a pen to take executive actions where Congress won't, and I've got a telephone to rally folks around the country on this mission.[30]

As we have explored with regard to immigration and climate, Obama's use of the pen brought mixed results. DACA did bring relief to many of the so-called "dreamers," but the courts effectively stymied DAPA, which would have afforded legal status to many more undocumented immigrants, and the Clean Power Plan, which would have restricted emissions from coal-burning power plants. Many other less high-profile measures were introduced through various executive actions, including some environmental regulations, minor gun control measures and adjustments to the implementation of the ACA.[31] These were of varying consequence and legality in their own right, and then of limited durability from January 2017.

The 2016 election: no third term

Overall, and not just with the benefit of hindsight, it was always naïve to think that the Obama presidency would leave a wide-ranging legacy that would be smoothly embedded. The abrupt change of political direction that came with the 2016 presidential election was, however, more of a surprise. Given the electoral reversals suffered by Democrats in 2010 and 2014, it was evident that Obama's winning electoral coalition had not taken the form of a new political majority in the country for his party. Hence a strong Republican challenge for the White House in 2016 was always likely—but until votes were actually counted in the Republican primaries, few expected that challenge to come from a candidate so far outside the established political framework as Donald Trump. And that outsider status was reflected not just in the fact that he had never competed for political office, but also in the way that he seemed to revel in trampling on the rules of acceptable behavior, explicitly deploying divisive language that played on racial and ethnic tensions and questioned the very legitimacy of his political opponents.

Thus, as the campaign unfolded and the general election shaped up with nearly all opinion polls suggesting a win for Hillary Clinton, Democrats understandably looked toward a new president who would reinforce the legacies of the Obama administration. In short, victory for Obama's former secretary of state would have been as close as possible to a third term in the White House. Michael Wolff exaggerated when he wrote of Democrats as being "so intoxicated with the righteousness of their cause" that they never saw defeat coming, but it was nevertheless a shock when the electoral college's math meant that after eight years with a progressive African American in the Oval Office, it turned out that demography was not destiny, or not yet at least.[32]

One similarity between Obama and Trump was that they both used social media in innovative ways on the campaign trail in their attempts to reach directly to voters. Advances in communications technology made such efforts possible, and the result powerful. In Obama's case, he utilized the new media of the day to good effect, offering tailored YouTube and MySpace videos to specific voter demographics and signing any personal Twitter messages with "BO." Compared to what came later, this approach was highly structured. Donald Trump caught the wave of increased public Twitter usage and utilized it in an unprecedented way. His engagement was visceral and, for many, addictive. This bypassing of the gatekeeping "fake news media" and communicating directly with followers via the intimacy of their phones allowed the President to connect in a radical and unprecedented way. Taking the new technology baton from his predecessor and running so successfully with it allowed him to publicize every aspect of his de-Obamafication plans directly to his followers. From disparaging comments while Obama was still in office, rising to an onslaught on the 2016 campaign trail, Trump successfully convinced supporters that he would revert, reduce and roll back key aspects of the Obama legacy. It also worked to Trump's great advantage that Fox News reinforced and amplified his message, regularly trampling on the traditional fourth estate boundaries. Former Fox contributor and conservative intellectual William Kristol blamed the network for escalating its "whipping up of ethnic resentments, racial resentments and the deep state."[33]

In this context, it was hardly surprising that Obama predicted dire consequences should Trump defeat Clinton, as he warned rallies when campaigning: "All the progress we made over the last eight years goes out the window if we don't win this election."[34] After the election, the outgoing president offered a more considered reflection, insisting that most achievements do "stick." His earlier admonishments were not, however, without justification. Pushback from a presidential successor of the other party is a natural part of political process and it is inevitable, expected even, that certain aspects of a legacy will be overturned. The early days of a new administration often involve rollback-related executive actions, offering a political sorbet between one administrative course and the next. At times, a highly symbolic act may occur, providing an early nod to voters anxious to see an immediate sign of change in a new presidency. The Mexico City reproductive rights ruling is a case in point, used as a political football by Republican and Democratic administrations since Ronald Reagan. For voters, such actions can act as a barometer of a president's policy position, as comforting to some as it is unnerving to others.

The "Mogul" in power

Donald Trump chose the name "Mogul" as his Secret Service moniker. The Cambridge online dictionary defines this term as "an important person who is very rich or powerful."[35] It is evident from observing the New Yorker's words and deeds that it matters greatly to him to be perceived as both. Clearly, being a billionaire and president of the United States ticked these boxes, but as a newcomer to any political office his capacity to wield power effectively was uncertain.

Our focus in this book has not been to assess President Trump's own legacy, but his success in reversing the path set by his predecessor. As we have seen, this proved to be a wide-ranging effort but with a mixed record of accomplishment. As the midterm elections of November 2018 saw the Democrats take control of the House, thus severely limiting the chances of further rolling back the Obama era through the legislative process, important elements of Obama's legacy remained in place. The ACA was still the law of the land, if somewhat battered and bruised. Further, while battles raged over transgender rights and questions of whether those providing wedding services could be compelled to serve a same-sex wedding, there seemed little public appetite for a full frontal attack on the right to same-sex marriage itself.

On the other hand, if progress toward national-level climate action was halting under Obama, the very notion of government acting to check global warming was mocked by the Trump administration. Similarly, while Obama's legacy on immigration reform was thinner than he had promised it would be as he entered office, DACA illustrated a preferred direction of travel. In the Trump era liberals could scoff at Mexico's unwillingness to pay for a border wall, and administrative sloppiness left DACA intact and protected by the courts for longer than may have been anticipated; but again, the reversal of policy was quite distinct. Further, the appearance of an Obama legacy could be deceptive. For example, the CFPB still existed in 2019, but it was a hollowed-out institution that was not performing the same functions as it had been doing three years earlier.

In some cases reversal was easy for the Trump administration since Obama had established legacy in a manner that might be, albeit harshly, characterized as "in name only." Certainly the commitment to the Trans Pacific Partnership and the Paris climate accords were not much more than paper pledges without binding mechanisms placed on US participation. The Iran nuclear deal clearly had more weight to it than these agreements, since it was a multilateral deal that had gone into effect. Hence, pulling the US out of this deal would have real-world consequences for ongoing international politics: It would not only aggravate the Iranians, but also alienate the US's European allies who had been party to the agreement. Nevertheless, despite some pushback from the State Department, Trump did reverse this central if controversial aspect of Obama's foreign policy legacy.

As people who became presidents, Obama and Trump could barely be more different. From their personal stories to their conduct of public relations, the two reflect not just different political philosophies but alternative visions of what it means to live a "good life." Unsurprisingly, these differences translated into their styles of presidential leadership and how they communicated their values to the public. The "twitterer-in-chief" was a stark contrast to the studied approach of "no-drama" Obama. On the other hand, Obama did not bequeath a retiring executive branch to his successor. Obama had proved quite willing to use and stretch executive authority to, and sometimes beyond, the legal limit. Hence, while Trump's executive actions were often intended to reverse Obama-era policies, Trump's use of those powers should be seen as an extension rather than a reversal of his predecessor's behavior.

Contextualizing legacy

Presidents do not get to choose their own legacy, at least as judged over time. Truman is often cited as an example of someone who left office amidst discontent, but whose reputation has subsequently been restored. If not to the same extent, both Eisenhower and Lyndon Johnson are granted more credit for the accomplishments of their presidencies than was sometimes given in the immediate aftermath of their departure form office. Looking further back, Ulysses Grant, president from 1869 to 1877, has risen in recent rankings by scholars of US presidents. He has never made the top tier, but has moved well away from the bottom-of-the-table places that he occupied in mid-twentieth-century polls. While the corruption and faltering economy that marked his time in office cannot be revised away, there has been a greater appreciation of his support for reconstruction and recent writers "have given him high marks for his efforts on behalf of African Americans and Native Americans."[36] Hence, what might be thought of as the changing moral standards of those who judge presidents can impact on the place of presidents in history. On the flip side of Grant's re-evaluation, President Andrew Jackson's brutality toward Native Americans is now sometimes seen in sharper relief, serving as a lens into his presidency that was sometimes neglected by previous generations of historians in their emphasis on the transformative nature of his time in office.[37]

Even assessing the political success of more recent presidents is problematic. Reagan is sometimes cast as a transformative president, and he certainly helped shift the political discourse in a conservative direction, but the major welfare state entitlement programs survived his time in office.[38] Historians have been kinder to George H. W. Bush than the voters were in 1992, but however much his handling of international affairs may gain acclaim, he was a one-term president. Bill Clinton's two terms in office proved that Democrats could win presidential elections after a run of five defeats in the six elections from 1968 onwards; yet the "Third Way" did not prove to be a lasting political settlement, and the disintegration of his relationship with Vice President Gore as a consequence of the Lewinsky scandal prevented Clinton from being a campaign asset in 2000, thus undermining the chances of reinforcing what there was of his own legacy. George W. Bush must surely have expected to be remembered for tax cuts and perhaps Social Security reform, rather than for initiating America's longest war following the intervention in Afghanistan.

A president's legacy is shaped by contingency as well as by deliberation. More than a shopping list to be ticked off as the years progress, it is a messy and complex business with no fixed guarantee of durability. Presidential fortunes will fluctuate and in terms of legacy-building achievements there will inevitably be disappointment and opposition. Sometimes apparently popular initiatives will quickly prove to have little foundation or arouse sustained opposition during the implementation process. Conversely, policies that were underwater with the public in their early stages can gain traction over time and develop institutional resilience.

The early stages of the the Democratic primary campaign in 2019 provide some context for how perceptions of legacy can change over time, even over relatively short periods. When enacted, the 1994 Crime Bill was acknowledged to contain a number of controversial elements. In one sharp analysis written at the end of the 1990s, Ann Chih Lin commented that the Clinton administration's efforts to portray the bill as showing that the Democratic Party understood public concern about high levels of crime worked to some extent, but that Republican efforts to "paint it as full of failed Great Society programs had succeeded as well."[39] In his 1995 State of the Union address, when reflecting on the loss of so many Democrats in the 1994 midterm elections, Clinton lamented that "several" had been defeated due to the efforts of the NRA in response to the assault weapons ban.[40] Twenty-five years later, however, one of the prime sponsors of that law in the Senate, Joe Biden, came under fire for his part in pushing the bill through. The debates of the merits of the 1994 law, however, paid little attention to the gun control measures but focused on the "tough on crime" clauses that helped expand the federal prison population and reinforce the era of mass incarceration. Hence, ironically, Clinton's effort to use rhetoric on crime to reposition the Democrats, in the context of the early to mid-1990s, as a party that could be as tough as the GOP on criminal behavior resonated more singularly amongst Democrats a quarter-century later than at the time. Further, as a lesson in rollback, the fact that this was the last significant piece of federal legislation that had gun control as a centerpiece caused little comment in the 2019 debate as President George W. Bush had let the assault weapons ban die a natural death at the end of 2004, since that measure had been time-limited.

In Greg Barker's documentary on Obama's final year, the President talks, as he had done before, about how history has a tendency to zig-zag. As his watch drew to a close, he reflected: "one of the things that I have been telling my younger staff, who in some cases have only known politics through my presidency, is history doesn't travel in a straight line. And it zigs and it zags and sometimes you take two steps forward and then you take a step back."[41] For Obama's champions his positive legacy was one of substantial achievement, such as the ACA, and of a putting in place a road map for where the country should go next on issues such as climate change, immigration, and LGBT rights. Whether President Trump's time in office represents a zig and zag or a fundamental re-routing is a profound question for the future of the nation.

Notes

1. Oxford Dictionary Online, <https://www.lexico.com/en/definition/renegade> (last accessed January 8, 2019).
2. "Barack Obama's Keynote Address at the 2004 Democratic National Convention," *PBS Newshour*, July 27, 2004, <https://www.pbs.org/newshour/show/barack-obamas-keynote-address-at-the-2004-democratic-national-convention> (last accessed January 8, 2020).
3. Frank Newport, "Americans See Obama Election as Race Relations Milestone," Gallup, November 7, 2008, <https://news.gallup.com/poll/111817/americans-see-obama-election-race-relations-milestone.aspx> (last accessed January 8, 2020).
4. Ta-Nehisi Coates, "Fear of a Black President," *The Atlantic*, September 2012, <https://www.theatlantic.com/magazine/archive/2012/09/fear-of-a-black-president/309064/> (last accessed January 8, 2020).
5. Southern Poverty Law Center, "Terror From the Right," 2019, <https://www.splcenter.org/20180723/terror-right> (last accessed January 8, 2020).
6. See for example Ron Kessler, *In the President's Secret Service: Behind the Scenes With Agents in the Line of Fire And the Presidents They Protect* (New York: Three Rivers, 2009).
7. Jennifer Senior, "The Paradox of the First Black President," *New York Magazine*, October 7, 2015, <http://nymag.com/intelligencer/2015/10/paradox-of-the-first-black-president.html> (last accessed January 8, 2020)
8. Glenn Beck, "Obama Has a Deep-Seated Hatred for White People," *YouTube*, July 28, 2009, <https://www.youtube.com/watch?v=MIZDnpPafaA> (last accessed January 8, 2020).
9. Theda Skocpol and Vanessa Williamson, *The Tea Party and the Remaking of Republican Conservatism* (New York: Oxford University Press, 2012).

10. Senior, "The Paradox of the First Black President."
11. John Sides, Lynn Vavreck, and Michael Tesler, *Identity Crisis: The 2016 Presidential Campaign and the Battle for the Meaning of America* (Princeton, NJ: Princeton University Press, 2018).
12. "Obama Leaving with High Approval Rating," *BBC News*, January 18, 2017, <https://www.bbc.co.uk/news/world-us-canada-38667115> (last accessed 8 January 18, 2020).
13. Senator Hillary Clinton voting record, <https://www.govtrack.us/congress/members/hillary_clinton/300022>; Senator Barack Obama voting record, <https://www.govtrack.us/congress/members/barack_obama/400629> (last accessed January 8, 2020).
14. Noam Chomsky, "Requiem for the American Dream with Amy Goodman," *YouTube*, September 2017, <https://www.youtube.com/watch?v=dlzODoqipT4> (last accessed January 8, 2020).
15. See for example Reed Hundt, *A Crisis Wasted* (New York: Rosetta Books, 2019) and Robert Kuttner, *A Presidency in Peril: The Inside Story of Obama's Promise, Wall Street's Power, and the Struggle to Control Our Economic Future* (Vermont: Chelsea Green Publishing, 2010).
16. "Mr Obama's Economic Advisors," *The New York Times*, November 25, 2008, A30.
17. Stephen Skowronek, *The Politics Presidents Make: Leadership From John Adams to Bill Clinton* (Cambridge, MA: Harvard University Press, 1993).
18. Rahm Emmanuel, "The Opportunities of Crisis," *YouTube*, November 19, 2008, <https://www.youtube.com/watch?v=_mzcbXi1Tkk> (last accessed January 8, 2020).
19. *Time* cover page, November 24, 2008, <http://content.time.com/time/covers/0,16641,20081124,00.html> (last accessed January 8, 2020).
20. Theda Skocpol and Lawrence Jacobs (eds.), *Reaching for a New Deal: Ambitious Governance, Economic Meltdown, and Polarized Politics in Obama's First Two Years* (New York: Russell Sage Foundation, 2011).
21. Steven Brill, *America's Bitter Pill* (New York: Random House, 2015), 92–3.
22. Rhodes Cook, "Not Your Father's Democratic Congress," *Sabato's Crystal Ball*, February 19, 2009, <http://www.centerforpolitics.org/crystalball/articles/frc2009021901/> (last accessed January 8, 2020).
23. The filibuster-proof sixty votes only finally crystalized in summer of 2009, as Minnesota's Al Franken was not formally sworn in for

several months owing to his 2008 election opponent contesting the 312-vote winning margin. Prior to that, Democrats got to fifty-nine seats in the Senate when Republican Arlen Specter of Pennsylvania switched parties in April 2009. Technically there were two Independent senators: Bernie Sanders from Vermont and Joe Lieberman from Connecticut, who caucused with the Democrats.

24. For a fuller discussion of the Clinton presidency, see Alex Waddan, *Clinton's Legacy? A New Democrat in Governance* (Basingstoke: Palgrave Macmillan, 2002).
25. Sheryl Gay Stolberg and Robert Pear, "Obama Signs Health Care Overhaul Bill, with a Flourish," *The New York Times*, March 23, 2010, <https://www.nytimes.com/2010/03/24/health/policy/24health.html> (last accessed December 12, 2019).
26. For a full discussion of ARRA see Eddie Ashbee, "Fiscal Policy Responses to the Economic Crisis in the UK and US," in Terrence Casey (ed.), *The Legacy of the Crash: How the Financial Crisis Changed America and Britain* (New York: Palgrave Macmillan, 2011), 79–98.
27. Sean Wilentz, *The Age of Reagan: A History, 1974–2008* (New York: Harper Collins, 2008), 308.
28. Liz Halloran, "Obama Humbled by Election 'Shellacking,'" *NPR*, November 3, 2010, <https://www.npr.org/templates/story/story.php?storyId=131046118> (last accessed January 8, 2020).
29. Matt Bai, "Obama vs. Boehner: Who Killed the Debt Deal," *The New York Times Magazine*, March 28, 2012, <https://www.nytimes.com/2012/04/01/magazine/obama-vs-boehner-who-killed-the-debt-deal.html> (last accessed January 8, 2020).
30. Tamara Keith, "Wielding a Pen and a Phone, Obama Goes it Alone," *NPR*, January 20, 2014, <https://www.npr.org/2014/01/20/263766043/wielding-a-pen-and-a-phone-obama-goes-it-alone> (last accessed January 8, 2020).
31. Andrew Rudalevige, "The Obama Administrative Presidency: Some Late Term Patterns," *Presidential Studies Quarterly*, 46.4 (December 2016): 868–90.
32. Michael Wolff, *Fire and Fury: Inside the Trump White House* (London: Little, Brown, 2018), 235. For a sophisticated but accessible analysis of the changes that persuaded many of truth of the idea of "demography as destiny" see John Kenneth White, *Barack Obama's America: How New Conceptions of Race, Family, and Religion Ended the Reagan Era* (Ann Arbor: University of Michigan Press, 2009).

33. Sabrina Siddiqui, "Fox News: How an Anti-Obama Fringe Set the Stage for Trump," *The Guardian*, March 19, 2019, <https://www.theguardian.com/media/2019/mar/18/fox-news-donald-trump-barack-obama-election> (last accessed January 8, 2020).
34. Peter Baker, "Trump's Ascendance Upends Obama's Vision for America," *The New York Times*, November 13, 2016, A1.
35. Cambridge Dictionary, <https://dictionary.cambridge.org/dictionary/english/mogul> (last accessed January 8, 2020).
36. Ronald Feinman, "The GOP President Historians Say They Like More and More," *History News Network*, June 10, 2018, <https://historynewsnetwork.org/article/168907> (last accessed January 8, 2020).
37. Jonathan Chait, "The Party of Andrew Jackson vs. the Party of Obama," *New York Magazine*, July 5, 2015, <http://nymag.com/intelligencer/2015/06/party-of-jackson-vs-the-party-of-obama.html> (last accessed January 8, 2020).
38. On Reagan as a transformative president, see Wilentz, *The Age of Reagan*. On the limits to the reconstruction of the welfare state in the 1980s see Paul Pierson (2010), *Dismantling the Welfare State? Reagan, Thatcher and the Politics of Retrenchment* (Cambridge: Cambridge University Press).
39. Ann Chih Lin, "The Troubled Success of Crime Policy," in Margaret Weir (ed.), *The Social Divide: Political Parties and the Future of Activist Government*, (Washington, DC: Brookings Institution Press, 1998), 312–57, at 312.
40. William Clinton, "Address Before a Joint Session of the Congress on the State of the Union," January 24, 1995, at Gerhard Peters and John T. Woolley, *The American Presidency Project*, <http://www.presidency.ucsb.edu/ws/?pid=51634> (last accessed January 8, 2020).
41. In Greg Barker (dir.), *The Final Year*, HBO documentary, 2017, <https://www.hbo.com/documentaries/the-final-year> (last accessed January 8, 2020).

Index

Affordable Care Act, 7, 12, 21, 25, 38, 39–47, 58, 63–5, 237, 239, 242, 246; *see also* Obamacare
Afghanistan, 2, 20, 119–21, 141, 142, 176, 200, 244
AFL-CIO Political Action Committee, 101
Ahmadinejad, Mahmoud, 135
Al Arabiya, 135
Alito, Samuel, 158, 159, 165, 167
al Qaeda, 129, 177, 179
American Bar Association, 158
"America First" slogan, 84, 119, 143, 181, 215
American Israel Public Affairs Committee, 139
American Recovery and Reinvestment Act (ARRA), 44, 79, 237, 239
Amnesty International, 215
Apprentice, The, 203, 209
Arab Spring, 142
Arkansas Project, 204
Art of the Deal, The, 216
ASEAN, 121
Assad, Bashar al, 118, 130–4, 180
Atlantic, The, 23
Auchter, Thorne, 14

Aung San Suu Kyi, 124
Australia, 122
Auto Alliance, 87
Axelrod, David, 122, 156, 168

Bannon, Steve, 173, 201–5, 211
Barker, Greg, 245
Baucus, Max, 43
Bayh, Evan, 81
Beck, Glenn, 233
Benghazi, 169–71; *see also* Clinton, Hillary
Berg, John, 80, 82
Biden, Hunter, 185
Biden, Joe, 40, 56, 57, 79, 185, 237, 245
Bingham, Eula, 14
Birther (Birtherism), 4, 5, 6, 209, 234
Black Lives Matter, 207, 208
Boehner, John, 3, 49, 77, 91, 93, 104, 238
Bork, Robert, 17, 158, 174
Brat, Dave, 91
Breitbart, 171, 202–3
Brennan, William, 157
Brown, Michael, 22, 207
Brown, Scott, 2, 41, 48
Bryant, Kobe, 126
Burma, 120, 123–4, 142

INDEX

Bush, George H. W., 102, 109, 119, 206, 210, 221, 238, 244
   Supreme Court appointments, 17, 157–8
Bush, George W., 4, 14, 20, 25, 49, 79, 99, 104, 120, 121, 122, 128, 129, 138, 139, 173, 183, 200, 221, 245
   and American power, 175–7
   immigration policy of, 89, 90, 210, 211, 213
   Iraq war, 116–17, 125
   and judicial branch, 155, 158–9, 161, 162, 167
   LGBT+ policies of, 53–4, 58
   and No Child Left Behind law, 21–2
   Tax cuts of, 12, 244
Butler, Anthea, 233, 234

California, 18, 51, 59, 87, 96, 97
Cambridge Analytica, 203
Cameron, David, 131
Campbell, Kurt, 123
Cantor, Eric, 91
Card, Andrew, 183
Carson, Ben, 63
Carter, Ashton, 219, 220
Carter, Jimmy, 17, 102, 157
Castro, Fidel, 140
Central Intelligence Agency (CIA), 169, 176, 178, 182
Charlottesville, 210
China, 101, 102, 105 121, 122, 123, 134, 136, 141
Choice, The (documentary), 60, 209
Chollet, Derek, 133, 171
Chomsky, Noam, 234
Citizens United v Federal Election Commission, 18, 167
Civil Rights Act of 1964, 13

Clean Power Plan (CPP), 77, 82–4, 239
Climate Action Plan, 82
climate change, 1, 26, 77–87, 104, 139, 235, 246
Clinton, Bill, 4, 97, 98, 158, 173, 175, 236, 244
   health care policy of, 39, 237
   and judicial branch, 17, 158, 161, 162
   LGBT+ policies of, 14–15, 54, 55, 57, 58, 183, 219
   welfare reform policy of, 13–14
Clinton, Hillary, 84, 98, 118, 182, 234, 240,
   Benghazi scandal, 170–1
   Election 2016, 4, 102, 123, 129, 171, 202–5
   and Obama's legacy, 3, 5, 6, 142, 154, 211, 241
   as Secretary of State, 120–1, 123, 125, 178
Coates, Ta-Nehisi, 233
Cobb, Ty, 175
Cohen, Michael, 174
Cold War, 140
Colombia, 98
Columbia University, 86
Comey, James, 173
Comprehensive Immigration Reform Act, 89
Confessore, Nick, 64
Conservative Political Action Conference, 44
Consumer Finance Protection Bureau (CFPB), 22, 25, 38, 39, 48, 49–52, 63–5, 237, 242
Contract with the American Voter, 84, 211
Cook, Tim, 61
Cordray, Richard, 49–53, 64
Corker, Bob, 177
Cotton, Tom, 136

Cox, Archibald, 174
Crimea, 177
Crines, Andrew, 213
Crowley, James (Sergeant), 207
Cruz, Ted, 60, 61, 62, 103, 204
Cuba, 26, 89, 120, 140–2
Cummings, Elijah, 208
Cuomo, Mario, 199

Daalder, Ivor, 127, 128
Daniels, Stormy, 174
Day O'Connor, Sandra, 17, 158, 159
Defense, Department of, 219
Defense of Marriage Act (DOMA), 15, 54, 57, 59, 169
Deferred Action for Childhood Arrivals (DACA), 6, 7, 16, 77, 92–7, 104, 239, 242
Deferred Action for Parents of Americans and Lawful Permanent Residents (DAPA), 6, 7, 16, 18, 77, 92–4, 239
Democrat National Convention of 2004, 232
Dempsey, Marty, 131
Development, Relief and Education for Alien Minors Act (DREAM), 90, 92, 104
Dodd, Christopher, 47
Dodd Frank Wall Street Reform and Consumer Protection Act, 25, 47, 48, 50, 51, 53, 64, 237
Dolowitz, David, 213
Don't Ask Don't Tell (DADT), 55, 57, 59, 219
Drones, 16, 120, 128, 177–9, 182

Earned Income Tax Credits (EITC), 38
Earnest, Josh, 83
Earth Day, 80
Economic Policy Institute, 103

Education, Department of, 62
Edwards, George C., 8
Eisenhower, Dwight, 116, 157, 243
election 2008, 55, 89, 235
elections 2010, 2, 81, 202
election 2012, 56, 104, 170
elections 2014, 160, 162
election 2016, 4, 84, 94, 172, 209, 211, 214, 215, 218, 239
election 2018, 27, 40
electoral college, 16, 240
Emmanuel, Rahm, 40, 235
Employment Non-Discrimination Act, 55
English, Leandra, 51
Environmental Protection Agency, 50, 80, 86
Equal Access Rule, 58, 63
European Union (EU), 105, 134
Every Student Succeeds Act (ESSA), 22

Facebook, 87
Federal Bureau of Investigation (FBI), 173, 174, 233
Federal Deposit Insurance Commission, 49
Federal Reserve, 48, 49
Federalist Society, 158
Ferguson, Missouri, 22, 207
Fitzgerald, Patrick, 173
fivethirtyeight.com, 165
Flood, Emmet, 175
Forbes, 84, 85
Ford, Gerald, 14, 102
Fox News, 138, 171, 233, 241
France, 134, 136, 137
Francisco, Neal, 62
Frank, Barney, 47
Friends of the Earth, 80
Frotman, Seth, 52
Frum, David, 221, 222

INDEX

G-20, 121
Gallup, 215, 233
Garland, Merrick, 160, 161, 163
Garner, Eric, 208
Gates, Henry Louis, 206, 207
Gates, Robert, 127, 168
gay marriage, 54–7, 59–61, 155, 164, 217, 218; *see also* same sex marriage
Geithner, Timothy, 234
Gerard, Leo, 99
Giuliani, Rudy, 175
Global Gag, 214–16; *see also* Mexico City ruling
Goldberg, Jeffrey, 23, 119,
Goldberg, Jonah, 181
Golden Valley, 51
Goldsmith, Jack, 177
Google, 87
Gorbachev, Mikhail, 19
Gore, Al, 175
Gorsuch, Neil, 163–5
Graham, Lindsay, 49, 81
Grant, Ulysses, 243
Great Recession, 89
Greatest Hoax, The, 82
green jobs, 200
Green, Michael, 121
Greenpeace, 80
Greenstein, Fred, 198, 212
Guantanamo, 167, 176
Guttmacher Institute, 215

Hagel, Chuck, 219
Hailey, Nikki, 139
Harris poll, 208
Hastert rule, 91
Hatch, Orrin, 101
Hate Crimes Prevention Bill, 58
Health and Human Services (HHS), 21, 27, 40, 63, 65

health care, 3, 21, 25, 27, 38–41, 44, 45, 47, 48, 55, 79, 89, 104, 200, 201, 204, 234–7
Health Security Act, 237
Heclo, Hugh, 10, 18
Heritage Foundation, 136, 203
Holder, Eric, 22, 57, 58
Homeland Security, Department of, 95, 96, 97
Horton, Willie, 206
Housing and Urban Development, Department of (HUD), 3, 58, 63
Howell, William, 8, 9
Huckabee, Mike, 217
Hurricane Katrina, 183, 210
Hussein, Saddam, 116

IBM, 87
Immigration, 16, 25, 77, 78, 88–95, 102, 104, 211, 213, 217, 239, 242, 246
Immigration and Customs Enforcement (ICE), 90
Indonesia, 121, 213
Indyk, Martin, 118
Infowars, 203
Inhofe, James, 82
Internal Revenue Service, 65
International Trade Commission, 99
Iran, 3, 4, 6, 7, 23, 25, 120, 124, 134–7, 140, 142, 179, 183, 217, 242, 243; *see also* Joint Comprehensive Plan of Action
Iran Contra, 183
Iraq, 2, 4, 116–21, 125–7, 129, 130, 132–3, 141–2, 176, 177, 200
ISIS, 125, 126, 129, 130, 132, 133
Israel, 135, 139

Jackson, Andrew, 243
Jacksonian, 143
Jacobs, Meg, 82, 104
Jane Doe v Trump, 220
Japan, 4, 121, 141
Johnson, Lyndon, 5, 9, 13, 39, 58, 116, 206, 243
Johnson, Richard, 206
Joint Comprehensive Plan of Action (JCPOA), 3, 7, 134–7, 140, 142, 143, 179–80, 205
Joint Plan of Action, 135
Justice, Department of, 18, 22, 27, 57, 62, 173, 185

Kaepernick, Colin, 222
Kagan, Elena, 159, 160, 218
Karmarck, Elaine, 211
Kasich, John, 103
Kavanaugh, Brett, 164–5
Kelly, John, 183
Kennedy, Anthony, 17, 155, 156, 158, 164
Kennedy, John F., 13, 116
Kerry, John, 54, 56, 81
Khomeini, Ayatollah, 135
Kim Jong-un, 181
Kimmel, Jimmy, 4
Kirk, Michael, 60, 209
Klein, Joe, 78, 158
Koch Brothers, 202
Koh, Harold, 128
Korea, North, 85, 181
Korea, South, 98, 99, 121
Korean War, 156
Kramar, David J., 124
Kranimger, Kathy, 52–3
Krieg, Andreas, 133, 179
Kristol, William, 241
Kuperman, Alan, 129
Kyoto Protocol, 79, 80

Labor, Department of, 65
Landler, Mark, 123, 140
Latin America, 19
Lauer, Matt, 211
Lawrence v Texas, 56
Lebanon, 19
Levin, Sander, 101
Lewinsky, Monica, 24, 183, 244
LGBT+, 3, 18, 25–7, 38, 39, 53, 57–63, 65, 199, 217, 219, 221, 246
Libby, Lewis, 173
Libya, 120, 125, 127–30, 132, 133, 143, 169, 177, 180
Lieberman, Joe, 41
Limbaugh, Rush, 233
Lin, Ann Chih, 245
Lizza, Ryan, 81
Lobbying Disclosure Act, 168
Log Cabin Republicans, 60
Luntz, Frank, 236
Lynch, Loretta, 22
Lynch, Marc, 142

McCain, John, 4, 45, 55, 81, 89, 167, 20, 233
McCain-Feingold Act, 167
McConnell, Mitch, 2, 160
McCurry, Michael, 15
McDonough, Denis, 131
McGahn, Don, 184
Make America Great Again (MAGA), 95, 213
Mar-a-Lago, 60
Martin, Trayvon, 207
Matthews, Chris, 214
Mattis, James General, 134, 220
Medicaid, 27, 39, 42–4, 47, 54
Medicare, 14, 21, 39, 201
Medicare Catastrophic Care Act, 21
Medicare Modernization Act, 13
Meet the Press, 4, 57

INDEX

Merkel, Angela, 131, 181
Mexico, 95, 210, 241, 242
Mexico City ruling, 241; *see also* Global Gag
Mercer, Robert, 204, 238
Miers, Harriet, 159
Michigan, 4, 9
Microsoft, 87
Middle East, 19, 137, 142
minimum wage, 19
Mitchell, Derek, 124
Moe, Terry, 8, 9
Moore, Johnnie, 65
Mueller investigation, 172–5, 185
Mueller, Robert, 172–4, 185
Mulvaney, Mick, 51–3, 64, 183
Munich Security Conference, 138
Murray, Donette, 127
Musharraf, Pervez, 178
Myanmar, 124; *see also* Burma

Napolitano, Janet, 97
National Defense University, 178
National Federation of Small Businesses v Sebelius, 42
National Security Council, 132, 133
NATO, 127, 128, 137, 138, 139
NBC, 61
Nelson, Ben, 104
Neustadt, Richard, 198
New Deal, 48, 82, 157, 235, 238
new "New Deal," 82, 235
Newsweek, 86
New Yorker, The, 5, 126, 217, 218, 242
New York Times, 60, 61, 64, 83, 84, 85, 86, 101, 123, 128, 162, 164, 166, 184, 209, 234
Nicaragua, 85
Nixon, Richard, 9, 14, 15, 39, 58, 121, 169, 174, 204
Nobel Peace Prize, 117, 118, 180
No Child Left Behind (NCLB), 21

North America Free Trade Association (NAFTA), 97–9, 102, 103, 237–8
Nuclear Proliferation Treaty, 135

Obama, Barack
  and American power, 23, 25, 175–80, 182
  Burma policy of, 120, 123–4
  climate change policy of, 78–84, 87, 104, 239, 242
  and Consumer Financial Protection Bureau, 38, 39, 47–51, 237, 242
  Cuba policy of, 120, 140–1
  health care policy of, 3, 4, 6, 12, 31, 38, 39–43, 44, 46, 165, 205, 237, 242; *see also* Affordable Care Act
  immigration policy of, 6, 88–94, 96, 104, 211, 239, 242
  Iran policy of, 3, 120, 134–6, 176, 179–80, 242–3; *see also* Joint Comprehensive Plan of Action
  Iraq policy of, 116, 125–6, 133, 142, 176
  and judicial branch, 159–62, 163, 166, 167
  Libya policy of, 120, 126–30, 133, 177, 180
  LGBT+ policies of, 3, 18, 54–60, 62, 155–6, 217–20; *see also* LGBT+; same sex marriage
  minimum wage policy of, 18–19
  and Pivot to Asia, 120–5, 141
  and racial justice, 199, 205–8, 232–4
  Syria policy of, 130–3, 176
  trade policy of, 98–102, 103, 121, 12; *see also* Trans-Pacific Partnership

Obamacare, 4, 6, 31, 38, 39, 43, 44, 46, 165, 205; *see also* Affordable Care Act
Obama Doctrine, 23, 25
Obergefell v. Hodges, 18, 55, 59, 52, 155, 218
Occupational and Safety Health Administration (OSHA), 14–15
O'Connor, Sandra Day, 17, 158, 159
Office of Information and Regulatory Affairs, 49
Oklahoma City bombing, 233
Operation Unified Protection, 128

Pakistan, 177–8, 182
Palin, Sarah, 201, 202, 234
Panetta, Leon, 122
Paris Climate Accord, 6, 7, 23, 83–7, 105, 205, 242
Pearl Harbour, 11
Pelosi, Nancy, 81, 96
Pence, Mike, 45, 61, 124, 163, 215, 218
Pennsylvania, 9, 98
Perot, Ross, 238
Perry, Rick, 85
Personal Responsibility and Work Opportunity Act (PRWOA), 13
Pew Research Center, 54, 161, 174
Philadelphia Eagles, 222
Phillips, Jack, 62
Pivot to Asia, 120–3, 124, 141
Planned Parenthood, 215, 216
Politico, 50, 138
Pompeo, Mike, 136, 137
Power, Samantha, 139
presidential legacy, 5, 7–20, 24–7, 243–6
Presidential Threat Task Force, 233

Priebus, Reince, 183
Proposition, 8, 18, 59
Pruitt, Scott, 86
Public Citizen, 169
Puerto Rico, 87
Pussygate tapes, 163, 216
Putin, Vladimir, 181

al-Qaddafi, Muammar, 128, 129

Rand Corporation, 219–20
Reagan, Ronald, 10, 12, 14, 17, 19, 21, 139, 158, 164, 183, 206, 210, 214, 241, 244
Reid, Harry, 161, 162, 164
Religious Freedom and Restoration Act, 61
Remnick, David, 5, 126
Republican National Committee (RNC), 6
Rhodes, Ben, 122, 124, 171
Rice, Susan, 139, 170
Roberts, John, 18, 155, 158, 166
Rockman, Bert, 10, 20
Roe v. Wade, 164, 215, 216
Rohingya, 124
rollback of presidential legacy, 20–6, 86, 134, 143, 201, 205, 209, 213, 241, 245
Roosevelt, Franklin D., 8, 10, 11, 156, 157, 235
Roper Center, 56
Rose, Gideon, 131
Ross, Wilbur, 141
Rouhani, Hassan, 135
Rubio, Marco, 103, 140
Rudalevige, Andrew, 16, 27
Rumsfeld, Donald, 2
Rusk, Dean, 121
Russia, 25, 132, 134, 136, 173–7, 181, 185
Ryan, Paul, 199, 203, 238

INDEX

Sabin Center for Climate Change Law, 86
same sex marriage, 17, 18, 38, 54–6, 155, 217, 218, 242; *see also* gay marriage
Sanders, Bernie, 102, 103, 234
Sanders, Sarah, 62
Santorum, Rick, 60, 217
Saturday Night Massacre, 174
Scales, Robert, 137
Scalia, Antonin, 160, 163
Schumer, Chuck, 96
Scowcroft, Brent, 119
Secret Service, 232, 241
Securities Exchange Commission, 49
September 11 2001 (9/11), 133, 175, 176
Sessions, Jeff, 22, 27, 62, 90
Shelby County decision, 18
Siver, Nate, 165
Skowronek, Stephen, 154
Skrentry, John, 90
Social Security Act, 11
Somalia, 177, 182
Sotomayor, Sonia, 159, 213, 218
Souter, David, 17, 157, 160
Southern Poverty Law Center, 233
State, Department of, 118, 128, 170, 171, 243
Stavridis, James, 127, 128
Stephanopoulos, George, 13
Stevens, Chris, 170
Stevens, John Paul, 160
Stoltenberg, Jens, 138
Stone v. Trump, 220
Stonewall National Monument, 59
Summers, Lawrence, 234
Sununu, John, 158
Supreme Court, 11, 16–18, 24, 43, 49, 55, 57, 59, 60, 62, 65, 89, 94, 97, 155–9, 161–7, 174, 213–15, 218, 221

Suri, Jeremi, 8, 117
Syria, 85, 118, 125, 126, 130–4, 143, 176, 181, 211

Tax Cut and Jobs Act, 46
Tea Party, 2, 91, 201, 202, 211, 234, 238
Terror From the Right report, 233
Texas v. Azar, 64
Texas v. US, 94
Thomas, Clarence, 165
Tierney, Dominic, 129
Time Magazine, 78, 235
Trade Adjustment Assistance (TAA), 100
Trade Promotion Authority (TPA), 78, 100, 101
Trans-Pacific Partnership, 6, 7, 78, 100–3, 105, 121, 141, 143, 242
Travel Ban, 183, 210, 211, 212
Treasury, Department of, 59, 65
Truman, Harry, 20, 39, 156, 200, 243
Trump Doctrine, 23, 119
Trump, Donald
  and America First, 84, 119, 181, 215
  and American power, 23, 180–2
  climate change policy of, 6, 84–7, 104, 242
  and Consumer Financial Protection Bureau, 53
  Cuba policy of, 140–1
  Election 2016, 9–10, 240
  health care policy of, 3, 44–7; *see also* Affordable Care Act
  immigration policy of, 6, 88, 90, 95–7, 104
  Iran policy of, 3, 4, 135–7, 243; *see also* Joint Comprehensive Plan of Action

257

Trump, Donald (*cont.*)
   and judicial branch, 162–8, 184, 212, 213, 215
   LGBT+ policies of, 60–3, 65, 217–21; *see also* LGBT+; same sex marriage
   and Mueller investigation, 172–5, 185
   and race issues, 199, 205, 208–10, 222, 234, 240; *see also* Birtherism
   reproductive rights, 214–16
   Syria policy of, 134
   trade policy of, 98, 102–3, 121, 123, 141, 142; *see also* North America Free Trade Association and Trans-Pacific Partnership
   travel ban of, 211–13
Twitter, 27, 173, 174, 213, 219, 220, 240

Ukraine, 177
Undefeated, The (documentary), 202
UN Framework Convention on Climate Change, 80, 84
United Nations (UN), 80, 124, 138, 139

United States Climate Alliance, 87
US v. Windsor, 57

Vietnam War, 9, 116
Violent Crime Control and Law Enforcement Act, 237
Voting Rights Act of 1965, 18

Wall Street, 7, 25, 47, 48, 237
Ward, Alex, 134
War on Terror, 120
War Powers Resolution, 128
Warren, Earl, 17, 157
Warren, Elizabeth, 48–50, 53
Washington, George, 10
Washington Post, 51, 124, 174
Watergate, 9, 24, 172, 174
Wheeler, Andrew, 86
Wolff, Michael, 240
World Health Organisation, 86

Xi Jinping, 122

Yemen, 177, 182
Yiannopolous, Milo, 203

Zelizer, Jualian, 63
Zimmerman, George, 207

EU representative:
Easy Access System Europe
Mustamäe tee 50, 10621 Tallinn, Estonia
Gpsr.requests@easproject.com

www.ingramcontent.com/pod-product-compliance
Lightning Source LLC
Chambersburg PA
CBHW070322240426
43671CB00013BA/2339